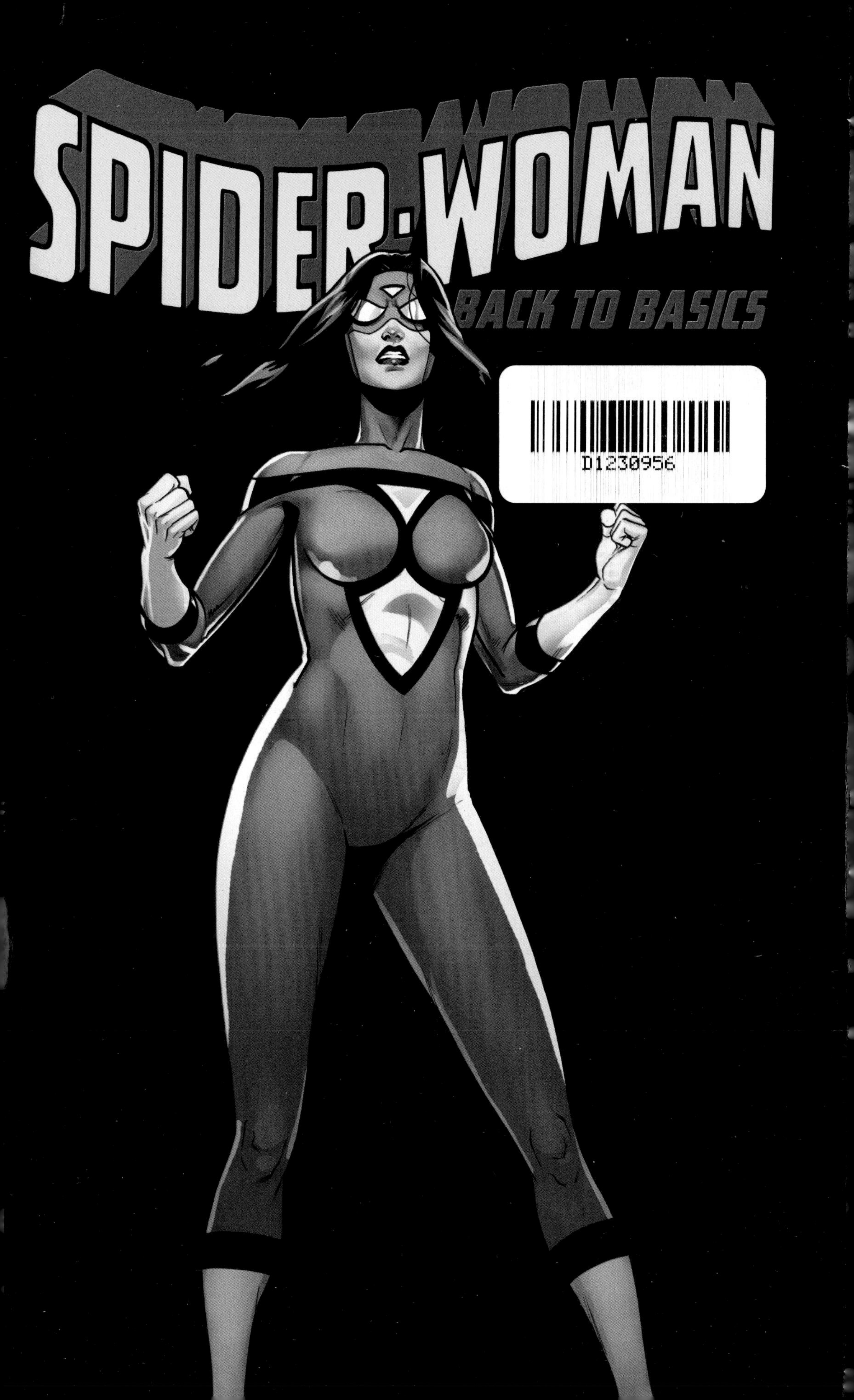
SPIDER-WOMAN
BACK TO BASICS

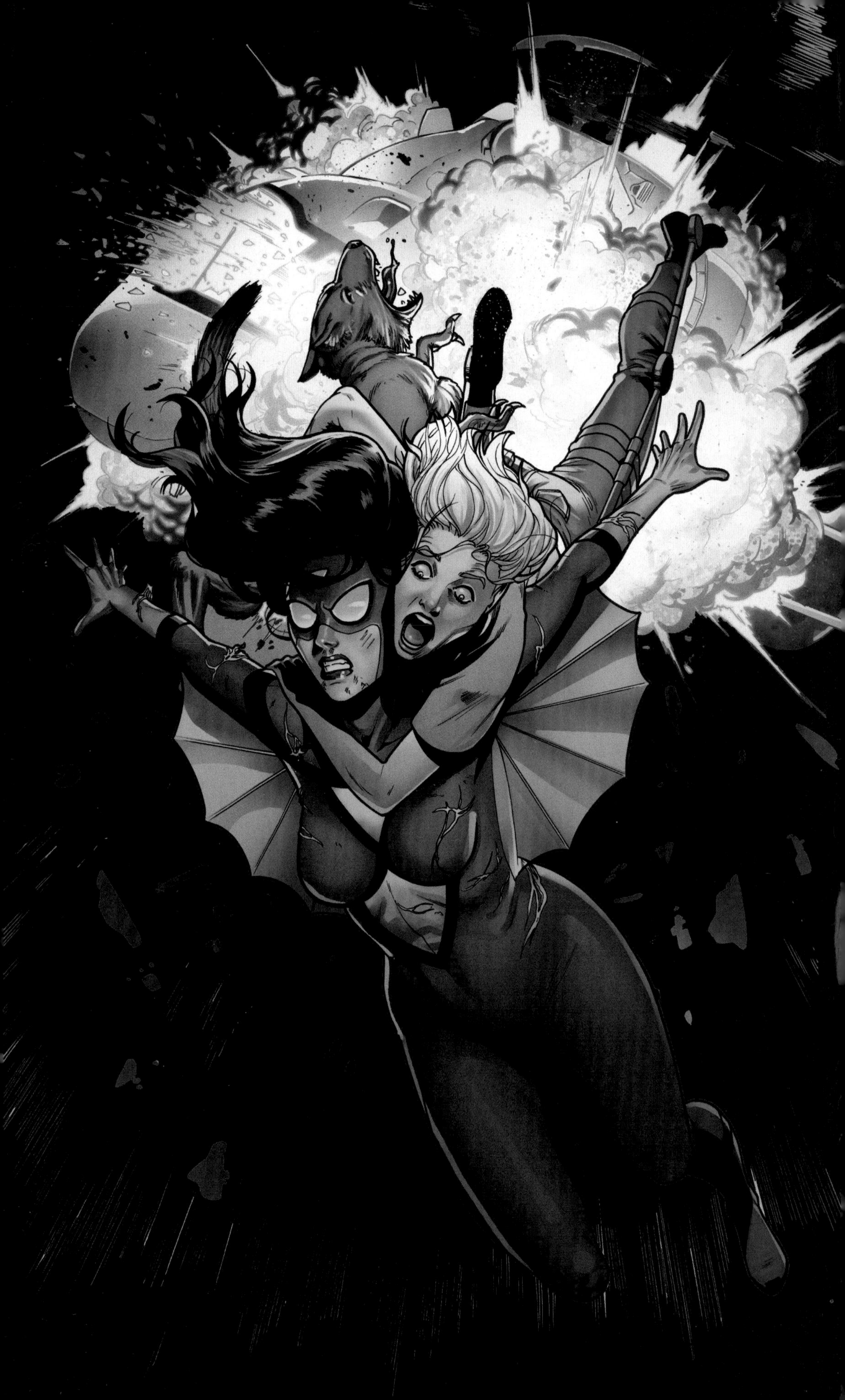

LETTERER *VC's TRAVIS LANHAM*
COVER ART *JUNGGEUN YOON*

ASSISTANT EDITOR *LINDSEY COHICK*
EDITOR *NICK LOWE*

COLLECTION EDITOR *JENNIFER GRÜNWALD*
ASSISTANT EDITOR *DANIEL KIRCHHOFFER*
ASSISTANT MANAGING EDITOR *MAIA LOY*
ASSISTANT MANAGING EDITOR *LISA MONTALBANO*

VP PRODUCTION & SPECIAL PROJECTS *JEFF YOUNGQUIST*
BOOK DESIGNERS *SARAH SPADACCINI* WITH *ADAM DEL RE*
SVP PRINT, SALES & MARKETING *DAVID GABRIEL*
EDITOR IN CHIEF *C.B. CEBULSKI*

SPIDER-WOMAN VOL. 3: BACK TO BASICS. Contains material originally published in magazine form as SPIDER-WOMAN (2020) #11-16. First printing 2021. ISBN 978-1-302-92905-3. Published by MARVEL WORLDWIDE, INC., a subsidiary of MARVEL ENTERTAINMENT, LLC. OFFICE OF PUBLICATION: 1290 Avenue of the Americas, New York, NY 10104. © 2021 MARVEL No similarity between any of the names, characters, persons, and/or institutions in this book with those of any living or dead person or institution is intended, and any such similarity which may exist is purely coincidental. **Printed in Canada.** KEVIN FEIGE, Chief Creative Officer; DAN BUCKLEY, President, Marvel Entertainment; JOE QUESADA, EVP & Creative Director; DAVID BOGART, Associate Publisher & SVP of Talent Affairs; TOM BREVOORT, VP, Executive Editor; NICK LOWE, Executive Editor, VP of Content, Digital Publishing; DAVID GABRIEL, VP of Print & Digital Publishing; JEFF YOUNGQUIST, VP of Production & Special Projects; ALEX MORALES, Director of Publishing Operations; DAN EDINGTON, Managing Editor; RICKEY PURDIN, Director of Talent Relations; JENNIFER GRÜNWALD, Senior Editor, Special Projects; SUSAN CRESPI, Production Manager; STAN LEE, Chairman Emeritus. For information regarding advertising in Marvel Comics or on Marvel. com, please contact Vit DeBellis, Custom Solutions & Integrated Advertising Manager, at vdebellis@marvel.com. For Marvel subscription inquiries, please call 888-511-5480. Manufactured between 11/5/2021 and 12/7/2021 by SOLISCO PRINTERS, SCOTT, QC, CANADA.

10 9 8 7 6 5 4 3 2 1

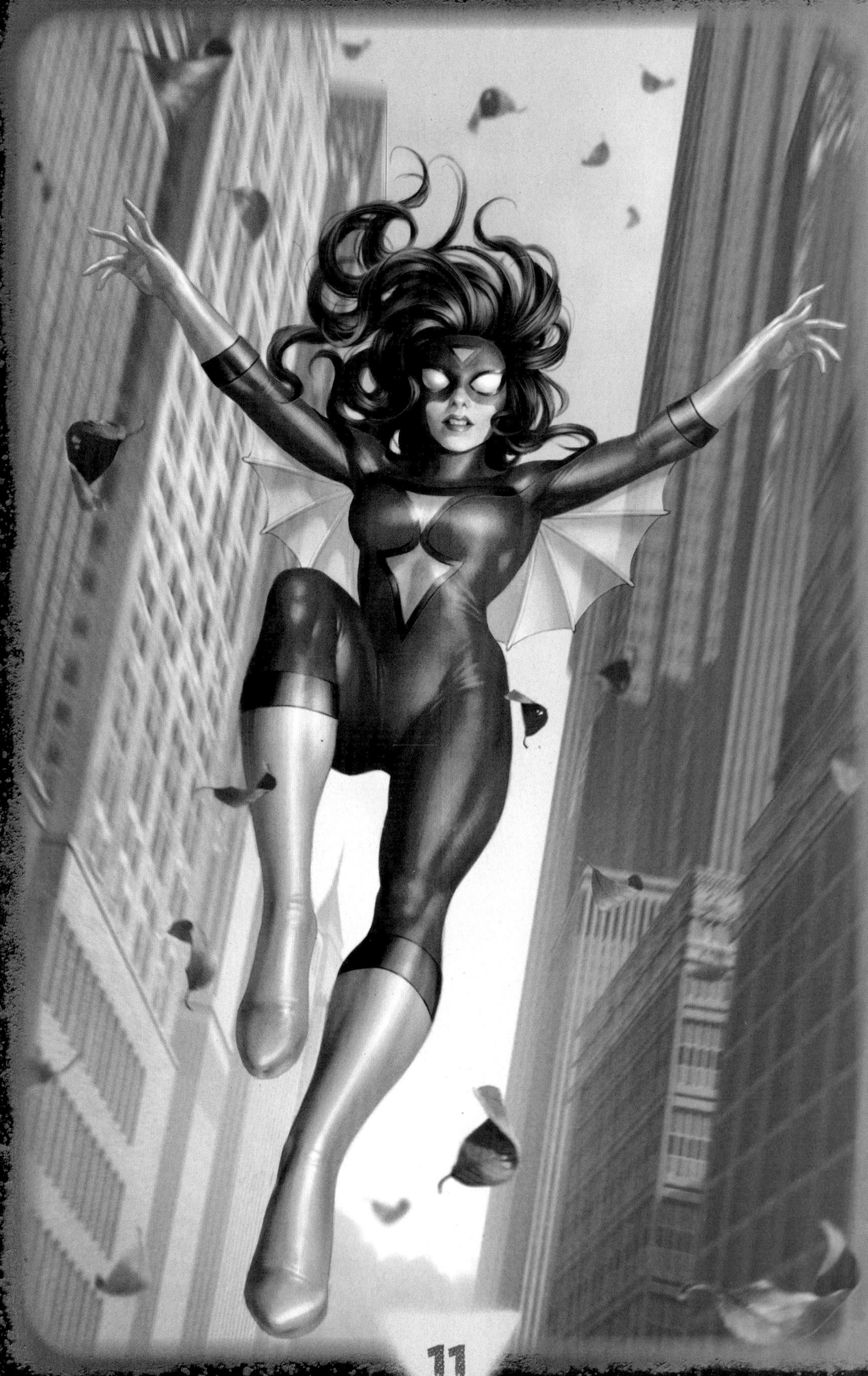

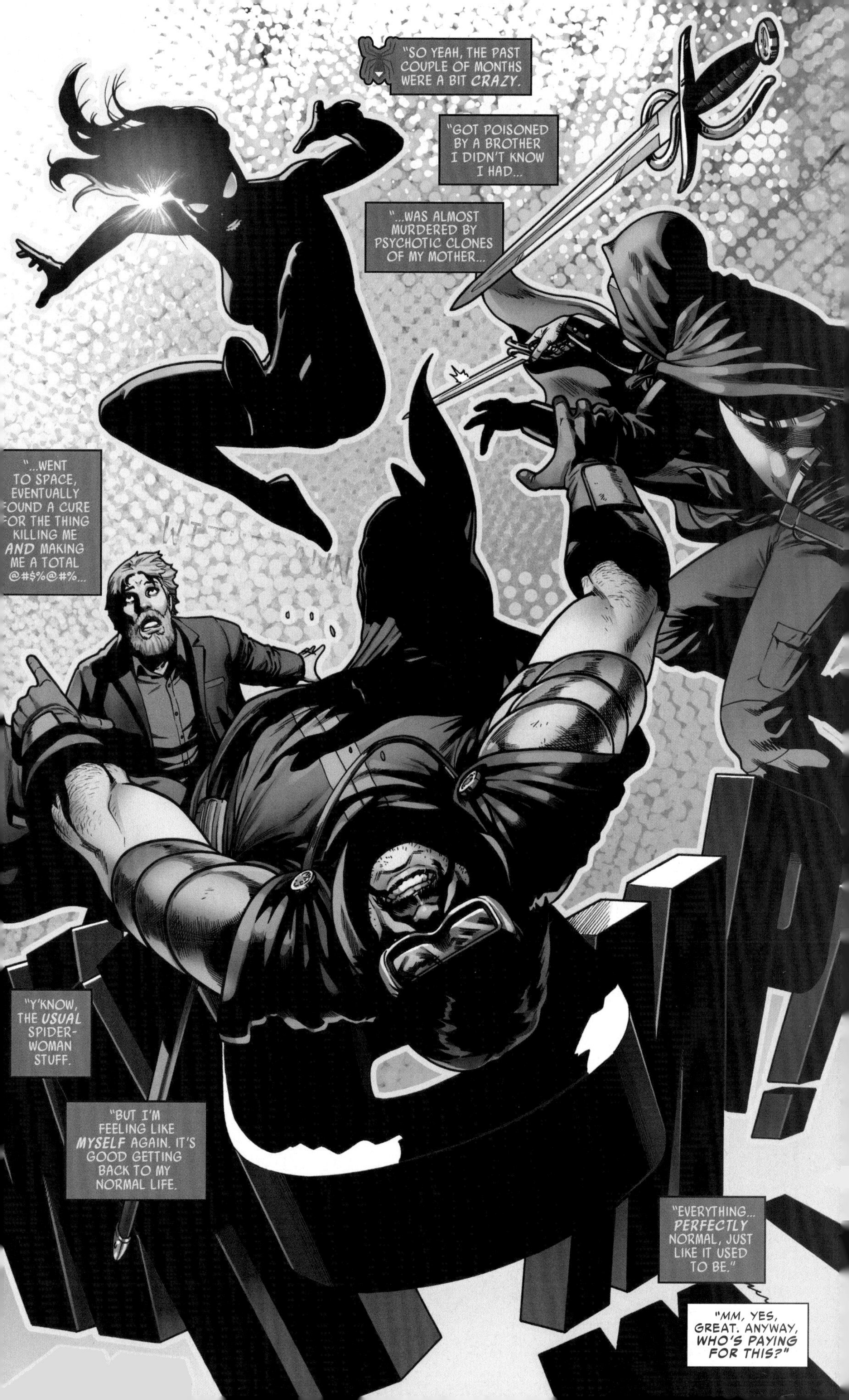
"SO YEAH, THE PAST COUPLE OF MONTHS WERE A BIT CRAZY.
"GOT POISONED BY A BROTHER I DIDN'T KNOW I HAD...
"...WAS ALMOST MURDERED BY PSYCHOTIC CLONES OF MY MOTHER...
"...WENT TO SPACE, EVENTUALLY FOUND A CURE FOR THE THING KILLING ME AND MAKING ME A TOTAL @#$%@#%...
"Y'KNOW, THE USUAL SPIDER-WOMAN STUFF.
"BUT I'M FEELING LIKE MYSELF AGAIN. IT'S GOOD GETTING BACK TO MY NORMAL LIFE.
"EVERYTHING... PERFECTLY NORMAL, JUST LIKE IT USED TO BE."
"MM, YES, GREAT. ANYWAY, WHO'S PAYING FOR THIS?"

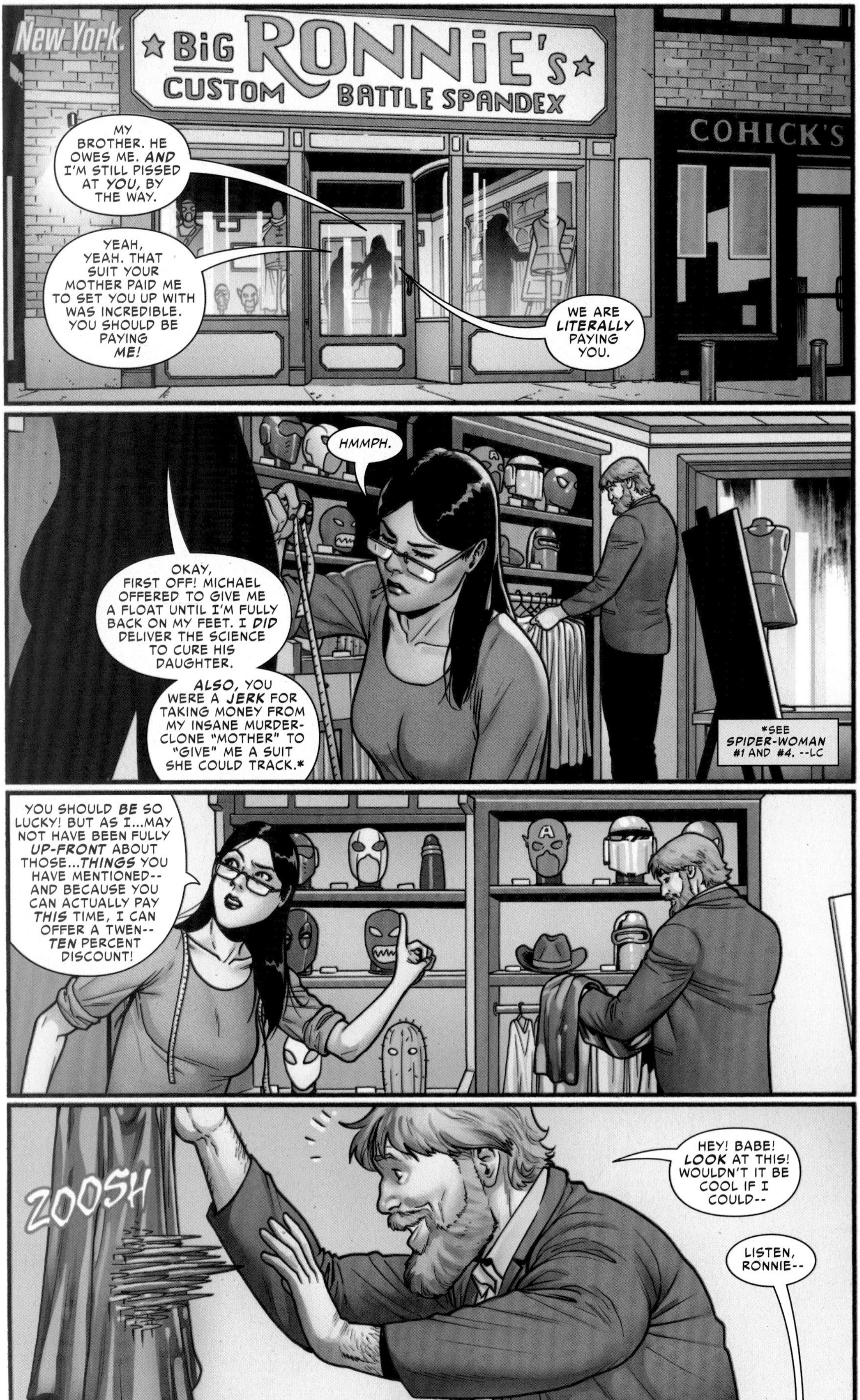
New York.
BIG RONNIE'S CUSTOM BATTLE SPANDEX
COHICK'S
MY BROTHER. HE OWES ME. AND I'M STILL PISSED AT YOU, BY THE WAY.
YEAH, YEAH. THAT SUIT YOUR MOTHER PAID ME TO SET YOU UP WITH WAS INCREDIBLE. YOU SHOULD BE PAYING ME!
WE ARE LITERALLY PAYING YOU.
HMMPH.
OKAY, FIRST OFF! MICHAEL OFFERED TO GIVE ME A FLOAT UNTIL I'M FULLY BACK ON MY FEET. I DID DELIVER THE SCIENCE TO CURE HIS DAUGHTER.
ALSO, YOU WERE A JERK FOR TAKING MONEY FROM MY INSANE MURDER-CLONE "MOTHER" TO "GIVE" ME A SUIT SHE COULD TRACK.*
*SEE SPIDER-WOMAN #1 AND #4. --LC
YOU SHOULD BE SO LUCKY! BUT AS I...MAY NOT HAVE BEEN FULLY UP-FRONT ABOUT THOSE...THINGS YOU HAVE MENTIONED--AND BECAUSE YOU CAN ACTUALLY PAY THIS TIME, I CAN OFFER A TWEN--TEN PERCENT DISCOUNT!
ZOOSH
HEY! BABE! LOOK AT THIS! WOULDN'T IT BE COOL IF I COULD--
LISTEN, RONNIE--

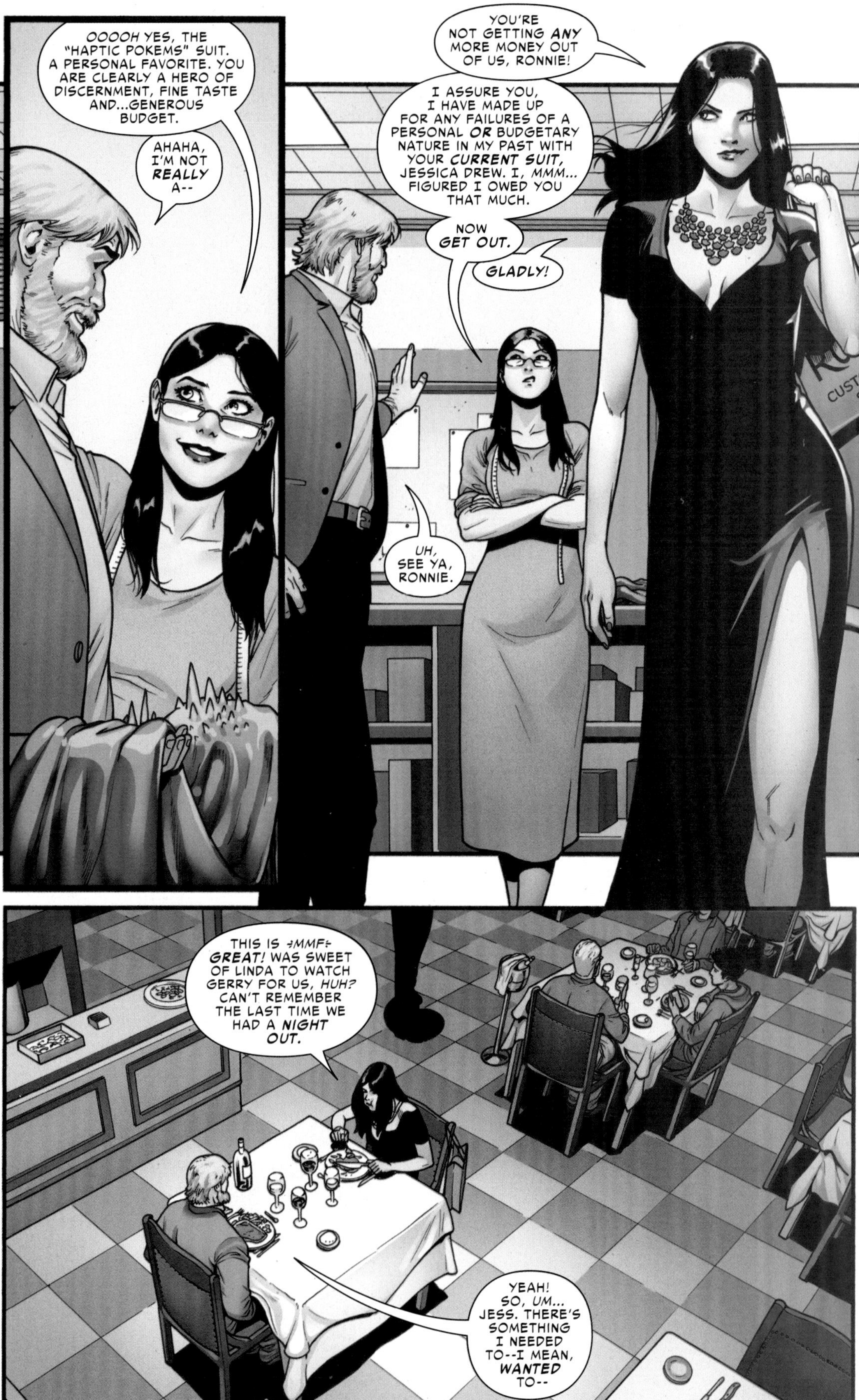
OOOOH YES, THE "HAPTIC POKEMS" SUIT. A PERSONAL FAVORITE. YOU ARE CLEARLY A HERO OF DISCERNMENT, FINE TASTE AND...GENEROUS BUDGET.
AHAHA, I'M NOT REALLY A--
YOU'RE NOT GETTING ANY MORE MONEY OUT OF US, RONNIE!
I ASSURE YOU, I HAVE MADE UP FOR ANY FAILURES OF A PERSONAL OR BUDGETARY NATURE IN MY PAST WITH YOUR CURRENT SUIT, JESSICA DREW. I, MMM... FIGURED I OWED YOU THAT MUCH.
NOW GET OUT.
GLADLY!
UH, SEE YA, RONNIE.
CUSTOM BAT
SPANDE
THIS IS -MMF- GREAT! WAS SWEET OF LINDA TO WATCH GERRY FOR US, HUH? CAN'T REMEMBER THE LAST TIME WE HAD A NIGHT OUT.
YEAH! SO, UM... JESS. THERE'S SOMETHING I NEEDED TO--I MEAN, WANTED TO--

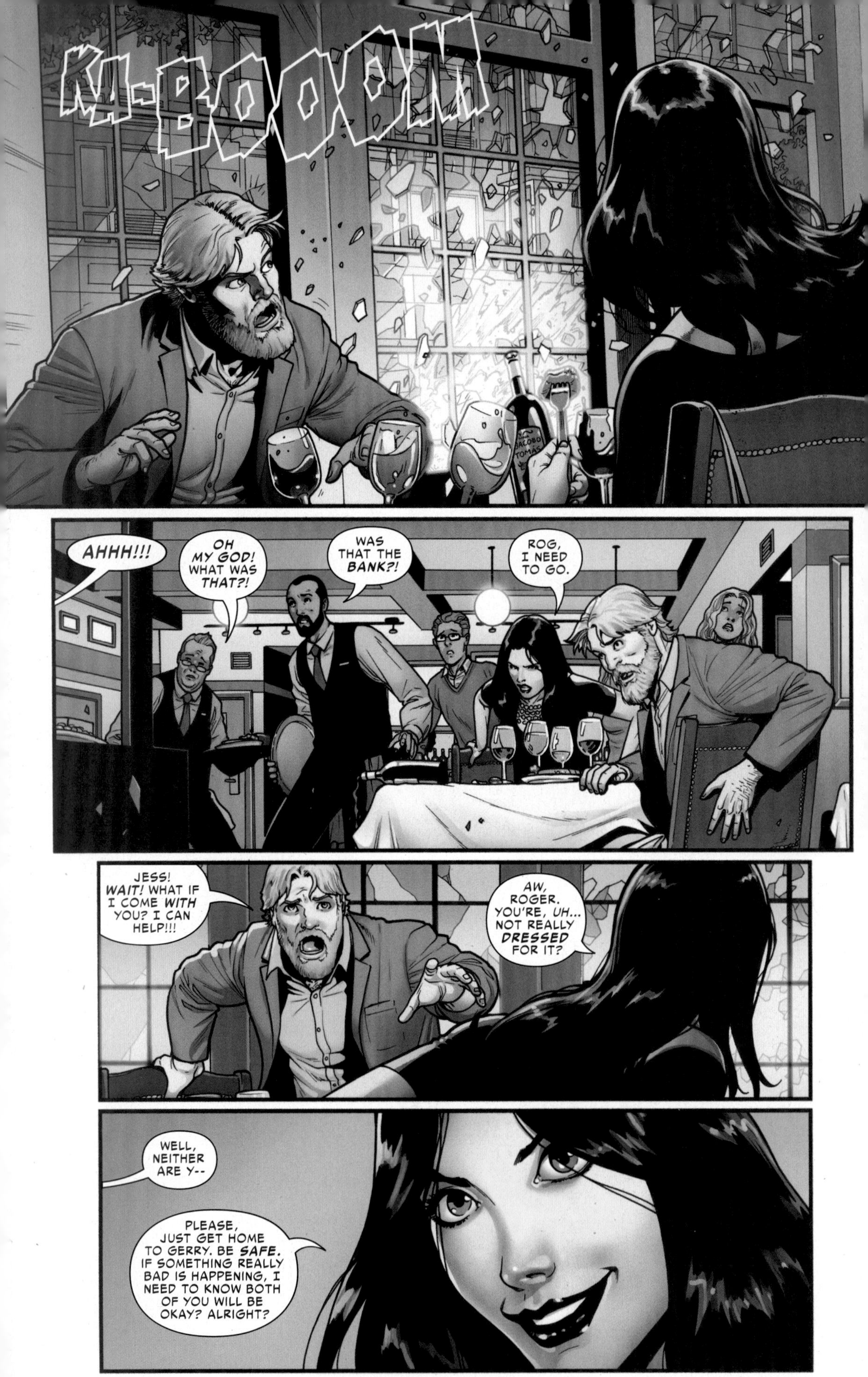
KA-BOOOM
AHHH!!!
OH MY GOD! WHAT WAS THAT?!
WAS THAT THE BANK?!
ROG, I NEED TO GO.
JESS! WAIT! WHAT IF I COME WITH YOU? I CAN HELP!!!
AW, ROGER. YOU'RE, UH... NOT REALLY DRESSED FOR IT?
WELL, NEITHER ARE Y--
PLEASE, JUST GET HOME TO GERRY. BE SAFE. IF SOMETHING REALLY BAD IS HAPPENING, I NEED TO KNOW BOTH OF YOU WILL BE OKAY? ALRIGHT?

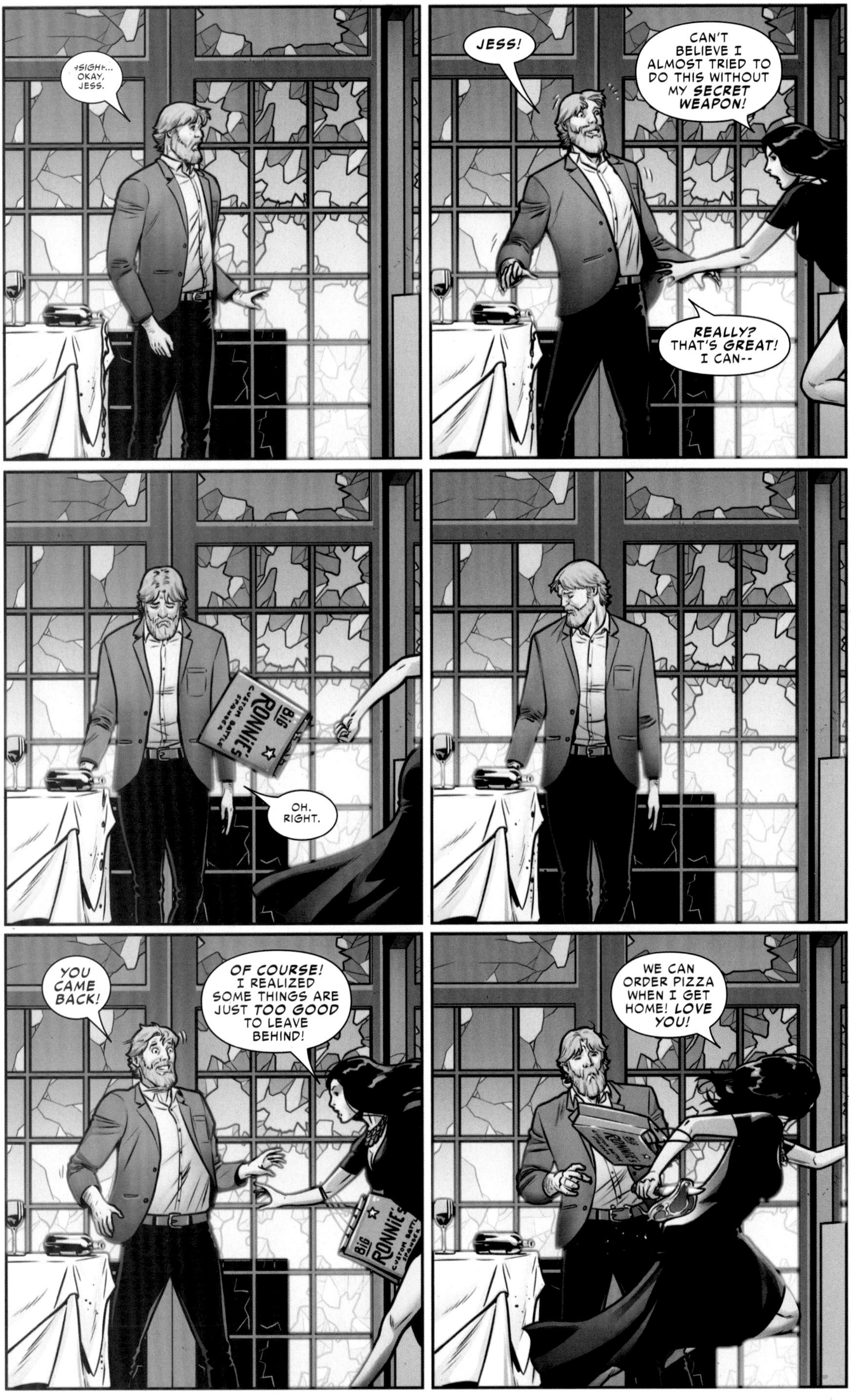
SIGH... OKAY, JESS.
JESS!
CAN'T BELIEVE I ALMOST TRIED TO DO THIS WITHOUT MY SECRET WEAPON!
REALLY? THAT'S GREAT! I CAN--
BIG RONNIE'S CUSTOM BATTLE SPONGES
OH. RIGHT.
YOU CAME BACK!
OF COURSE! I REALIZED SOME THINGS ARE JUST TOO GOOD TO LEAVE BEHIND!
BIG RONNIE'S CUSTOM BATTLE SPONGES
WE CAN ORDER PIZZA WHEN I GET HOME! LOVE YOU!

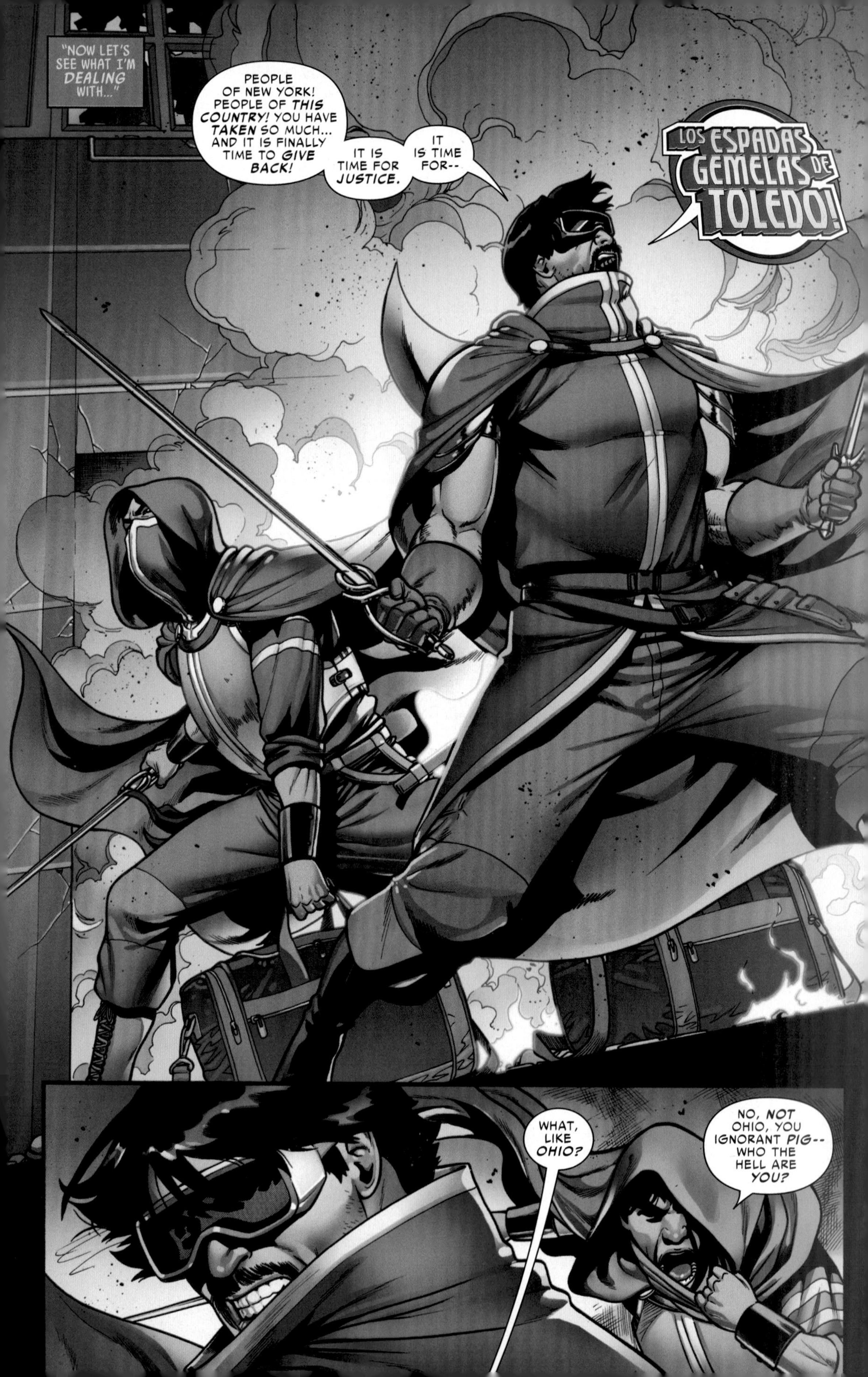
"NOW LET'S SEE WHAT I'M DEALING WITH..."
PEOPLE OF NEW YORK! PEOPLE OF THIS COUNTRY! YOU HAVE TAKEN SO MUCH... AND IT IS FINALLY TIME TO GIVE BACK!
IT IS TIME FOR JUSTICE.
IT IS TIME FOR--
LOS ESPADAS GEMELAS DE TOLEDO!
WHAT, LIKE OHIO?
NO, NOT OHIO, YOU IGNORANT PIG-- WHO THE HELL ARE YOU?

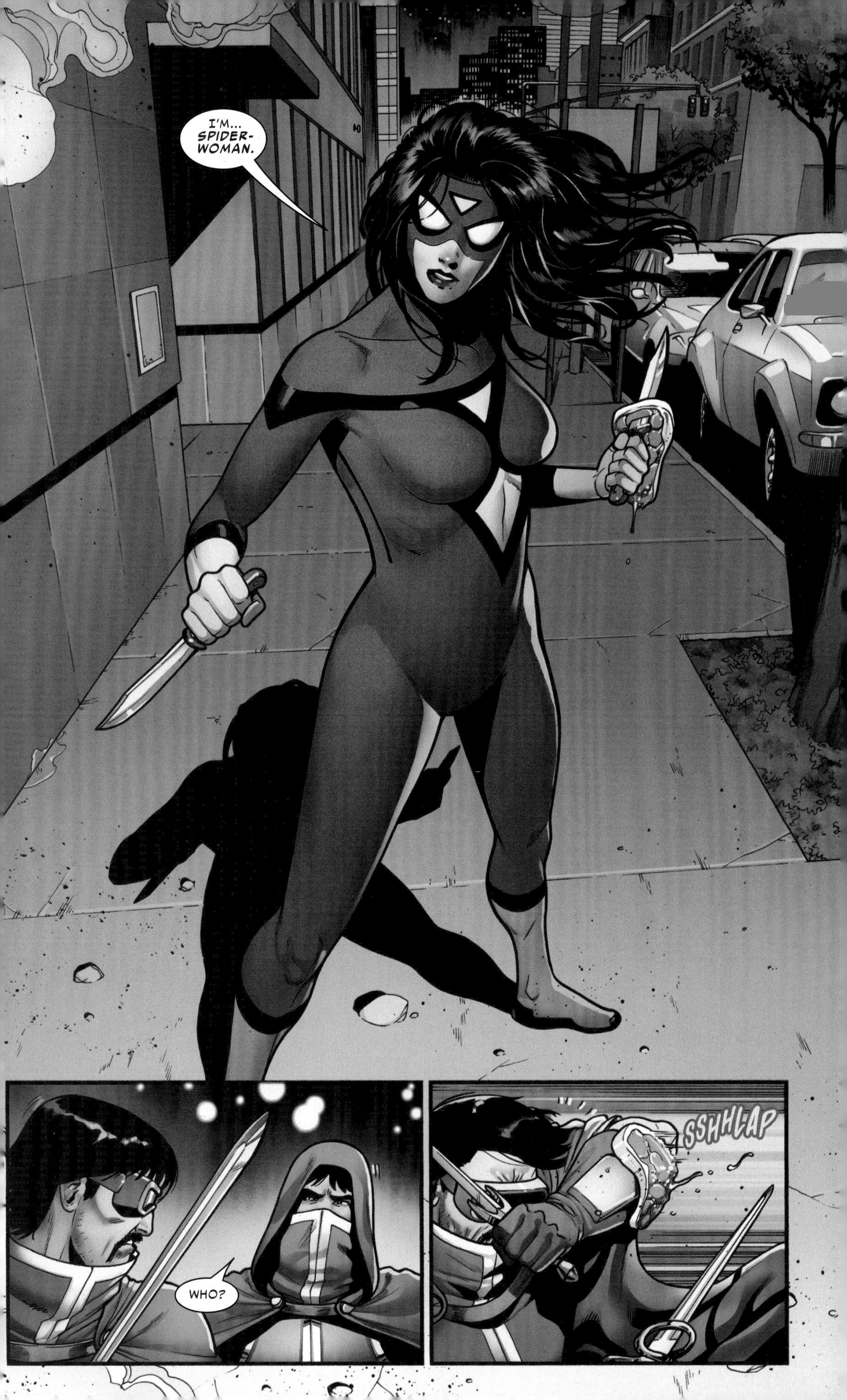
I'M... SPIDER-WOMAN.
WHO?
SSHHLAP

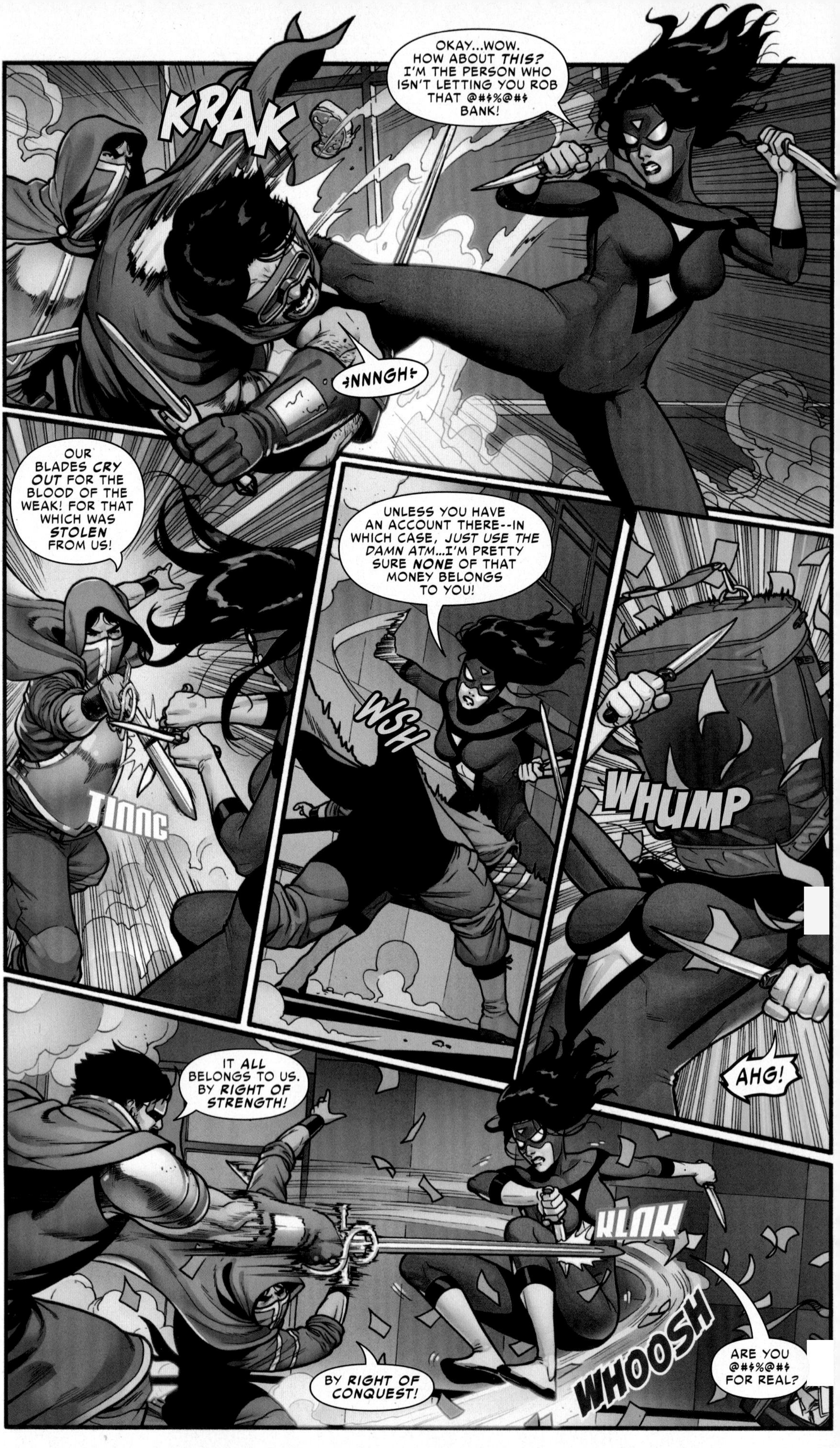

KRAK
OKAY...WOW. HOW ABOUT THIS? I'M THE PERSON WHO ISN'T LETTING YOU ROB THAT @#$%@#$ BANK!
NNNGH!
OUR BLADES CRY OUT FOR THE BLOOD OF THE WEAK! FOR THAT WHICH WAS STOLEN FROM US!
TINNG
UNLESS YOU HAVE AN ACCOUNT THERE--IN WHICH CASE, JUST USE THE DAMN ATM...I'M PRETTY SURE NONE OF THAT MONEY BELONGS TO YOU!
WSH
WHUMP
AHG!
IT ALL BELONGS TO US. BY RIGHT OF STRENGTH!
KLNK
BY RIGHT OF CONQUEST!
WHOOSH
ARE YOU @#$%@#$ FOR REAL?

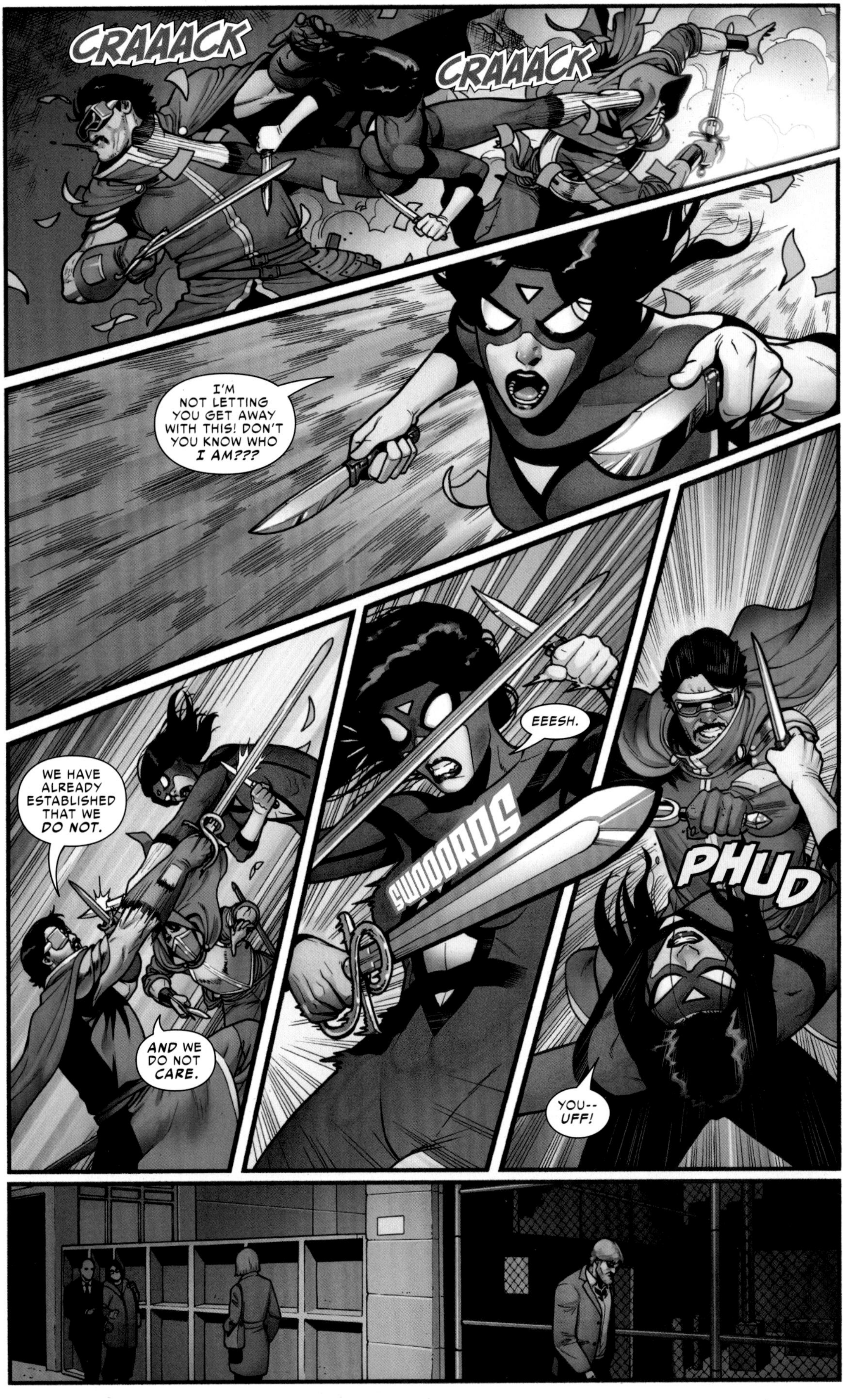
CRAAACK
CRAAACK
I'M NOT LETTING YOU GET AWAY WITH THIS! DON'T YOU KNOW WHO I AM???
WE HAVE ALREADY ESTABLISHED THAT WE DO NOT.
AND WE DO NOT CARE.
EEESH.
SWOOORDS
PHUD
YOU-- UFF!

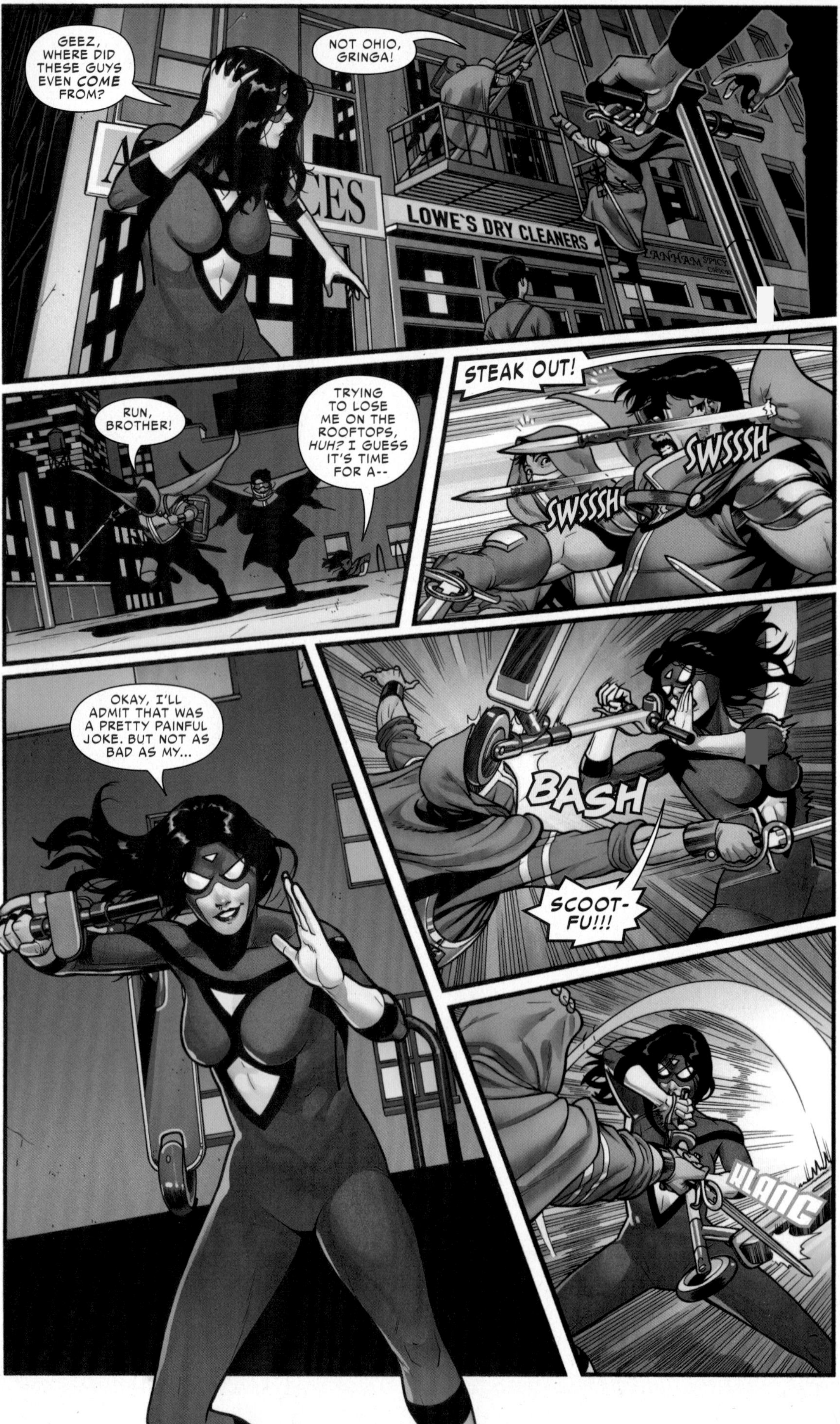
GEEZ, WHERE DID THESE GUYS EVEN COME FROM?
NOT OHIO, GRINGA!
LOWE'S DRY CLEANERS
RUN, BROTHER!
TRYING TO LOSE ME ON THE ROOFTOPS, HUH? I GUESS IT'S TIME FOR A--
STEAK OUT!
SWSSSH
SWSSSH
OKAY, I'LL ADMIT THAT WAS A PRETTY PAINFUL JOKE. BUT NOT AS BAD AS MY...
BASH
SCOOT-FU!!!
KLANG

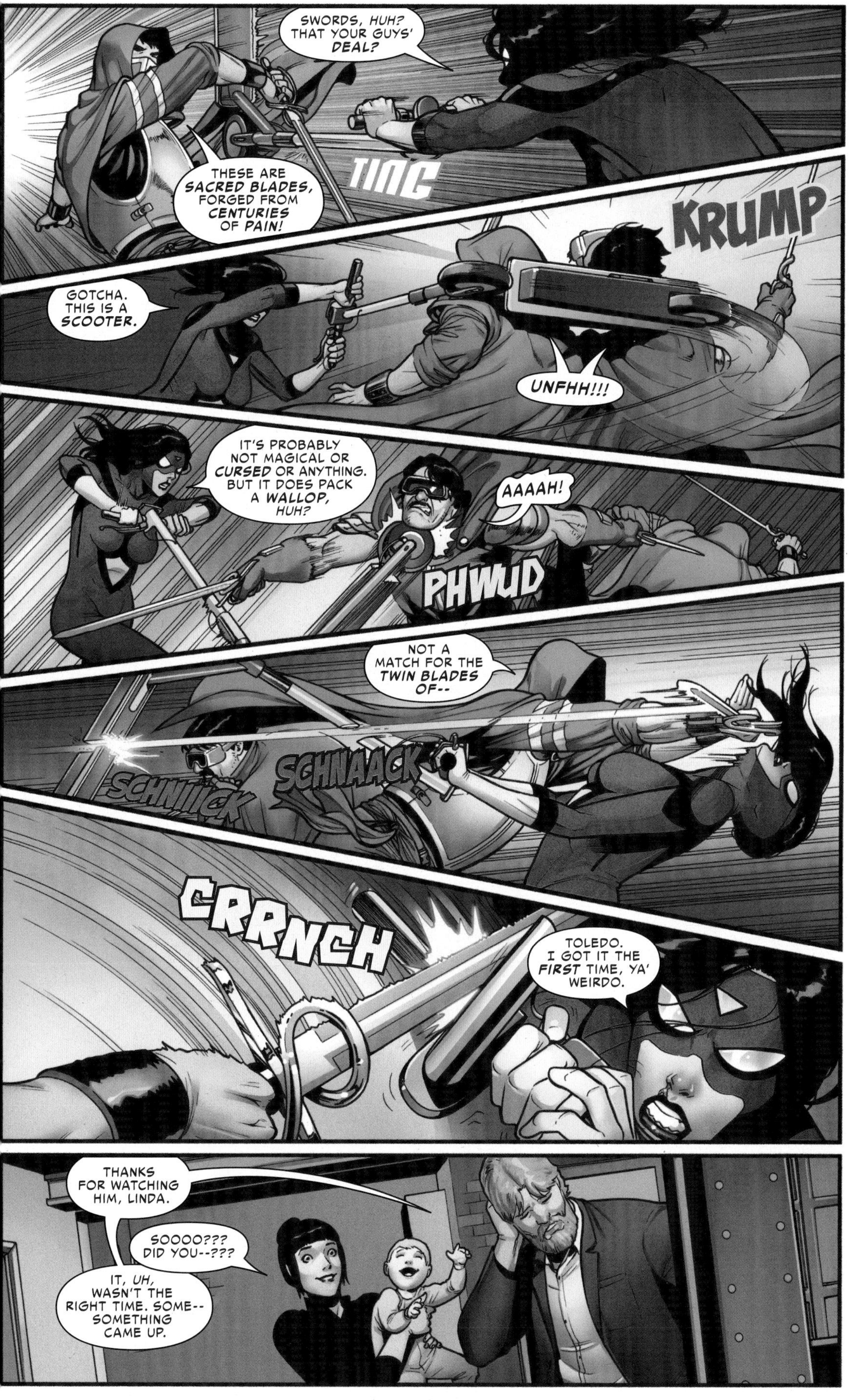
SWORDS, HUH? THAT YOUR GUYS' DEAL?
THESE ARE SACRED BLADES, FORGED FROM CENTURIES OF PAIN!
TINC
KRUMP
GOTCHA. THIS IS A SCOOTER.
UNFHH!!!
IT'S PROBABLY NOT MAGICAL OR CURSED OR ANYTHING. BUT IT DOES PACK A WALLOP, HUH?
AAAAH!
PHWUD
NOT A MATCH FOR THE TWIN BLADES OF--
SCHNIIICK
SCHNAAACK
CRRNCH
TOLEDO. I GOT IT THE FIRST TIME, YA' WEIRDO.
THANKS FOR WATCHING HIM, LINDA.
SOOOO??? DID YOU--???
IT, UH, WASN'T THE RIGHT TIME. SOME-- SOMETHING CAME UP.

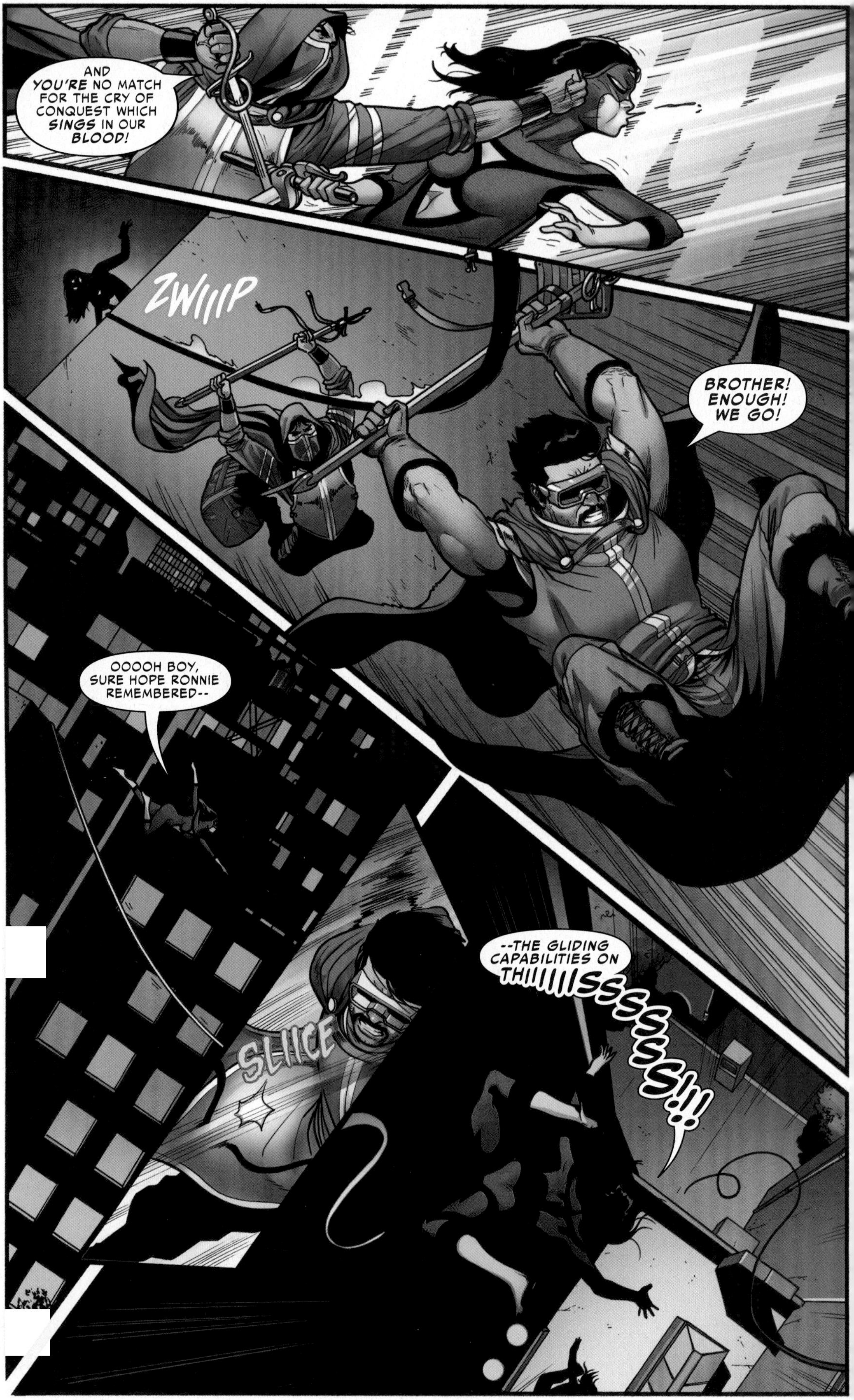
AND YOU'RE NO MATCH FOR THE CRY OF CONQUEST WHICH SINGS IN OUR BLOOD!
ZWIIIP
BROTHER! ENOUGH! WE GO!
OOOOH BOY, SURE HOPE RONNIE REMEMBERED--
--THE GLIDING CAPABILITIES ON THIIIIIISSSSSSS!!!
SLIICE

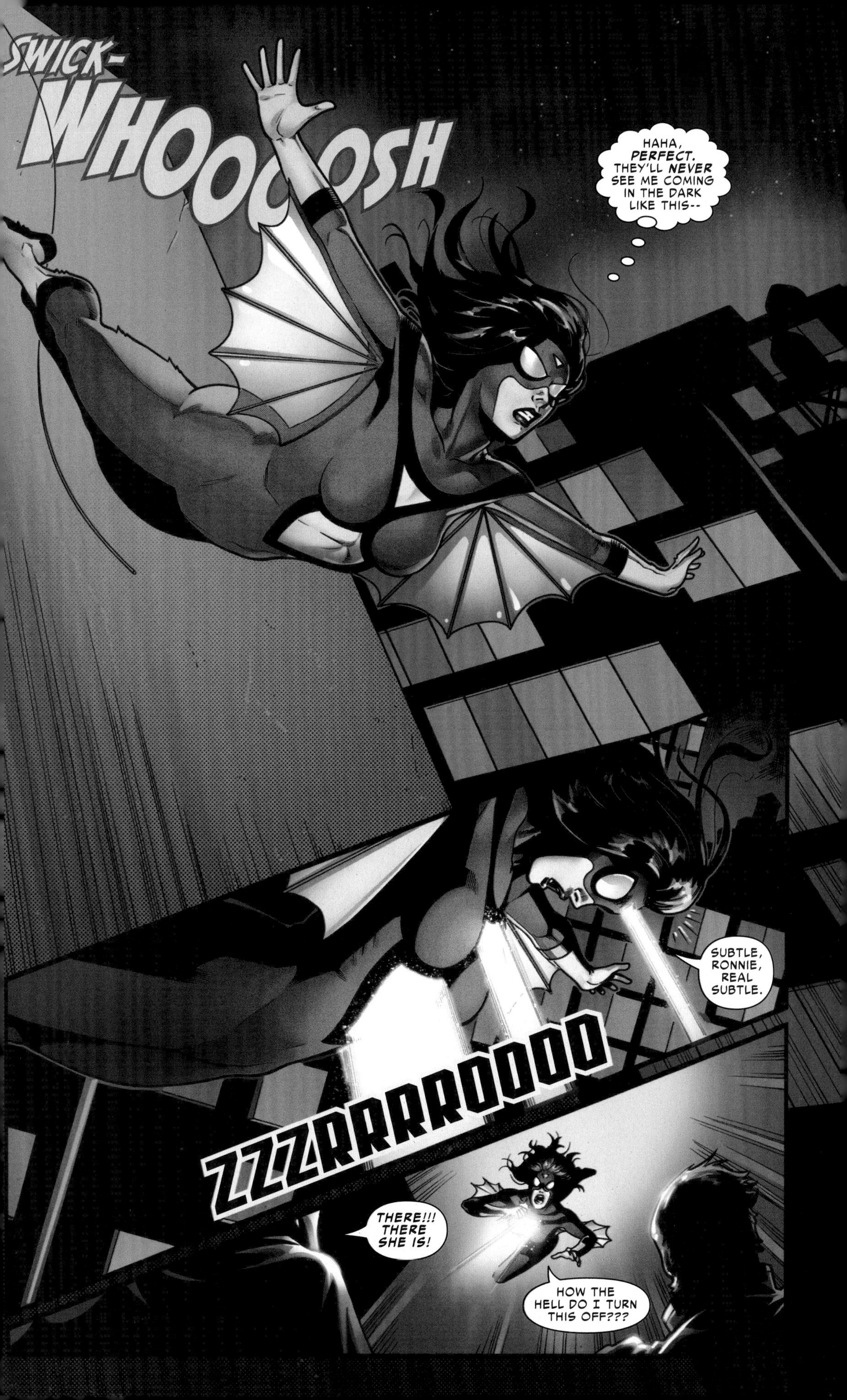
SWICK-WHOOOOOSH
HAHA, PERFECT. THEY'LL NEVER SEE ME COMING IN THE DARK LIKE THIS--
SUBTLE, RONNIE, REAL SUBTLE.
ZZZRRRROOOO
THERE!!! THERE SHE IS!
HOW THE HELL DO I TURN THIS OFF???

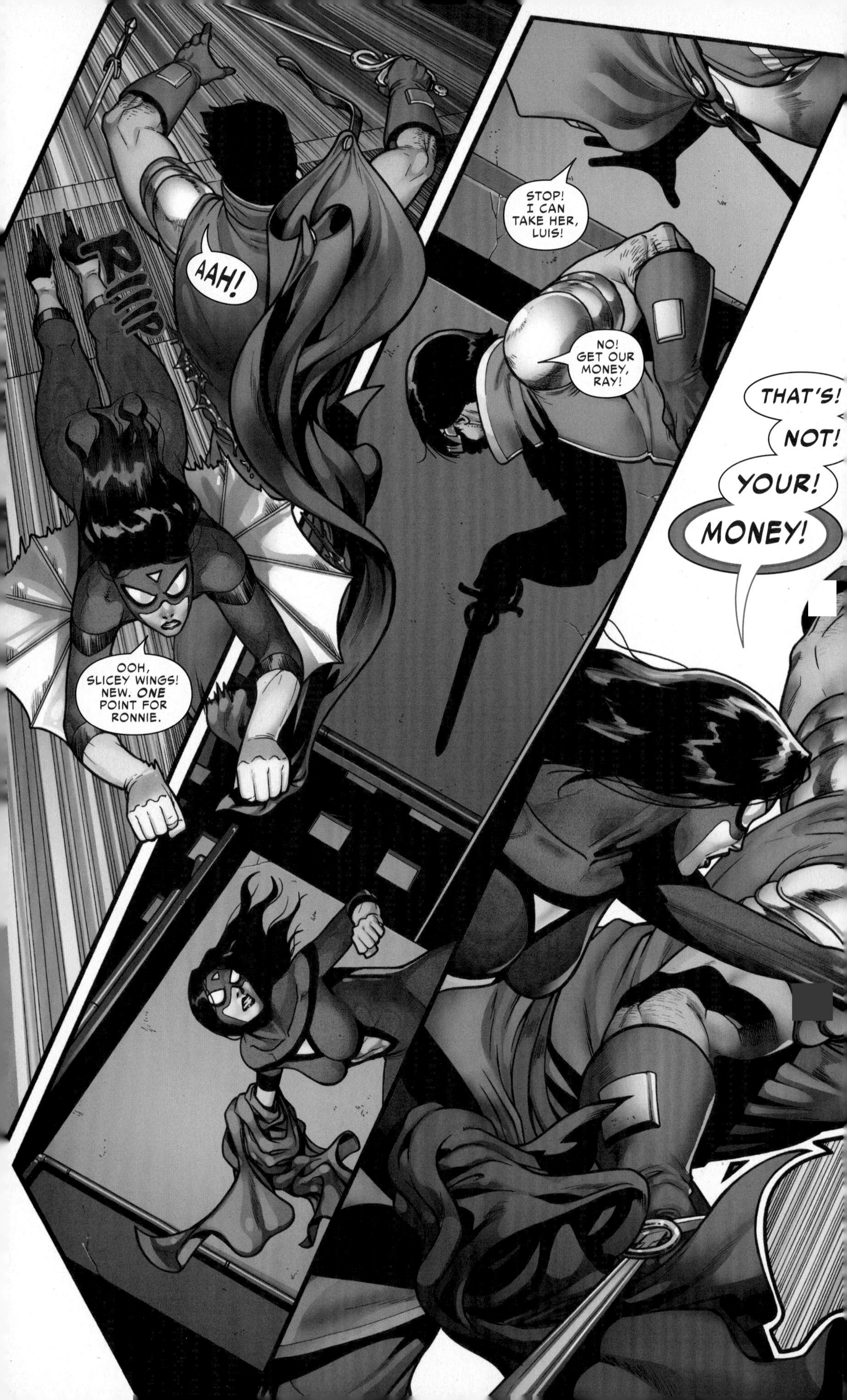
RIIIP
AAH!
OOH, SLICEY WINGS! NEW. ONE POINT FOR RONNIE.
STOP! I CAN TAKE HER, LUIS!
NO! GET OUR MONEY, RAY!
THAT'S! NOT! YOUR! MONEY!

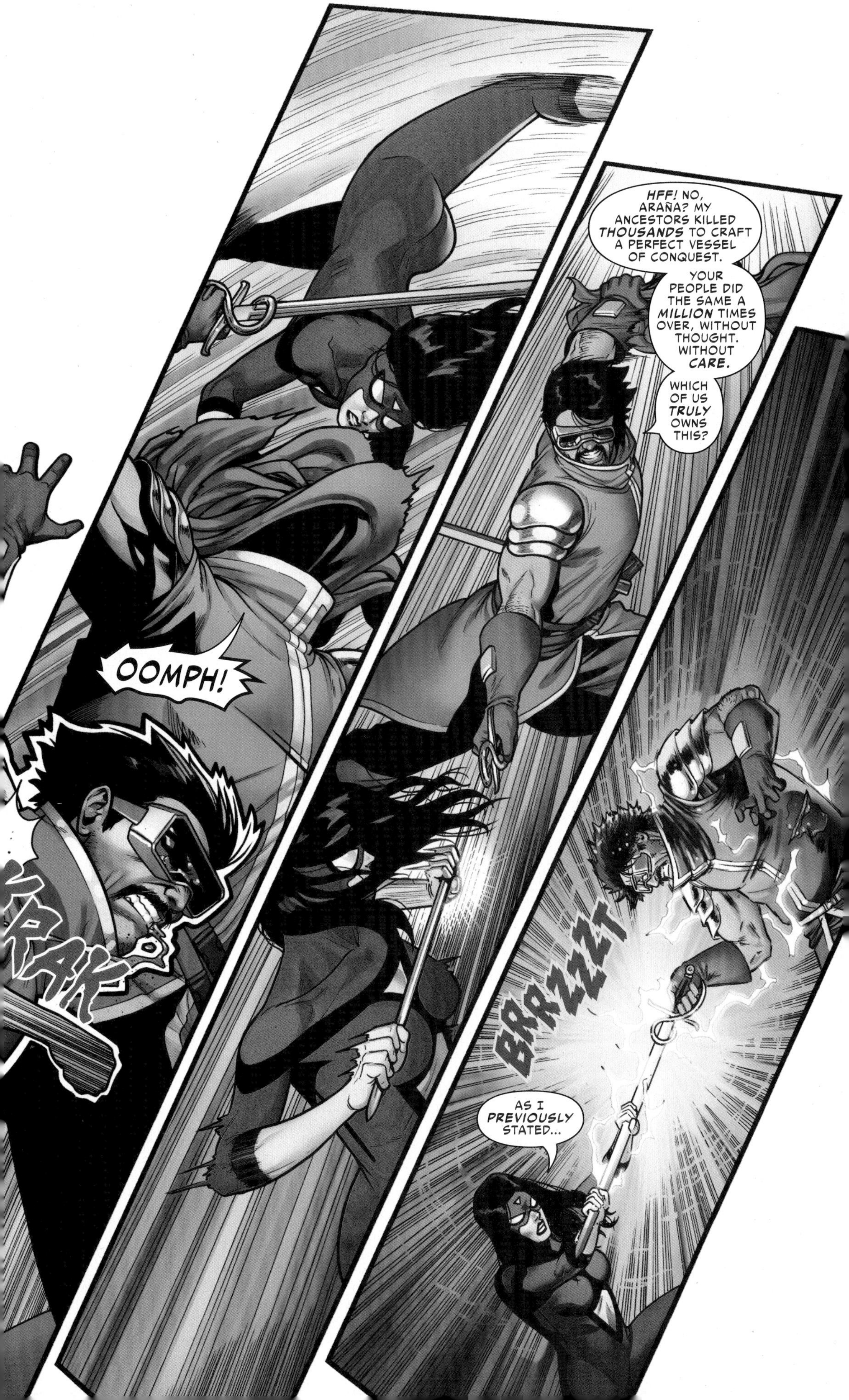
OOMPH!
KRAK
HFF! NO, ARAÑA? MY ANCESTORS KILLED THOUSANDS TO CRAFT A PERFECT VESSEL OF CONQUEST.
YOUR PEOPLE DID THE SAME A MILLION TIMES OVER, WITHOUT THOUGHT. WITHOUT CARE.
WHICH OF US TRULY OWNS THIS?
BRRZZZT
AS I PREVIOUSLY STATED...

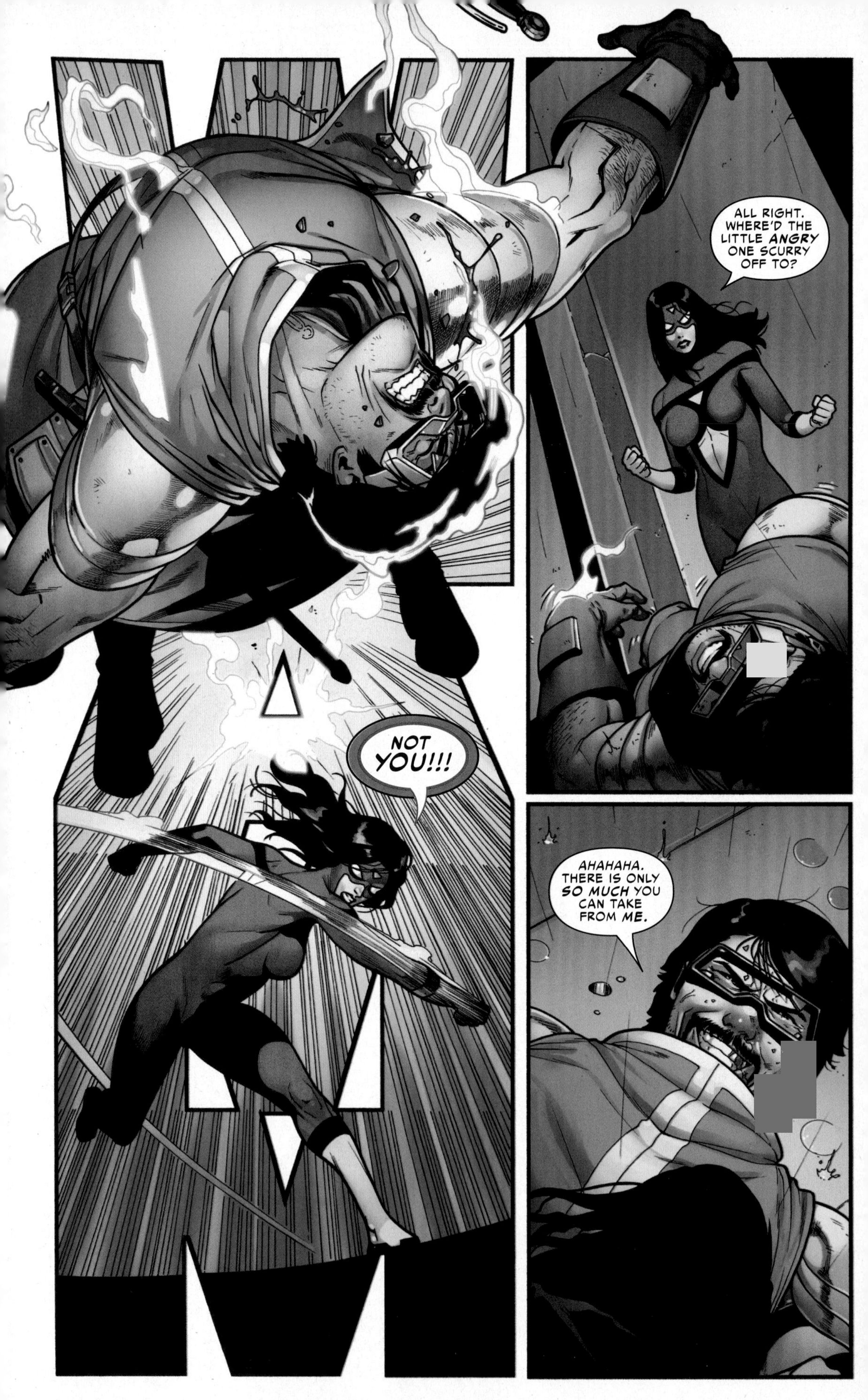
NOT YOU!!!
ALL RIGHT. WHERE'D THE LITTLE ANGRY ONE SCURRY OFF TO?
AHAHAHA. THERE IS ONLY SO MUCH YOU CAN TAKE FROM ME.

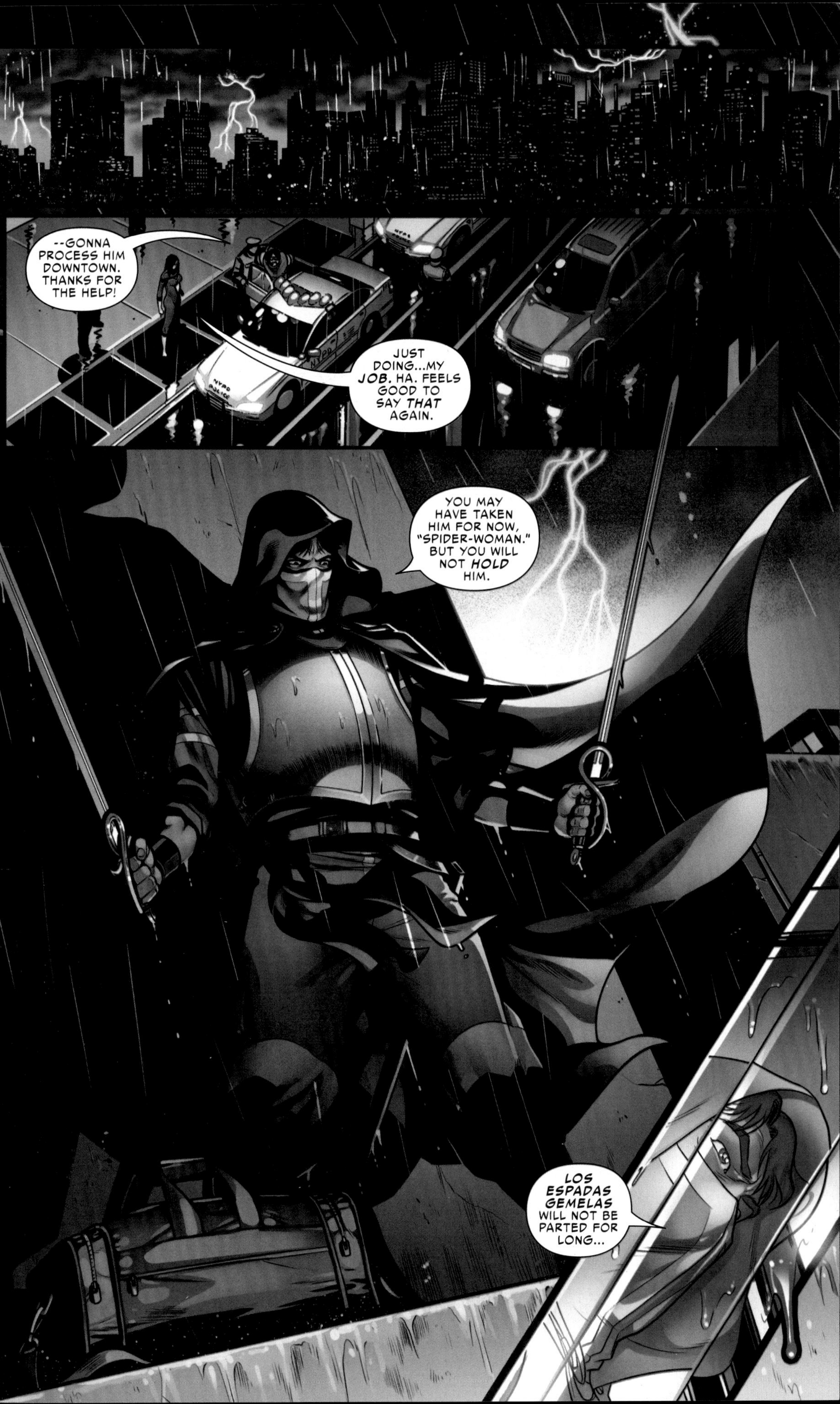
--GONNA PROCESS HIM DOWNTOWN. THANKS FOR THE HELP!
JUST DOING...MY JOB. HA. FEELS GOOD TO SAY THAT AGAIN.
YOU MAY HAVE TAKEN HIM FOR NOW, "SPIDER-WOMAN." BUT YOU WILL NOT HOLD HIM.
LOS ESPADAS GEMELAS WILL NOT BE PARTED FOR LONG...

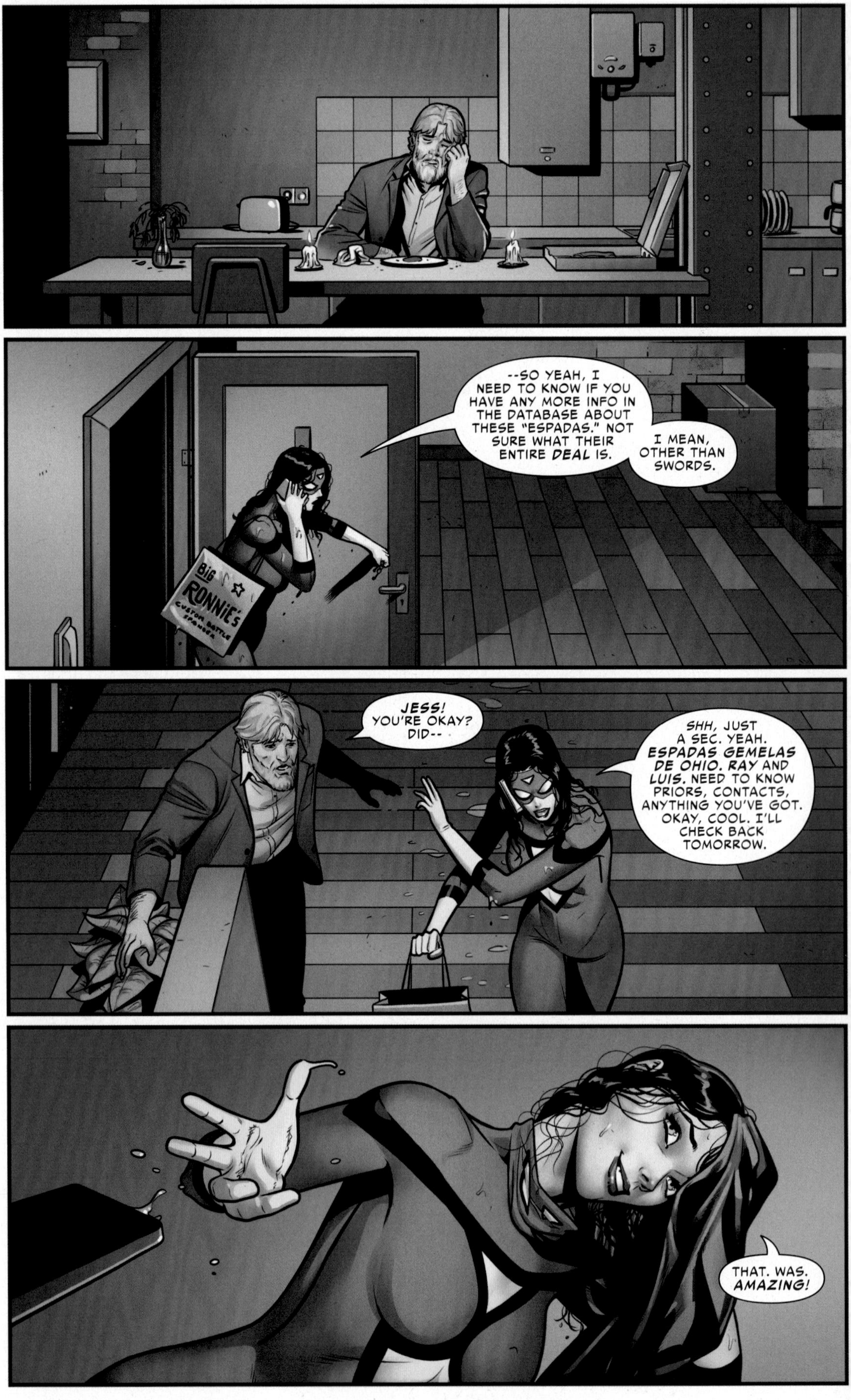
--SO YEAH, I NEED TO KNOW IF YOU HAVE ANY MORE INFO IN THE DATABASE ABOUT THESE "ESPADAS." NOT SURE WHAT THEIR ENTIRE *DEAL* IS.
I MEAN, OTHER THAN SWORDS.
BIG RONNIE'S
JESS! YOU'RE OKAY? DID--
SHH, JUST A SEC. YEAH. ***ESPADAS GEMELAS DE OHIO. RAY*** AND ***LUIS.*** NEED TO KNOW PRIORS, CONTACTS, ANYTHING YOU'VE GOT. OKAY, COOL. I'LL CHECK BACK TOMORROW.
THAT. WAS. ***AMAZING!***

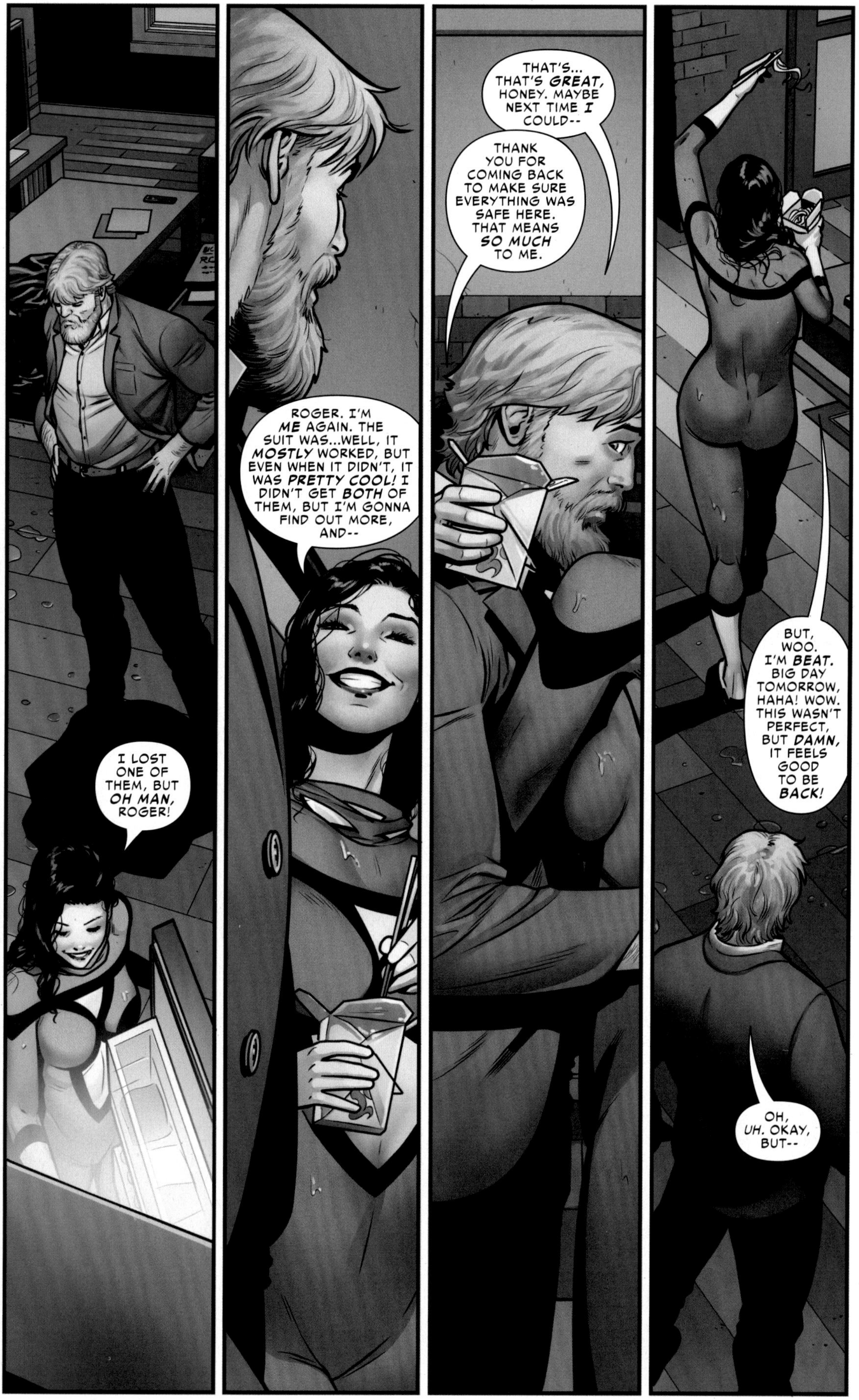
I LOST ONE OF THEM, BUT OH MAN, ROGER!
ROGER. I'M ME AGAIN. THE SUIT WAS...WELL, IT MOSTLY WORKED, BUT EVEN WHEN IT DIDN'T, IT WAS PRETTY COOL! I DIDN'T GET BOTH OF THEM, BUT I'M GONNA FIND OUT MORE, AND--
THAT'S... THAT'S GREAT, HONEY. MAYBE NEXT TIME I COULD--
THANK YOU FOR COMING BACK TO MAKE SURE EVERYTHING WAS SAFE HERE. THAT MEANS SO MUCH TO ME.
BUT, WOO. I'M BEAT. BIG DAY TOMORROW, HAHA! WOW. THIS WASN'T PERFECT, BUT DAMN, IT FEELS GOOD TO BE BACK!
OH, UH. OKAY, BUT--

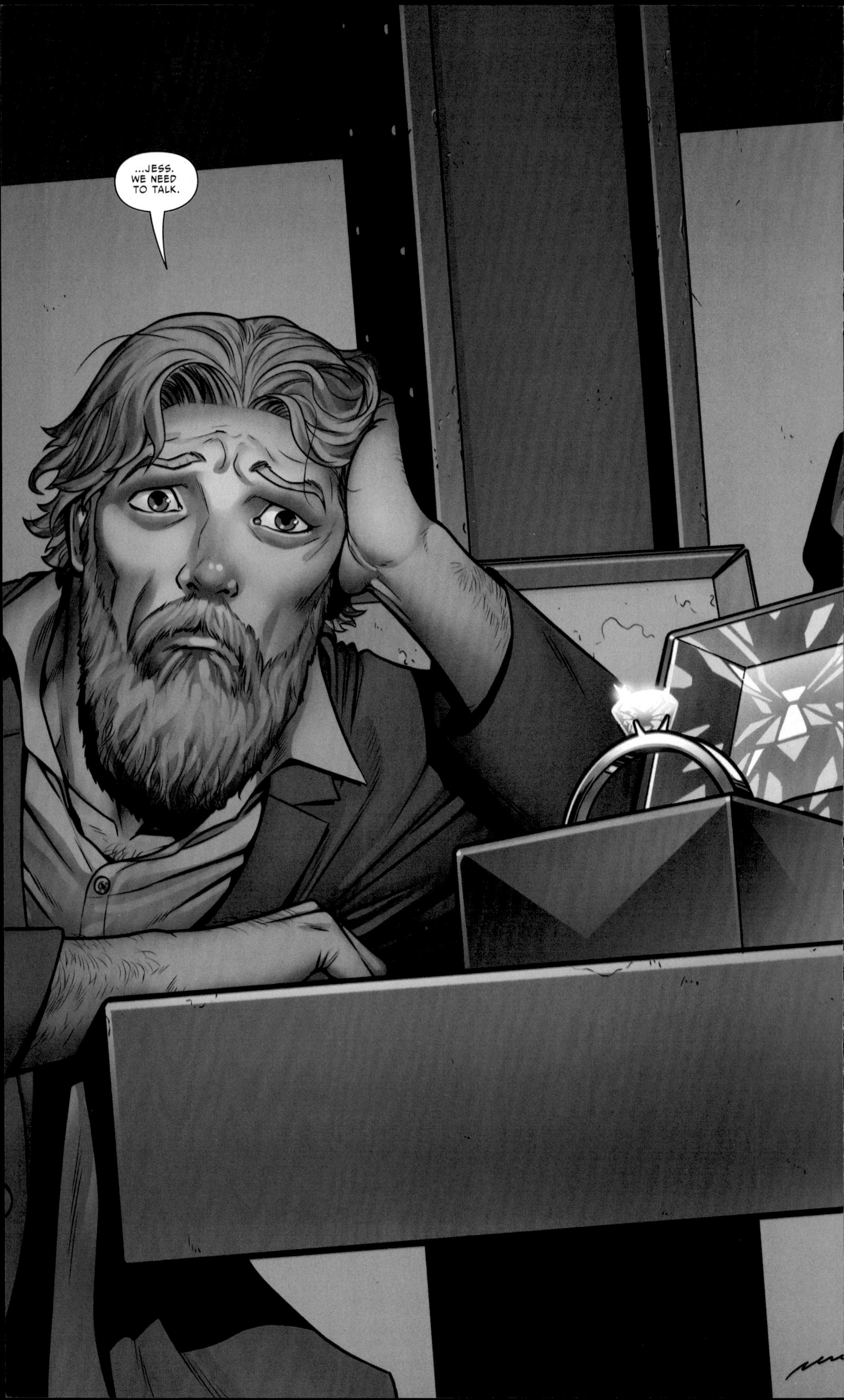
...JESS. WE NEED TO TALK.

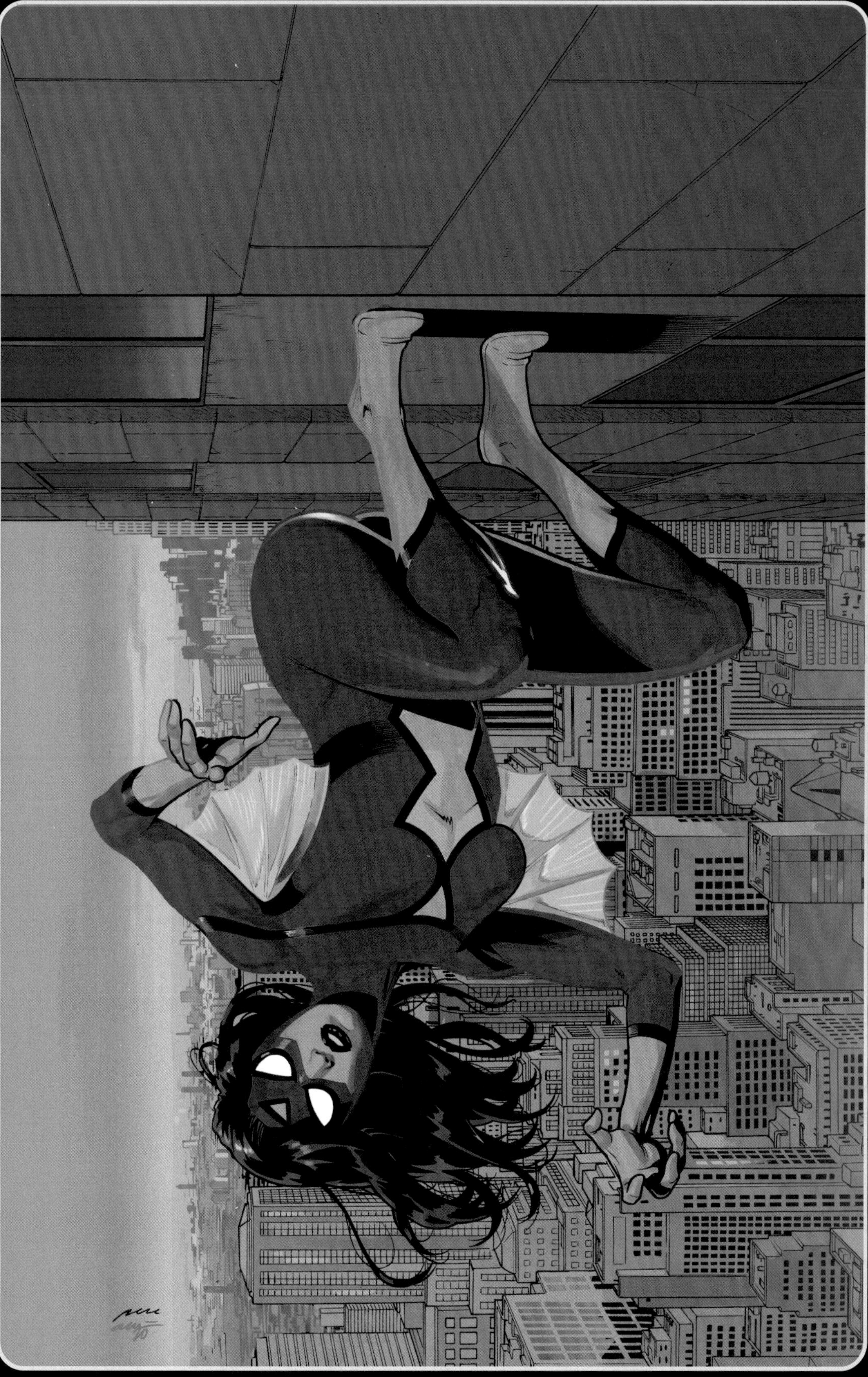

#11 VARIANT BY

PERE PÉREZ & DANIEL ACUÑA

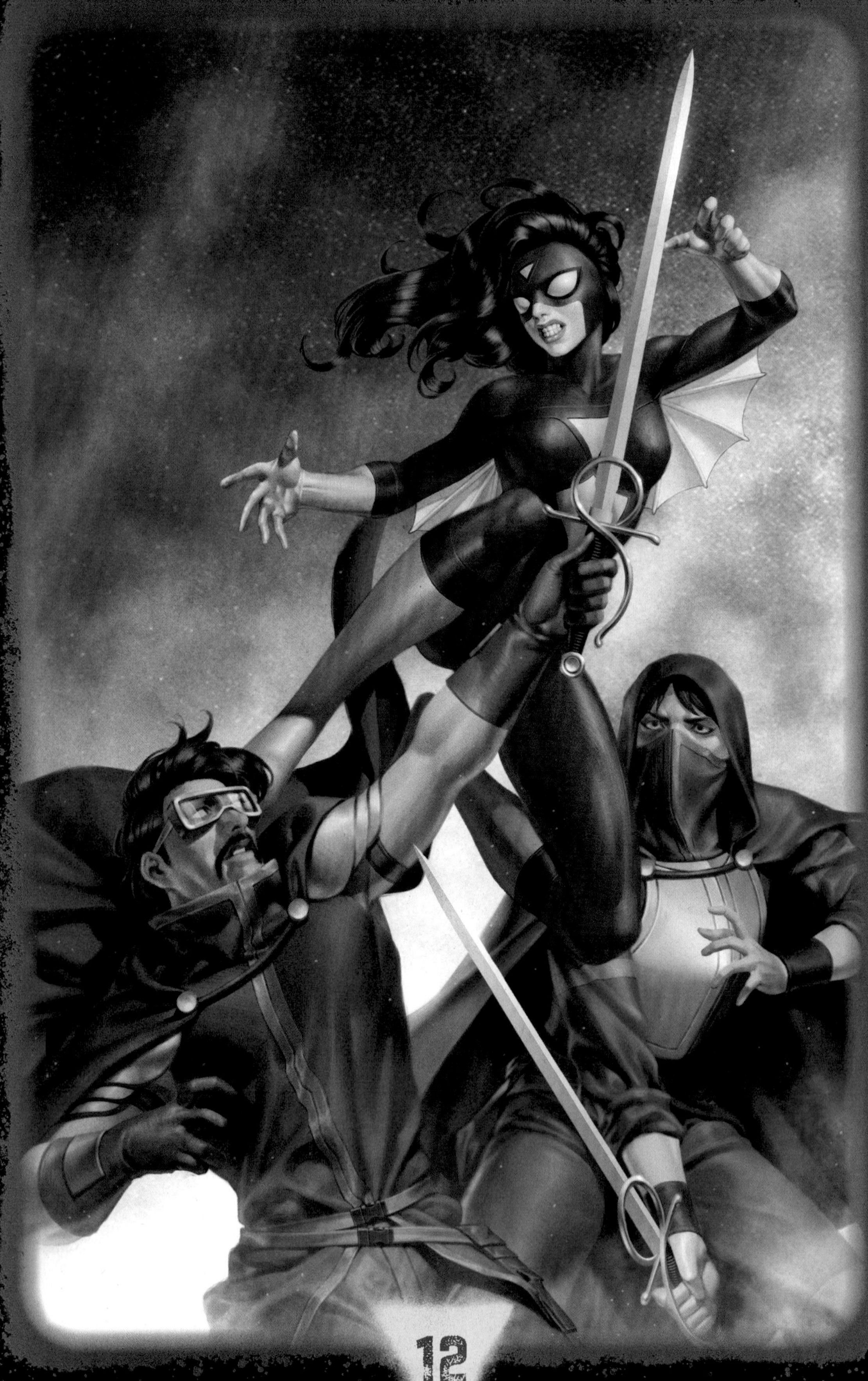

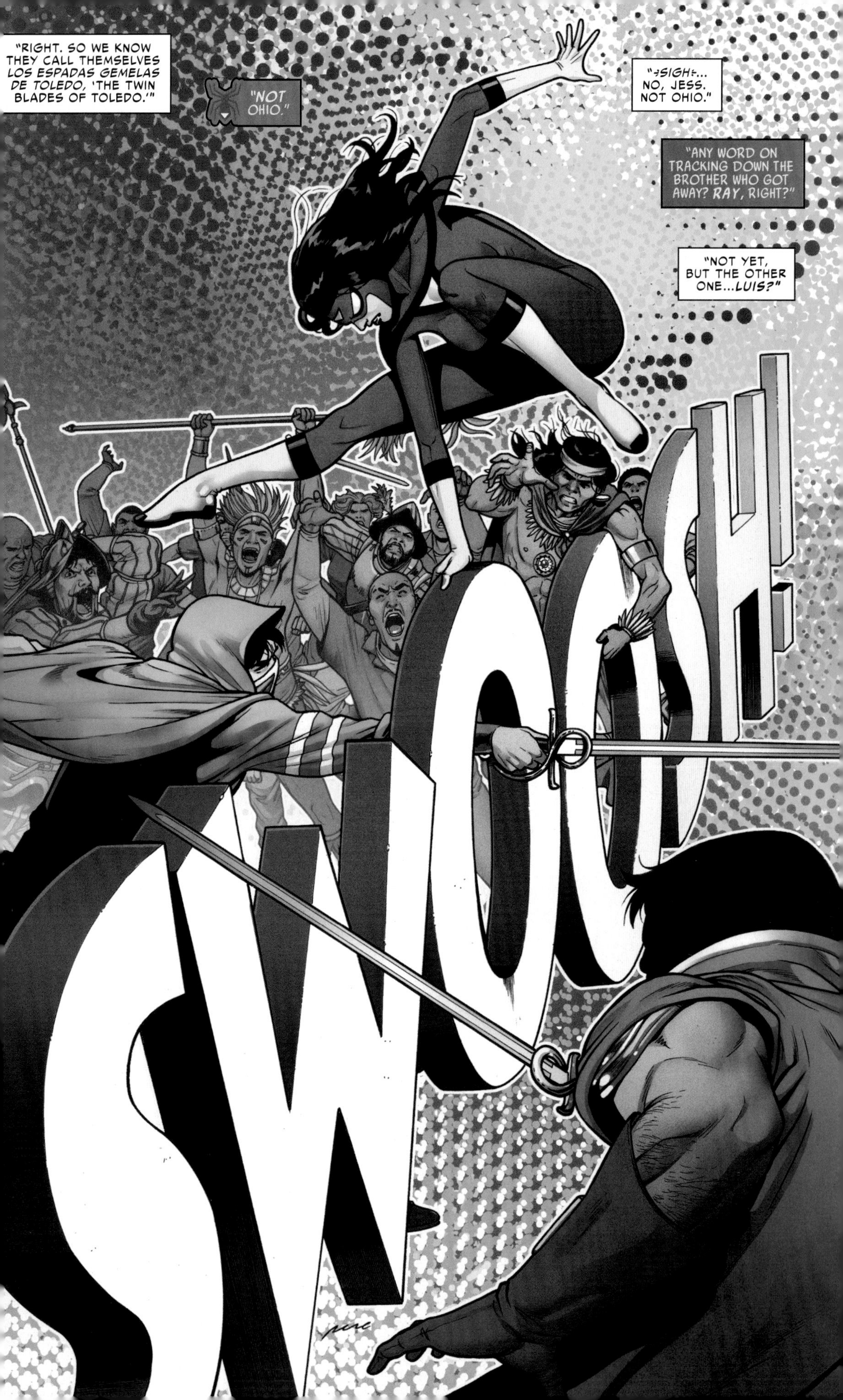
"RIGHT. SO WE KNOW THEY CALL THEMSELVES LOS ESPADAS GEMELAS DE TOLEDO, 'THE TWIN BLADES OF TOLEDO.'"
"NOT OHIO."
"*SIGH*... NO, JESS. NOT OHIO."
"ANY WORD ON TRACKING DOWN THE BROTHER WHO GOT AWAY? RAY, RIGHT?"
"NOT YET, BUT THE OTHER ONE...LUIS?"
SWOOSH

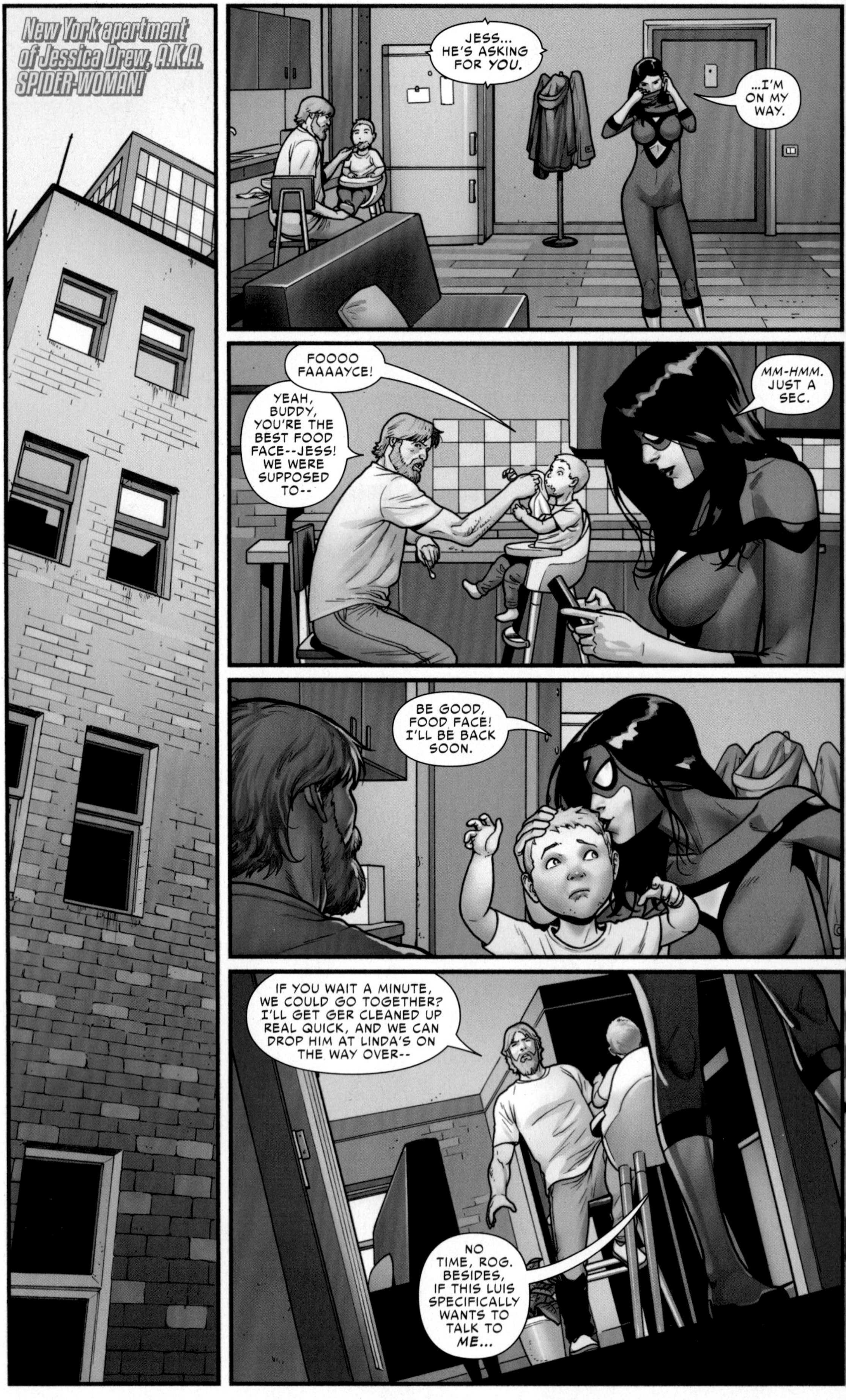
New York apartment of Jessica Drew, A.K.A. SPIDER-WOMAN!
JESS... HE'S ASKING FOR YOU.
...I'M ON MY WAY.
FOOOO FAAAAYCE!
YEAH, BUDDY, YOU'RE THE BEST FOOD FACE--JESS! WE WERE SUPPOSED TO--
MM-HMM. JUST A SEC.
BE GOOD, FOOD FACE! I'LL BE BACK SOON.
IF YOU WAIT A MINUTE, WE COULD GO TOGETHER? I'LL GET GER CLEANED UP REAL QUICK, AND WE CAN DROP HIM AT LINDA'S ON THE WAY OVER--
NO TIME, ROG. BESIDES, IF THIS LUIS SPECIFICALLY WANTS TO TALK TO ME...

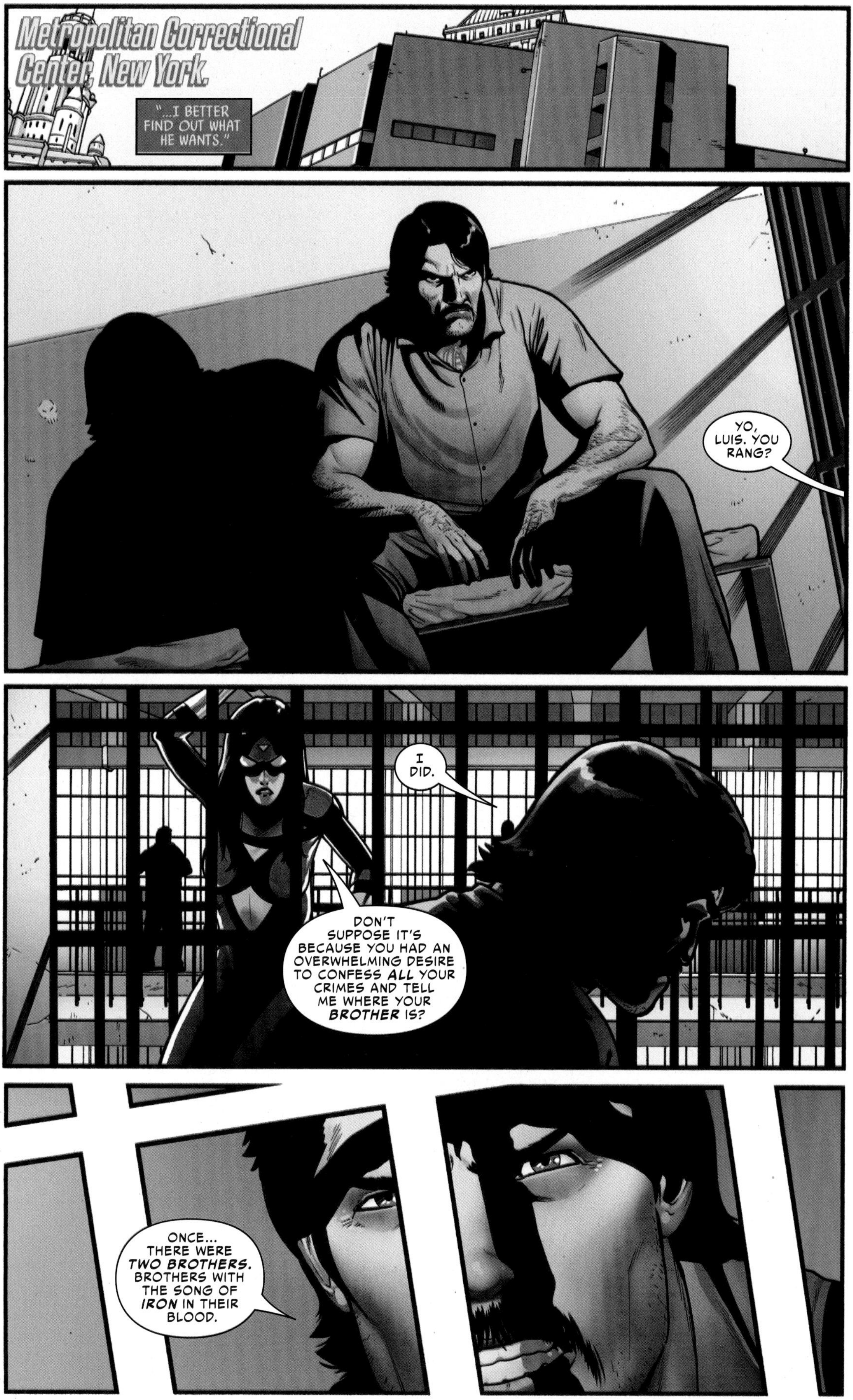
Metropolitan Correctional Center, New York.
"...I BETTER FIND OUT WHAT HE WANTS."
YO, LUIS. YOU RANG?
I DID.
DON'T SUPPOSE IT'S BECAUSE YOU HAD AN OVERWHELMING DESIRE TO CONFESS ALL YOUR CRIMES AND TELL ME WHERE YOUR BROTHER IS?
ONCE... THERE WERE TWO BROTHERS. BROTHERS WITH THE SONG OF IRON IN THEIR BLOOD.

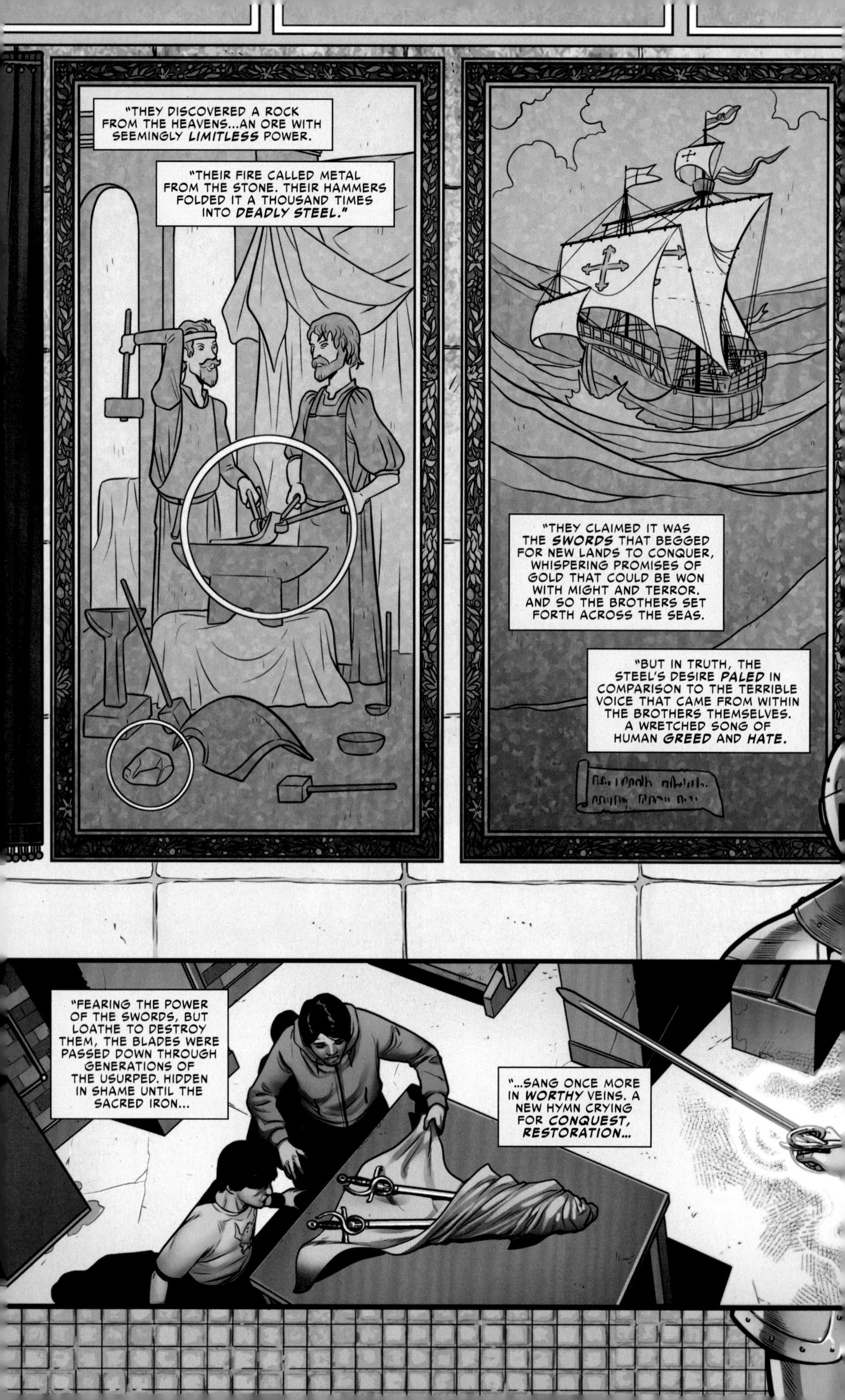
"THEY DISCOVERED A ROCK FROM THE HEAVENS...AN ORE WITH SEEMINGLY LIMITLESS POWER.
"THEIR FIRE CALLED METAL FROM THE STONE. THEIR HAMMERS FOLDED IT A THOUSAND TIMES INTO DEADLY STEEL."
"THEY CLAIMED IT WAS THE SWORDS THAT BEGGED FOR NEW LANDS TO CONQUER, WHISPERING PROMISES OF GOLD THAT COULD BE WON WITH MIGHT AND TERROR. AND SO THE BROTHERS SET FORTH ACROSS THE SEAS.
"BUT IN TRUTH, THE STEEL'S DESIRE PALED IN COMPARISON TO THE TERRIBLE VOICE THAT CAME FROM WITHIN THE BROTHERS THEMSELVES. A WRETCHED SONG OF HUMAN GREED AND HATE.
"FEARING THE POWER OF THE SWORDS, BUT LOATHE TO DESTROY THEM, THE BLADES WERE PASSED DOWN THROUGH GENERATIONS OF THE USURPED. HIDDEN IN SHAME UNTIL THE SACRED IRON...
"...SANG ONCE MORE IN WORTHY VEINS. A NEW HYMN CRYING FOR CONQUEST, RESTORATION...

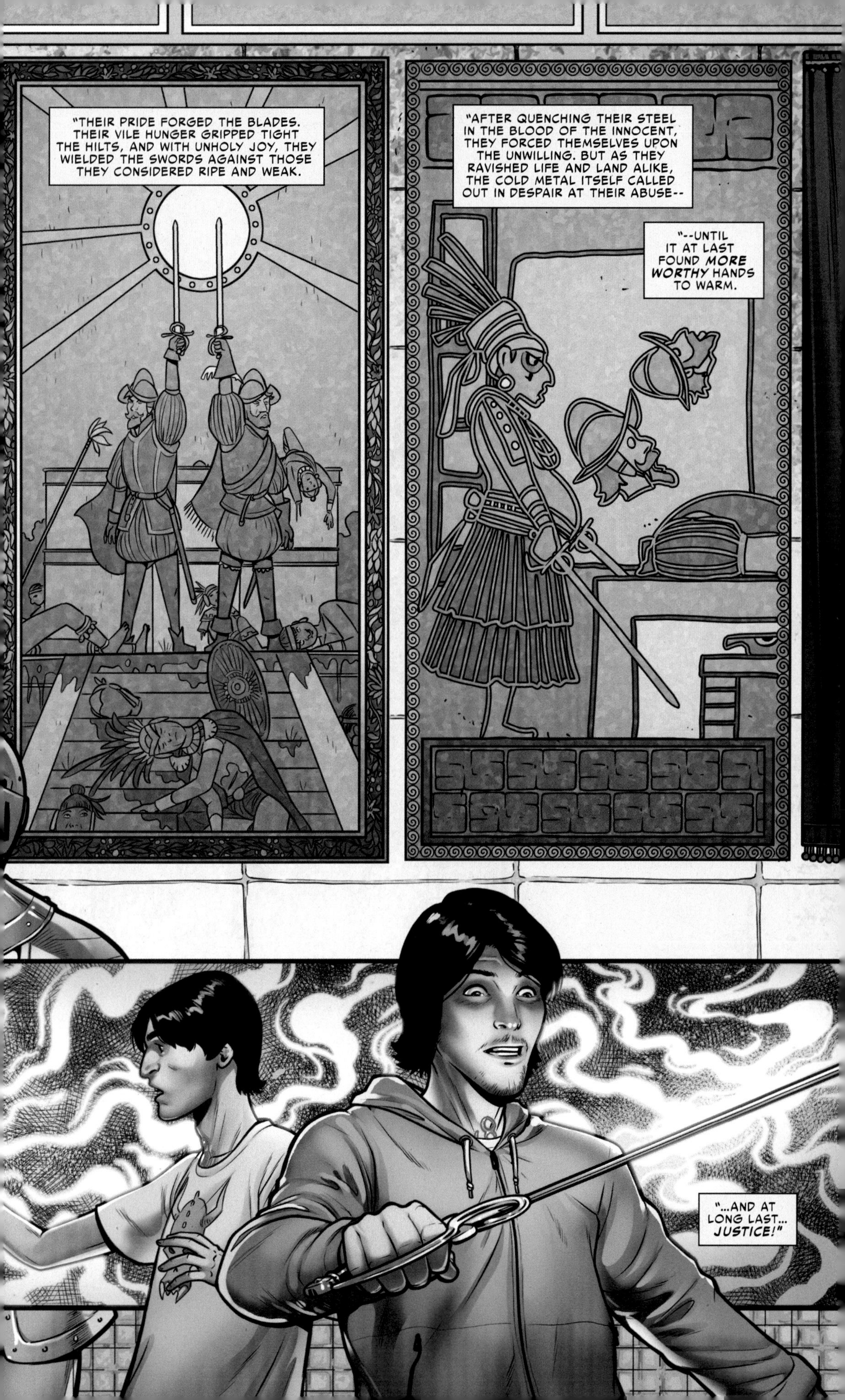
"THEIR PRIDE FORGED THE BLADES. THEIR VILE HUNGER GRIPPED TIGHT THE HILTS, AND WITH UNHOLY JOY, THEY WIELDED THE SWORDS AGAINST THOSE THEY CONSIDERED RIPE AND WEAK.
"AFTER QUENCHING THEIR STEEL IN THE BLOOD OF THE INNOCENT, THEY FORCED THEMSELVES UPON THE UNWILLING. BUT AS THEY RAVISHED LIFE AND LAND ALIKE, THE COLD METAL ITSELF CALLED OUT IN DESPAIR AT THEIR ABUSE--
"--UNTIL IT AT LAST FOUND ***MORE WORTHY*** HANDS TO WARM.
"...AND AT LONG LAST... ***JUSTICE!***"

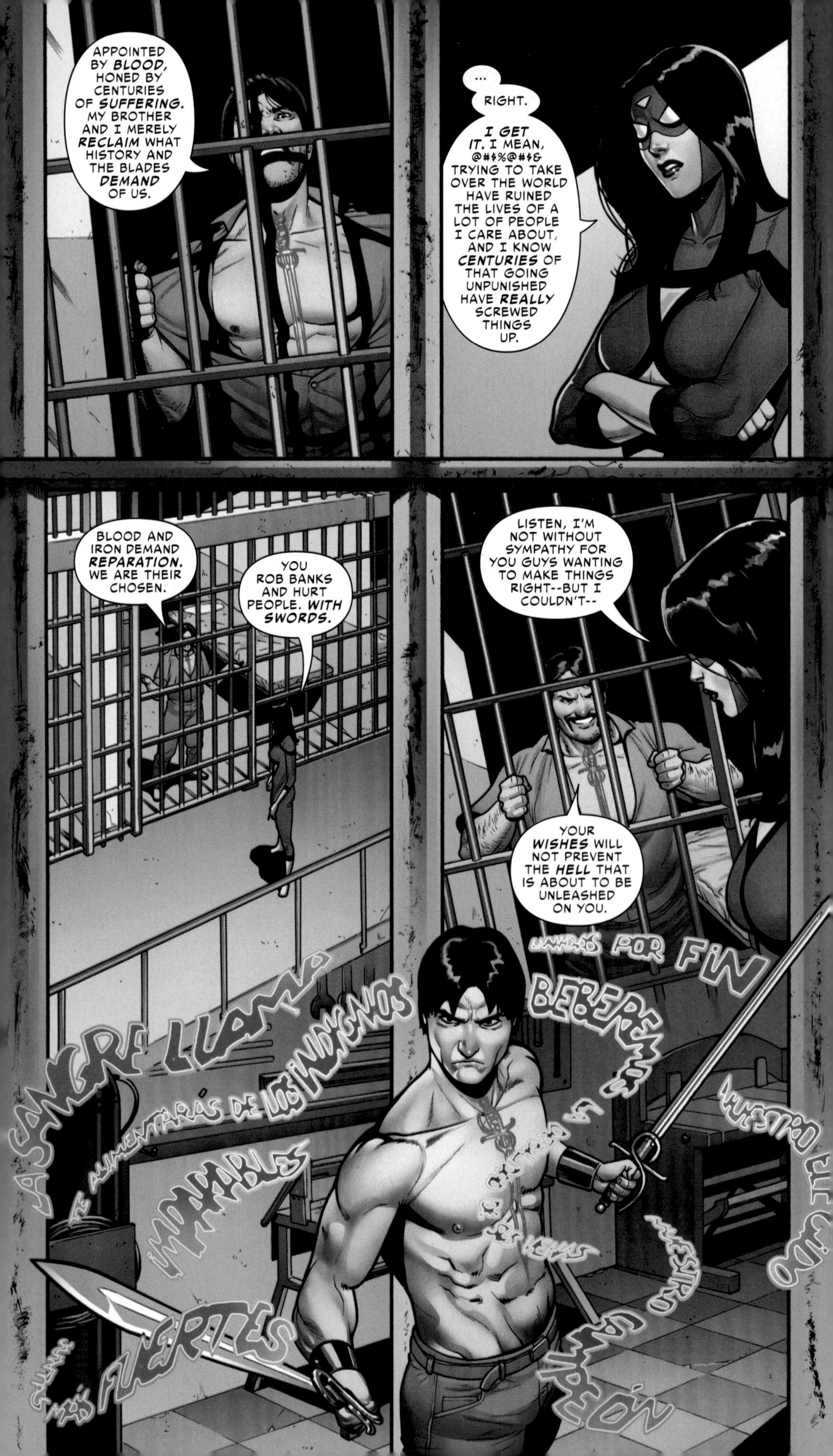
APPOINTED BY BLOOD, HONED BY CENTURIES OF SUFFERING. MY BROTHER AND I MERELY RECLAIM WHAT HISTORY AND THE BLADES DEMAND OF US.
...
RIGHT.
I GET IT. I MEAN, @#$%@#$& TRYING TO TAKE OVER THE WORLD HAVE RUINED THE LIVES OF A LOT OF PEOPLE I CARE ABOUT, AND I KNOW CENTURIES OF THAT GOING UNPUNISHED HAVE REALLY SCREWED THINGS UP.
BLOOD AND IRON DEMAND REPARATION. WE ARE THEIR CHOSEN.
YOU ROB BANKS AND HURT PEOPLE. WITH SWORDS.
LISTEN, I'M NOT WITHOUT SYMPATHY FOR YOU GUYS WANTING TO MAKE THINGS RIGHT--BUT I COULDN'T--
YOUR WISHES WILL NOT PREVENT THE HELL THAT IS ABOUT TO BE UNLEASHED ON YOU.

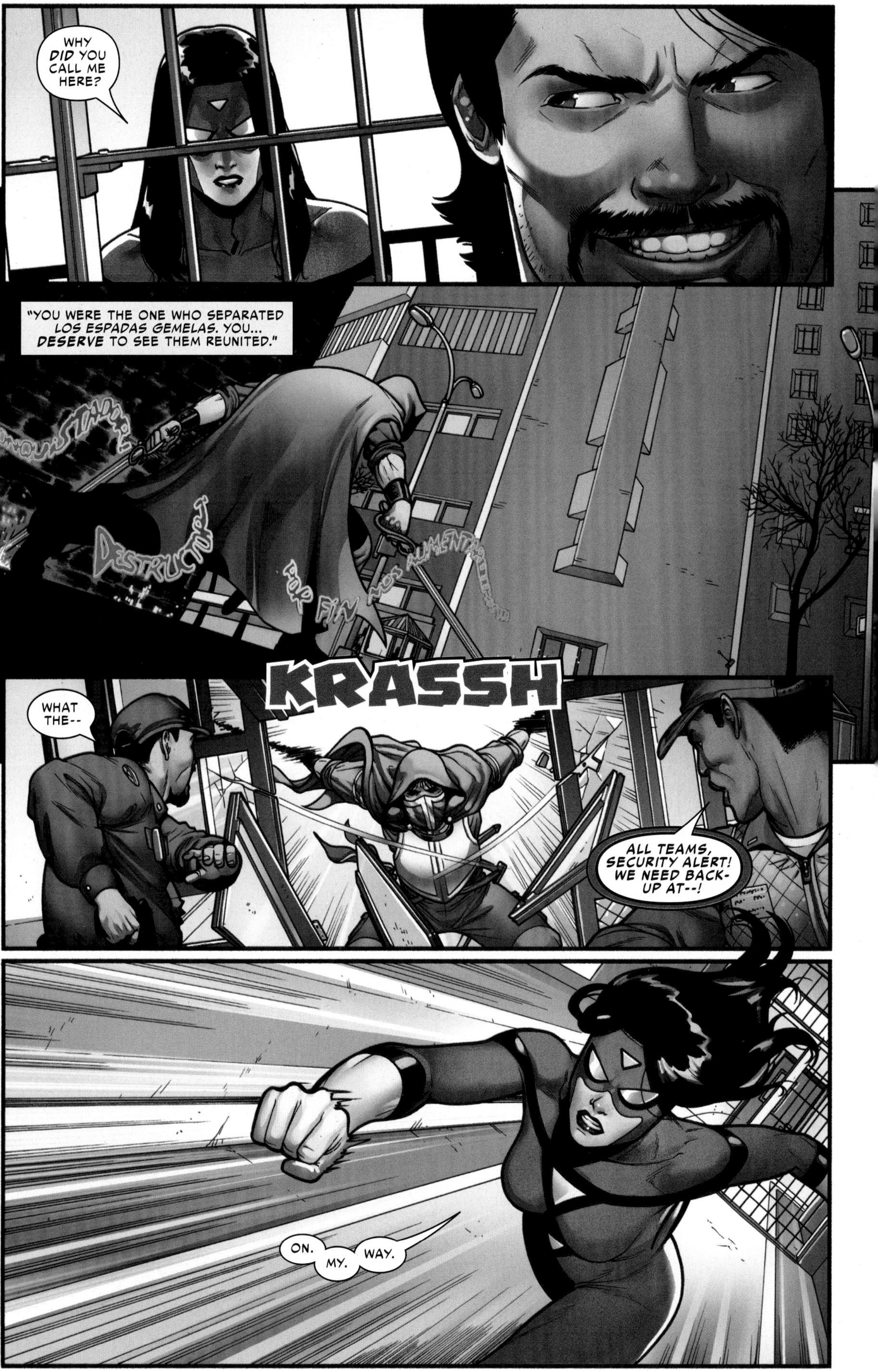
WHY *DID* YOU CALL ME HERE?
"YOU WERE THE ONE WHO SEPARATED *LOS ESPADAS GEMELAS*. YOU... ***DESERVE*** TO SEE THEM REUNITED."
DESTRUCCIÓN
POR FIN
KRASSH
WHAT THE--
ALL TEAMS, SECURITY ALERT! WE NEED BACK-UP AT--!
ON.
MY.
WAY.

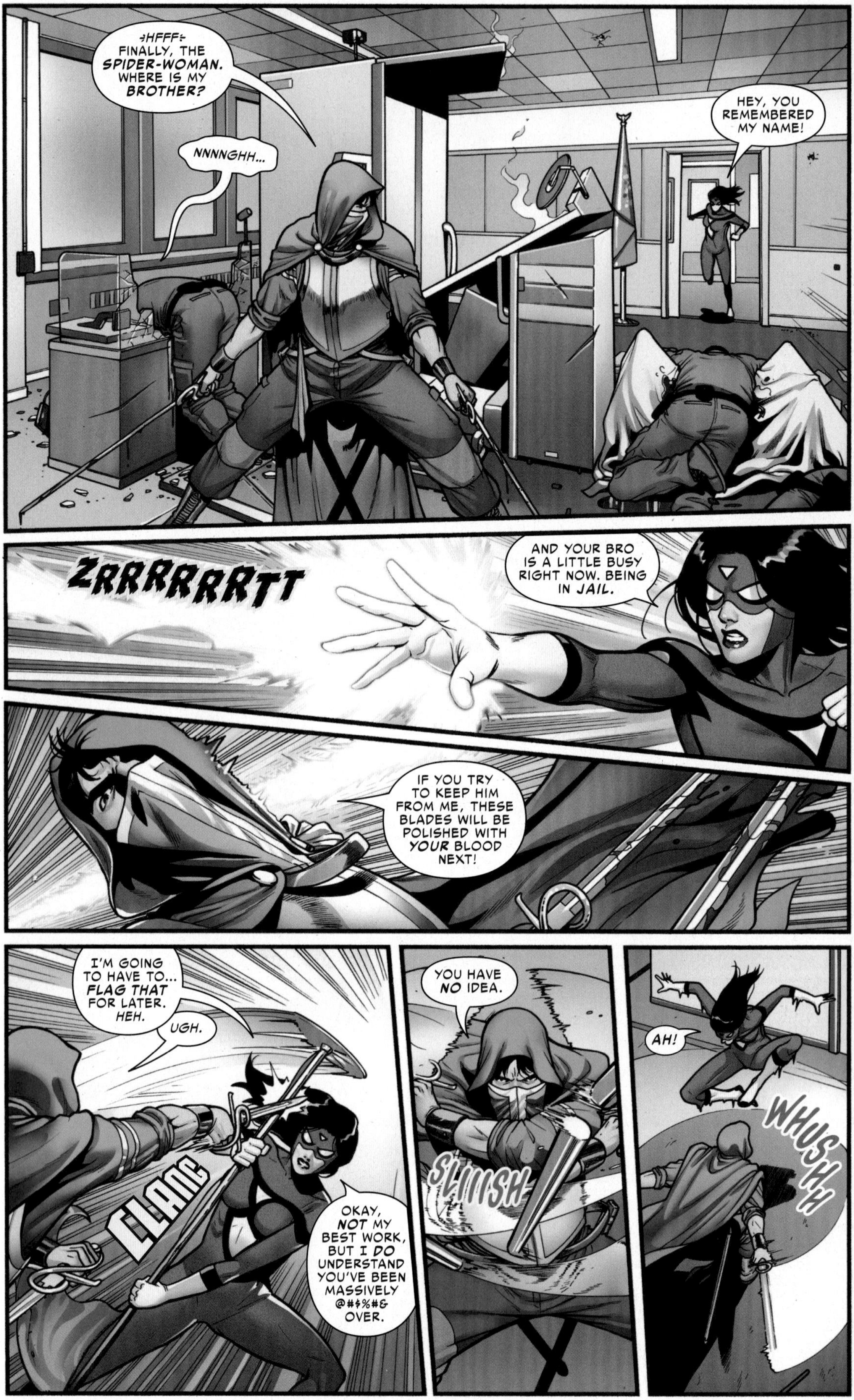
HFFF FINALLY, THE SPIDER-WOMAN. WHERE IS MY BROTHER?
NNNNGHH...
HEY, YOU REMEMBERED MY NAME!
ZRRRRRRRTT
AND YOUR BRO IS A LITTLE BUSY RIGHT NOW. BEING IN JAIL.
IF YOU TRY TO KEEP HIM FROM ME, THESE BLADES WILL BE POLISHED WITH YOUR BLOOD NEXT!
I'M GOING TO HAVE TO... FLAG THAT FOR LATER. HEH.
UGH.
CLANG
OKAY, NOT MY BEST WORK, BUT I DO UNDERSTAND YOU'VE BEEN MASSIVELY @#$%#& OVER.
YOU HAVE NO IDEA.
SLIIISH
AH!
WHUSHH

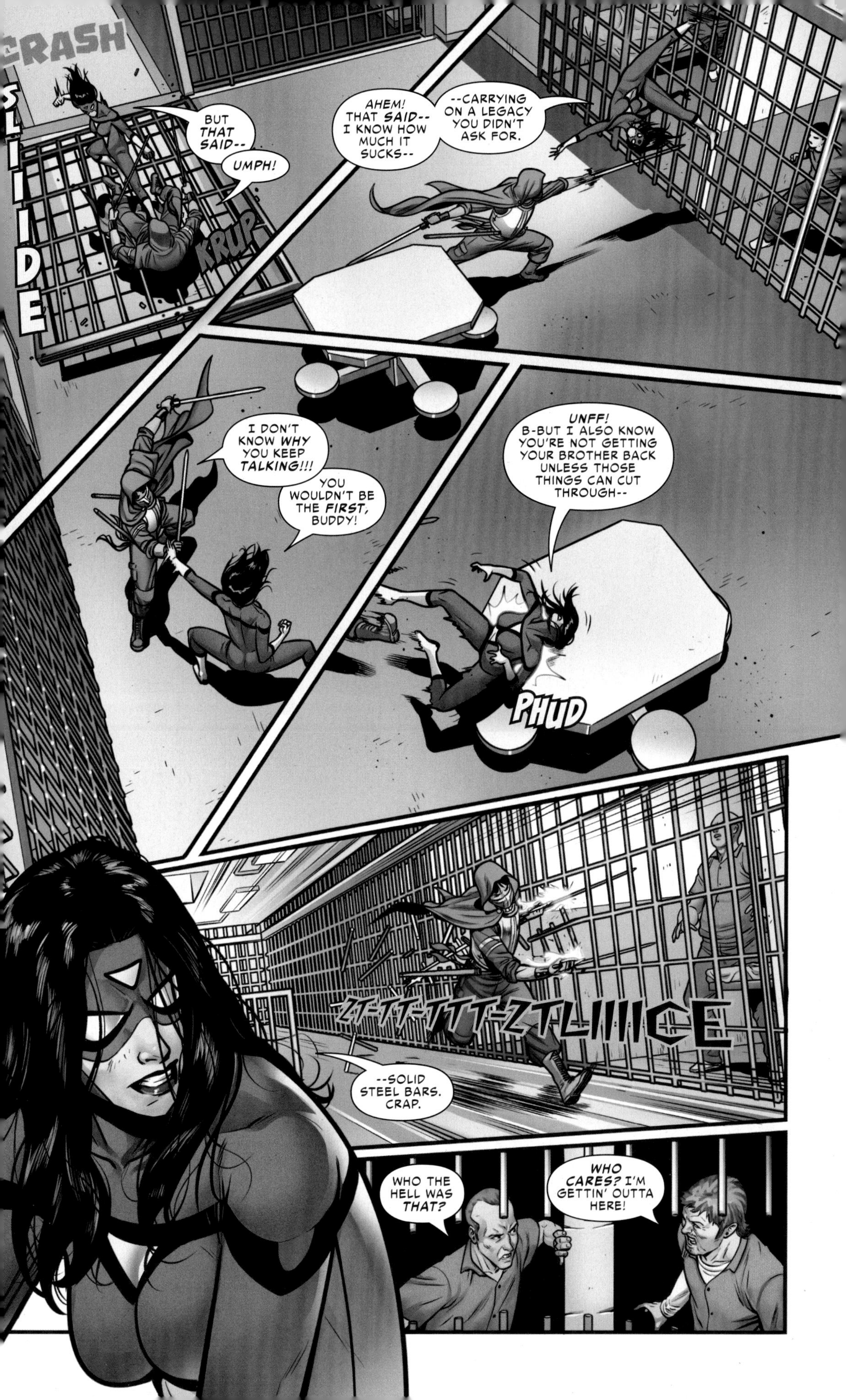
CRASH
SLIIIDE
BUT THAT SAID--
UMPH!
KRUP
AHEM! THAT SAID-- I KNOW HOW MUCH IT SUCKS--
--CARRYING ON A LEGACY YOU DIDN'T ASK FOR.
I DON'T KNOW WHY YOU KEEP TALKING!!!
YOU WOULDN'T BE THE FIRST, BUDDY!
UNFF! B-BUT I ALSO KNOW YOU'RE NOT GETTING YOUR BROTHER BACK UNLESS THOSE THINGS CAN CUT THROUGH--
PHUD
ZT-TT-TTT-ZTLIIIICE
--SOLID STEEL BARS. CRAP.
WHO THE HELL WAS THAT?
WHO CARES? I'M GETTIN' OUTTA HERE!

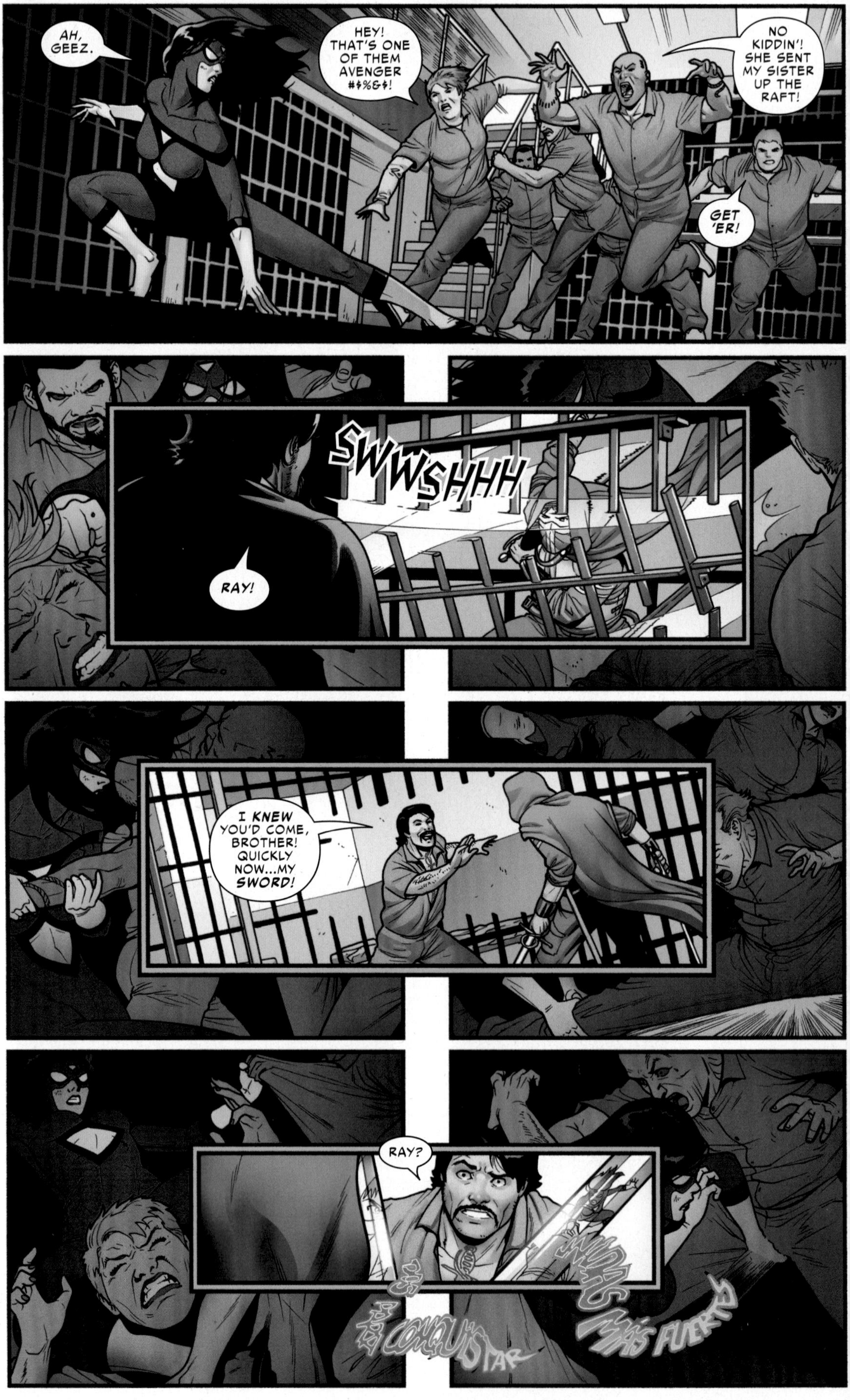
AH, GEEZ.
HEY! THAT'S ONE OF THEM AVENGER #$%&$!
NO KIDDIN'! SHE SENT MY SISTER UP THE RAFT!
GET 'ER!
SWWSHHH
RAY!
I KNEW YOU'D COME, BROTHER! QUICKLY NOW...MY SWORD!
RAY?
CONQUISTAR
MÁS FUERTES

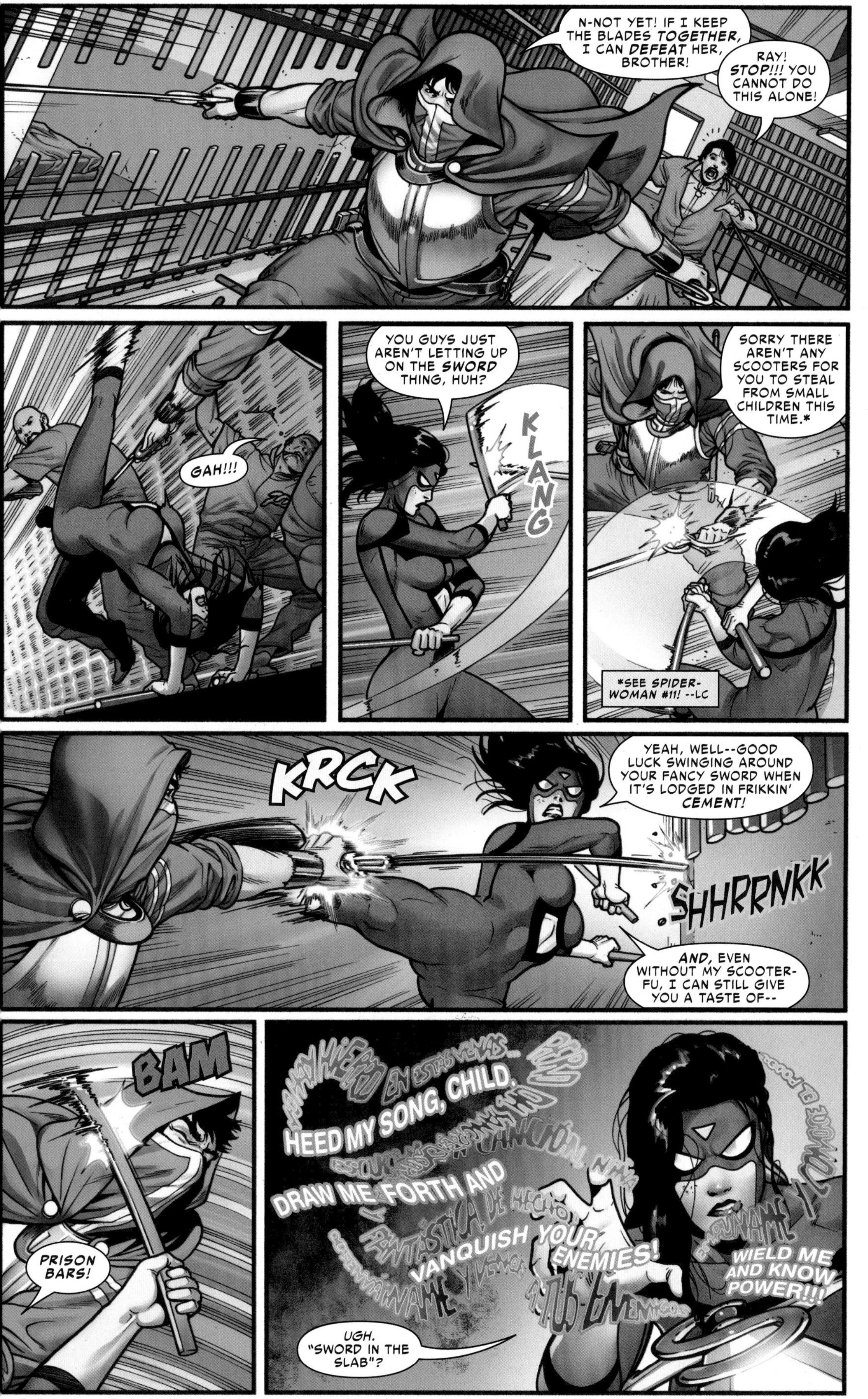
N-NOT YET! IF I KEEP THE BLADES TOGETHER, I CAN DEFEAT HER, BROTHER!
RAY! STOP!!! YOU CANNOT DO THIS ALONE!
GAH!!!
YOU GUYS JUST AREN'T LETTING UP ON THE SWORD THING, HUH?
KLANG
SORRY THERE AREN'T ANY SCOOTERS FOR YOU TO STEAL FROM SMALL CHILDREN THIS TIME.*
*SEE SPIDER-WOMAN #11! --LC
KRCK
YEAH, WELL--GOOD LUCK SWINGING AROUND YOUR FANCY SWORD WHEN IT'S LODGED IN FRIKKIN' CEMENT!
SHHRRNKK
AND, EVEN WITHOUT MY SCOOTER-FU, I CAN STILL GIVE YOU A TASTE OF--
BAM
PRISON BARS!
EN ESTAS VENAS...
HEED MY SONG, CHILD.
DRAW ME FORTH AND
VANQUISH YOUR ENEMIES!
WIELD ME AND KNOW POWER!!!
UGH. "SWORD IN THE SLAB"?

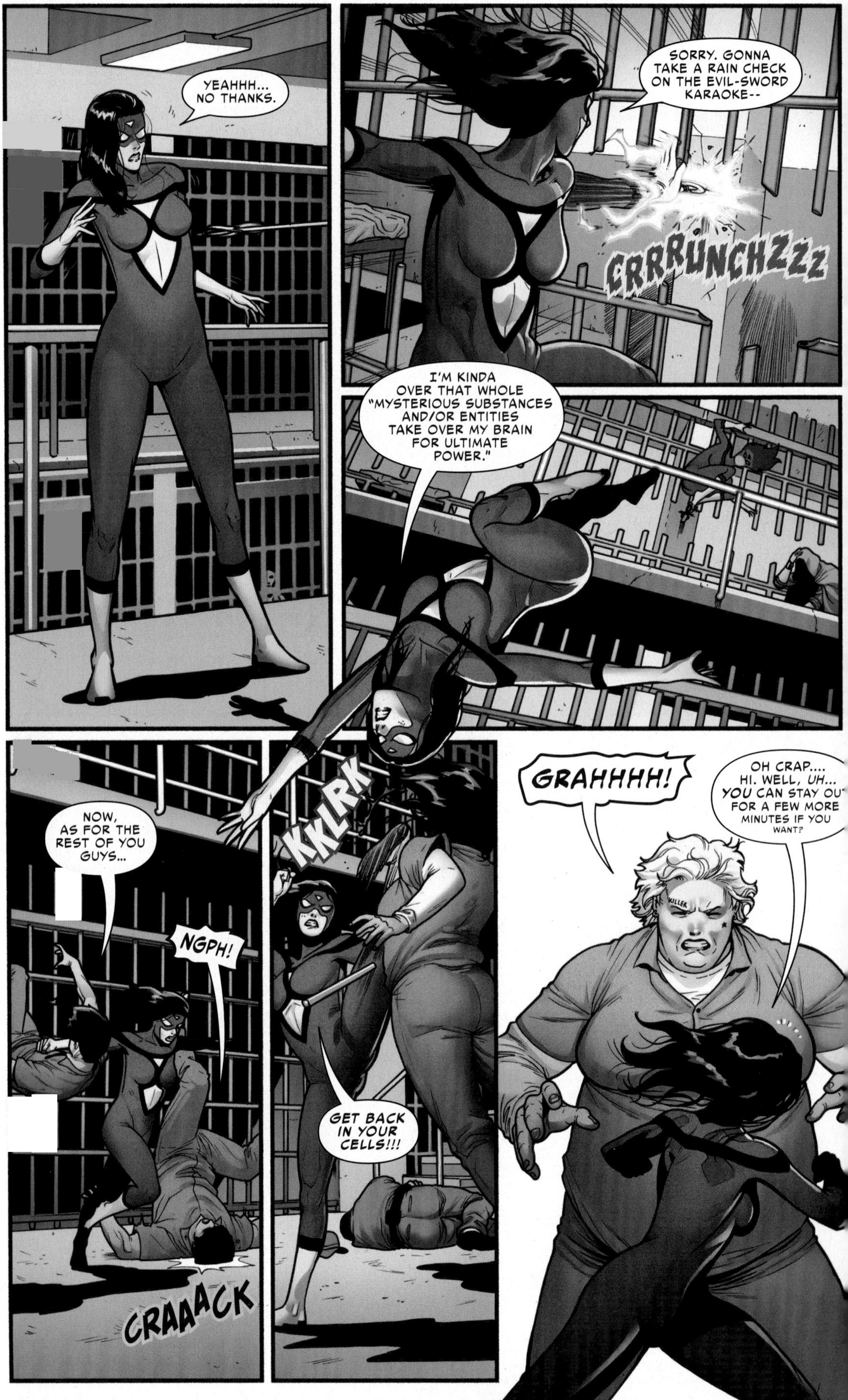
YEAHHH... NO THANKS.
SORRY. GONNA TAKE A RAIN CHECK ON THE EVIL-SWORD KARAOKE--
CRRRUNCHZZZ
I'M KINDA OVER THAT WHOLE "MYSTERIOUS SUBSTANCES AND/OR ENTITIES TAKE OVER MY BRAIN FOR ULTIMATE POWER."
NOW, AS FOR THE REST OF YOU GUYS...
NGPH!
CRAAACK
KKLRK
GET BACK IN YOUR CELLS!!!
GRAHHHH!
OH CRAP.... HI. WELL, UH... YOU CAN STAY OUT FOR A FEW MORE MINUTES IF YOU WANT?
KILLER

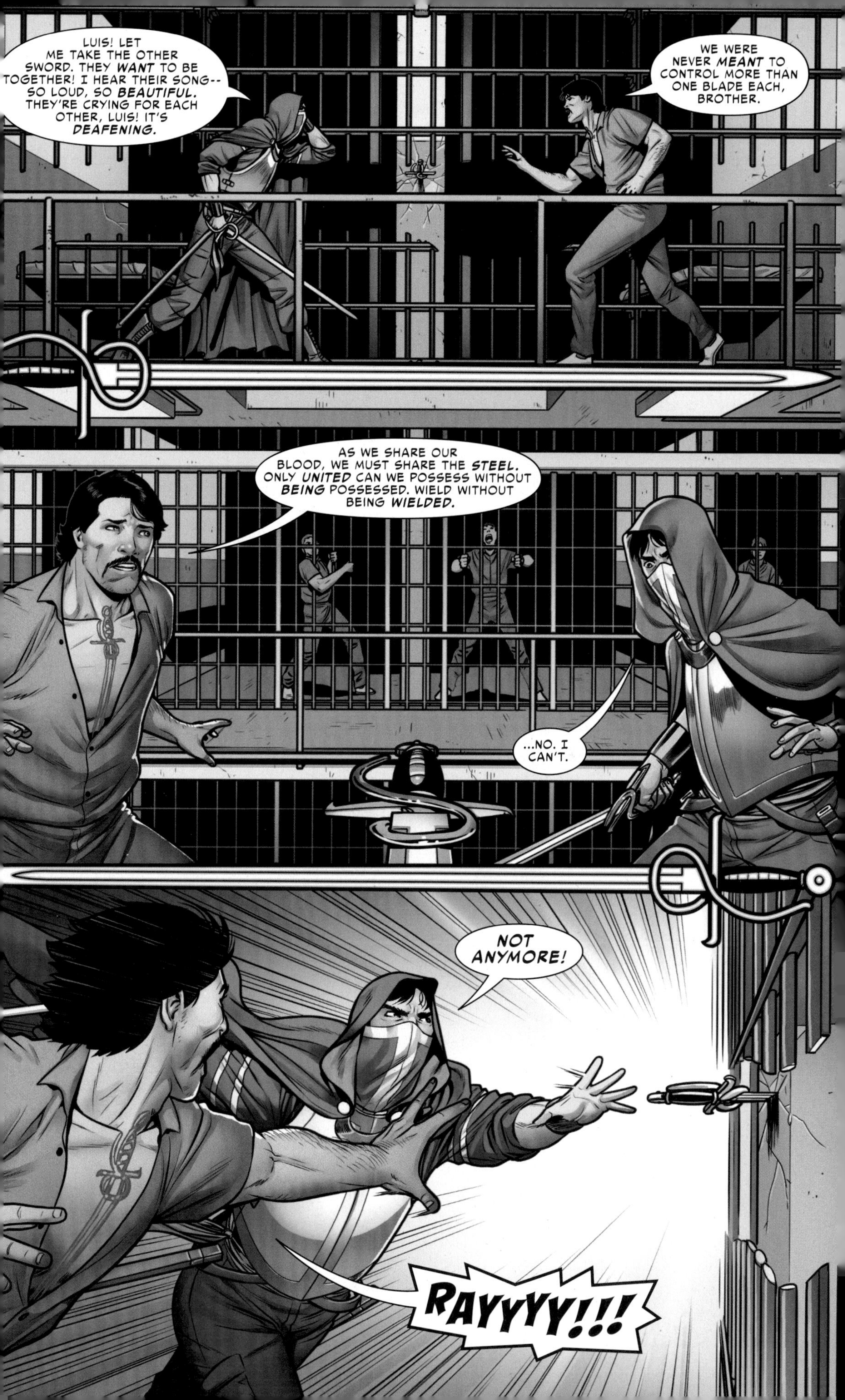

LUIS! LET ME TAKE THE OTHER SWORD. THEY *WANT* TO BE TOGETHER! I HEAR THEIR SONG-- SO LOUD, SO *BEAUTIFUL*. THEY'RE CRYING FOR EACH OTHER, LUIS! IT'S *DEAFENING*.
WE WERE NEVER *MEANT* TO CONTROL MORE THAN ONE BLADE EACH, BROTHER.
AS WE SHARE OUR BLOOD, WE MUST SHARE THE *STEEL*. ONLY *UNITED* CAN WE POSSESS WITHOUT *BEING* POSSESSED. WIELD WITHOUT BEING *WIELDED*.
...NO. I CAN'T.
NOT ANYMORE!
RAYYYY!!!

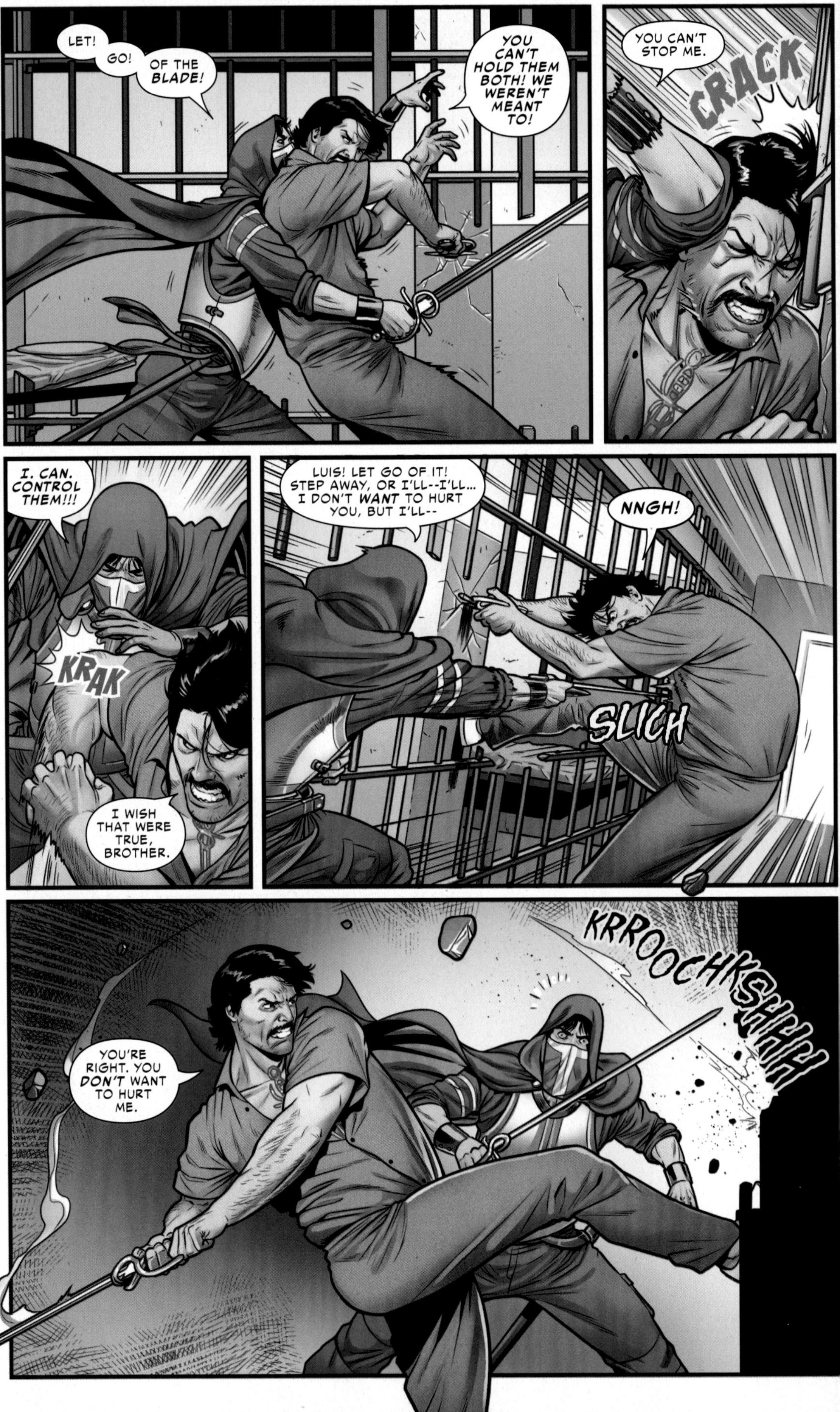
LET!
GO!
OF THE BLADE!
YOU CAN'T HOLD THEM BOTH! WE WEREN'T MEANT TO!
YOU CAN'T STOP ME.
CRACK
I. CAN. CONTROL THEM!!!
KRAK
I WISH THAT WERE TRUE, BROTHER.
LUIS! LET GO OF IT! STEP AWAY, OR I'LL--I'LL... I DON'T WANT TO HURT YOU, BUT I'LL--
NNGH!
SLICH
KRROOCHKSHHH
YOU'RE RIGHT. YOU DON'T WANT TO HURT ME.

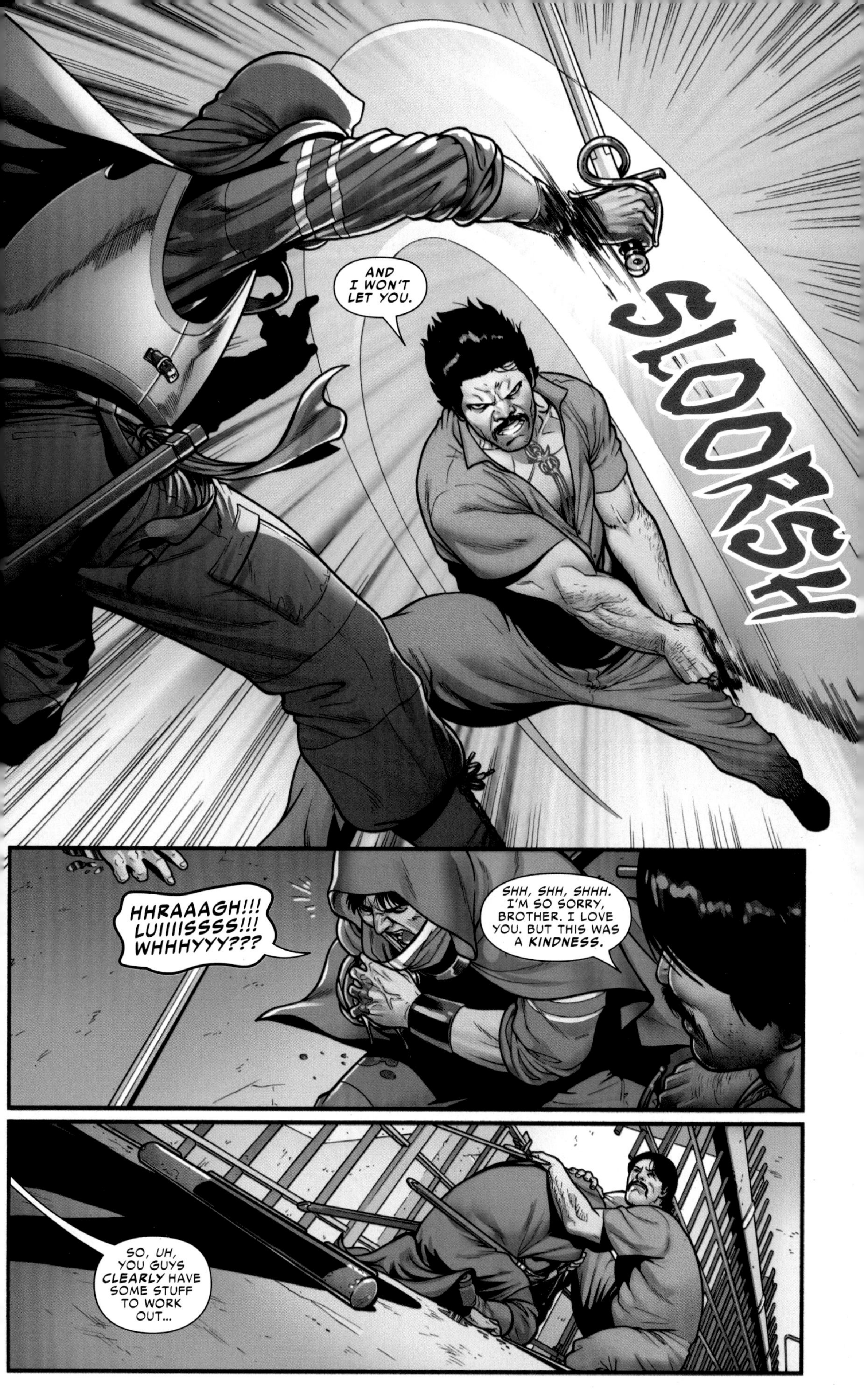
AND I WON'T LET YOU.
SLOORSH
HHRAAAGH!!! LUIIIISSSS!!! WHHHYYY???
SHH, SHH, SHHH. I'M SO SORRY, BROTHER. I LOVE YOU. BUT THIS WAS A KINDNESS.
SO, UH, YOU GUYS CLEARLY HAVE SOME STUFF TO WORK OUT...

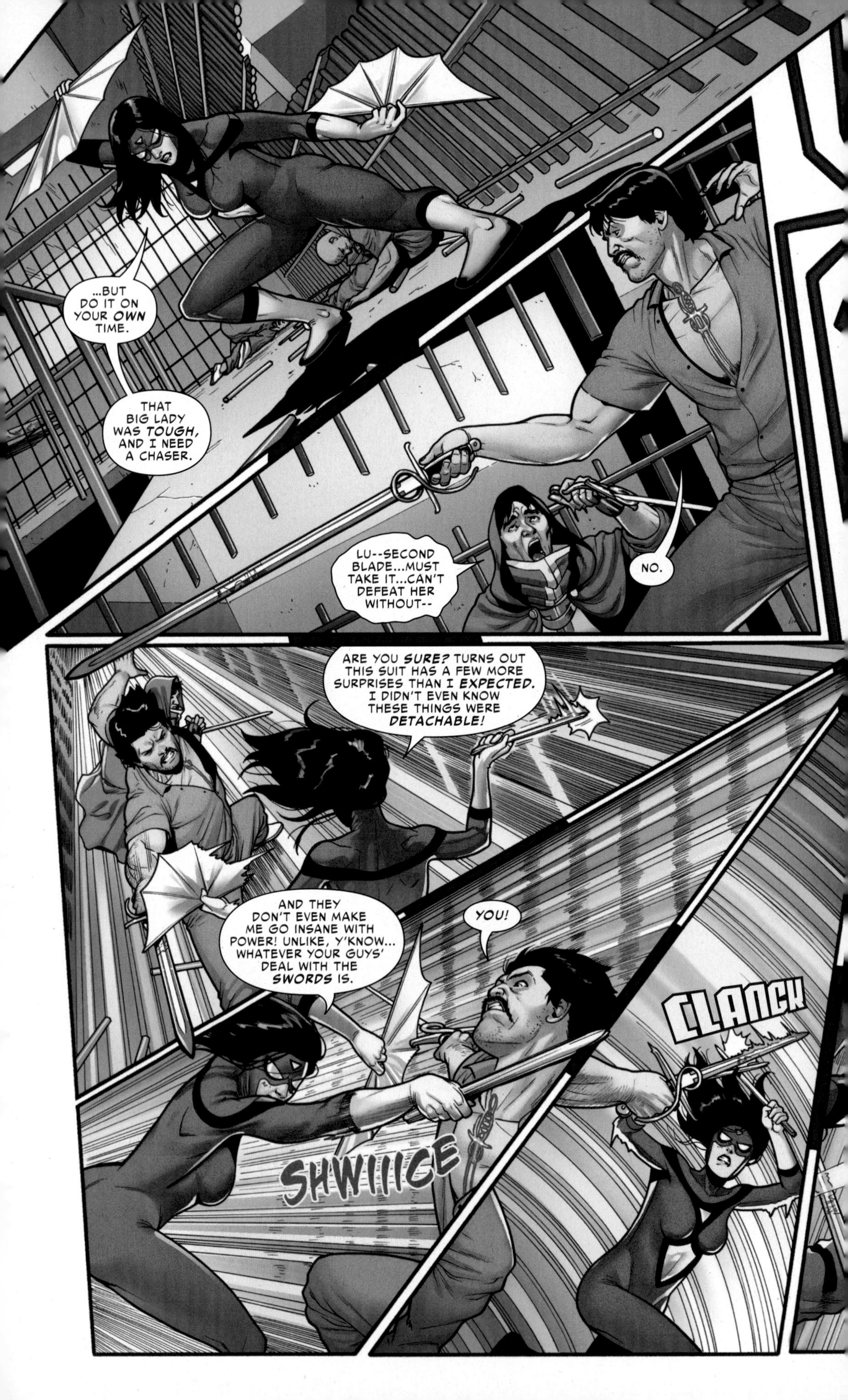
...BUT DO IT ON YOUR *OWN* TIME.
THAT BIG LADY WAS *TOUGH*, AND I NEED A CHASER.
LU--SECOND BLADE...MUST TAKE IT...CAN'T DEFEAT HER WITHOUT--
NO.
ARE YOU *SURE?* TURNS OUT THIS SUIT HAS A FEW MORE SURPRISES THAN I *EXPECTED*. I DIDN'T EVEN KNOW THESE THINGS WERE *DETACHABLE!*
AND THEY DON'T EVEN MAKE ME GO INSANE WITH POWER! UNLIKE, Y'KNOW... WHATEVER YOUR GUYS' DEAL WITH THE *SWORDS* IS.
YOU!
CLANCK
SHWIIICE

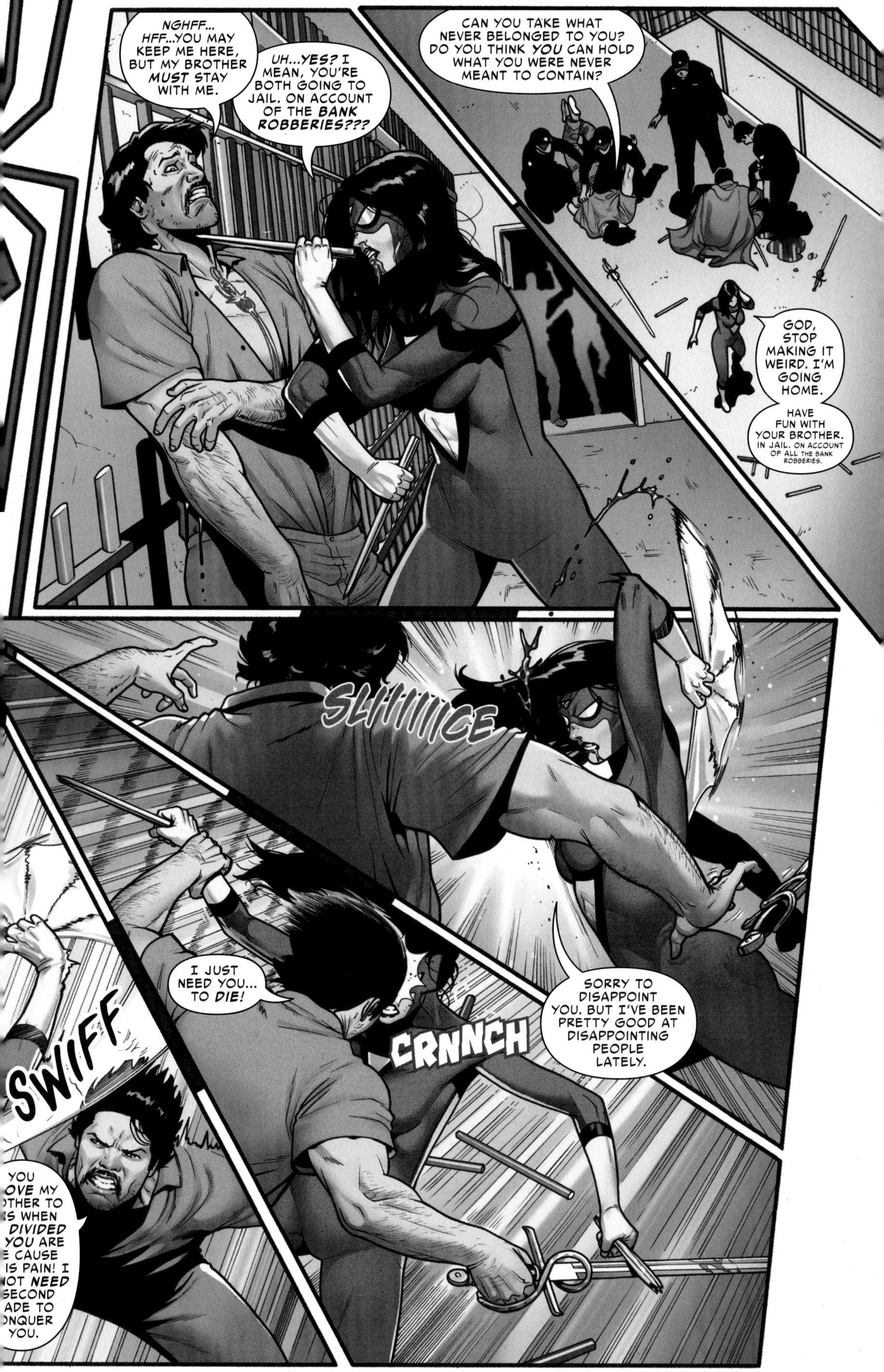
NGHFF... HFF...YOU MAY KEEP ME HERE, BUT MY BROTHER MUST STAY WITH ME.
UH...YES? I MEAN, YOU'RE BOTH GOING TO JAIL. ON ACCOUNT OF THE BANK ROBBERIES???
CAN YOU TAKE WHAT NEVER BELONGED TO YOU? DO YOU THINK YOU CAN HOLD WHAT YOU WERE NEVER MEANT TO CONTAIN?
GOD, STOP MAKING IT WEIRD. I'M GOING HOME.
HAVE FUN WITH YOUR BROTHER. IN JAIL. ON ACCOUNT OF ALL THE BANK ROBBERIES.
SLIIIIICE
I JUST NEED YOU... TO DIE!
SORRY TO DISAPPOINT YOU. BUT I'VE BEEN PRETTY GOOD AT DISAPPOINTING PEOPLE LATELY.
CRNNCH
SWIFF
YOU
OVE MY
OTHER TO
S WHEN
DIVIDED
YOU ARE
E CAUSE
IS PAIN! I
OT NEED
SECOND
ADE TO
NQUER
YOU.

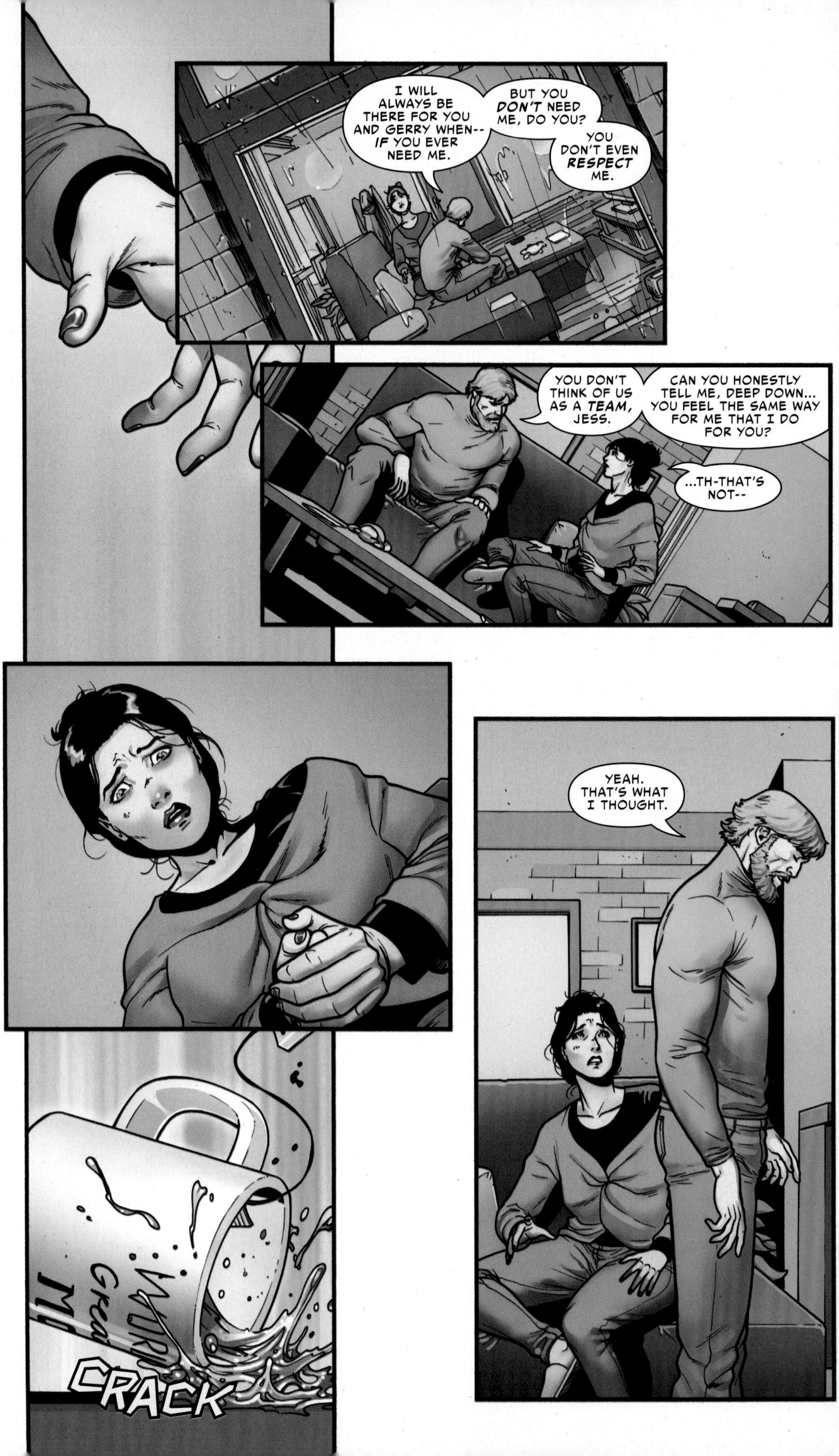
I WILL ALWAYS BE THERE FOR YOU AND GERRY WHEN-- IF YOU EVER NEED ME.
BUT YOU DON'T NEED ME, DO YOU?
YOU DON'T EVEN RESPECT ME.
YOU DON'T THINK OF US AS A TEAM, JESS.
CAN YOU HONESTLY TELL ME, DEEP DOWN... YOU FEEL THE SAME WAY FOR ME THAT I DO FOR YOU?
...TH-THAT'S NOT--
CRACK
YEAH. THAT'S WHAT I THOUGHT.

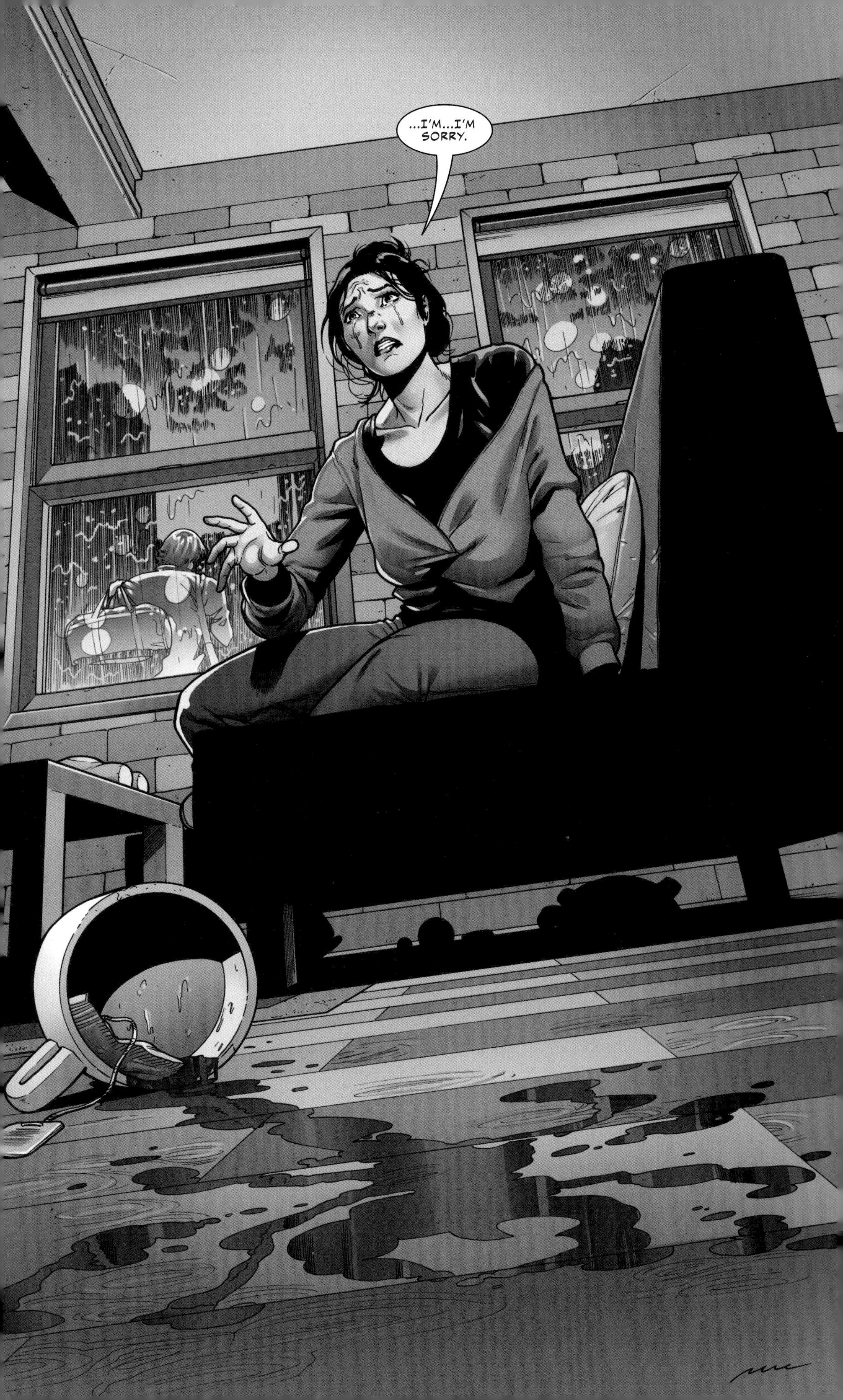
...I'M...I'M SORRY.

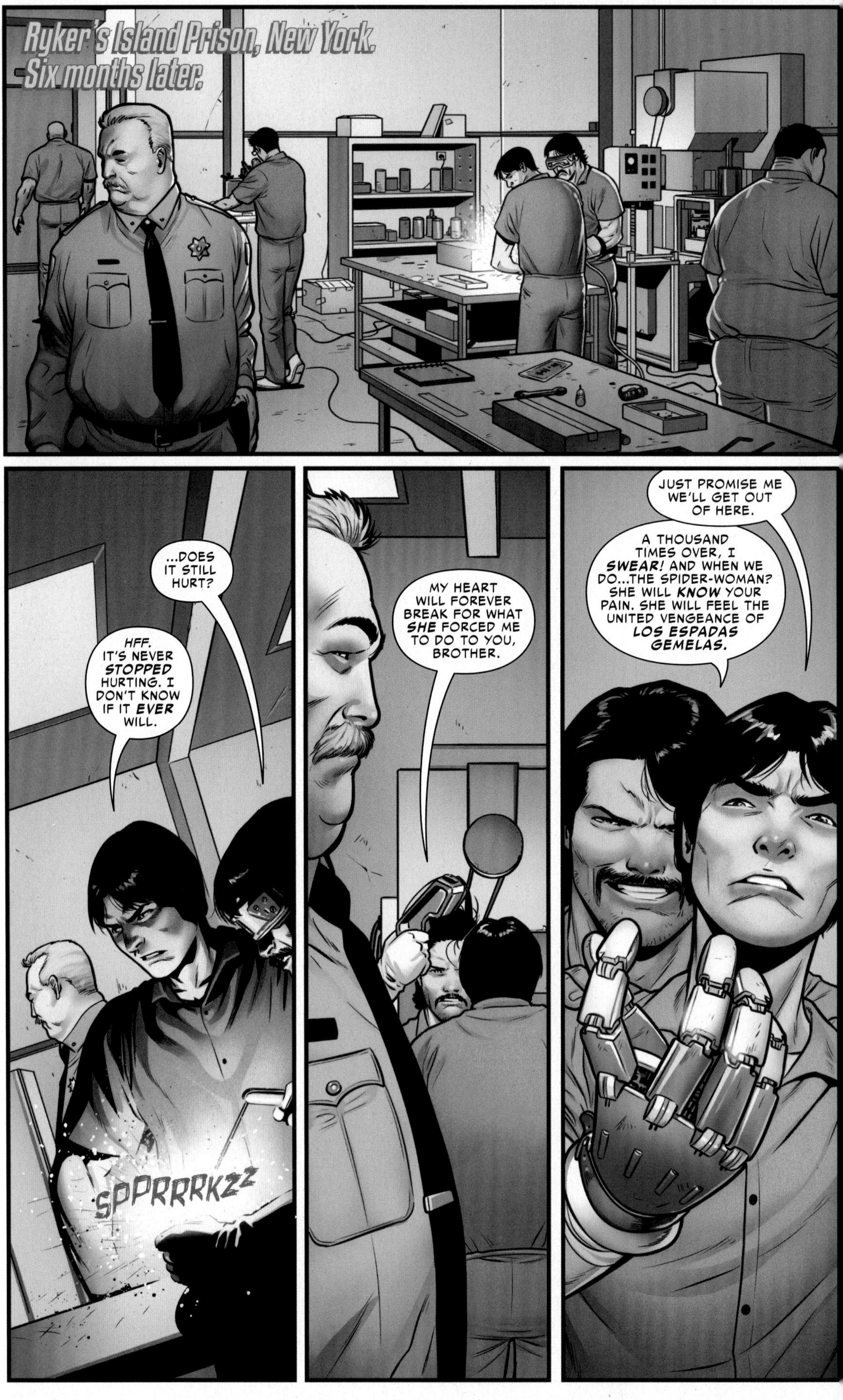
Ryker's Island Prison, New York.
Six months later.
...DOES IT STILL HURT?
HFF. IT'S NEVER STOPPED HURTING. I DON'T KNOW IF IT EVER WILL.
SPPRRRKZZ
MY HEART WILL FOREVER BREAK FOR WHAT SHE FORCED ME TO DO TO YOU, BROTHER.
JUST PROMISE ME WE'LL GET OUT OF HERE.
A THOUSAND TIMES OVER, I SWEAR! AND WHEN WE DO...THE SPIDER-WOMAN? SHE WILL KNOW YOUR PAIN. SHE WILL FEEL THE UNITED VENGEANCE OF LOS ESPADAS GEMELAS.

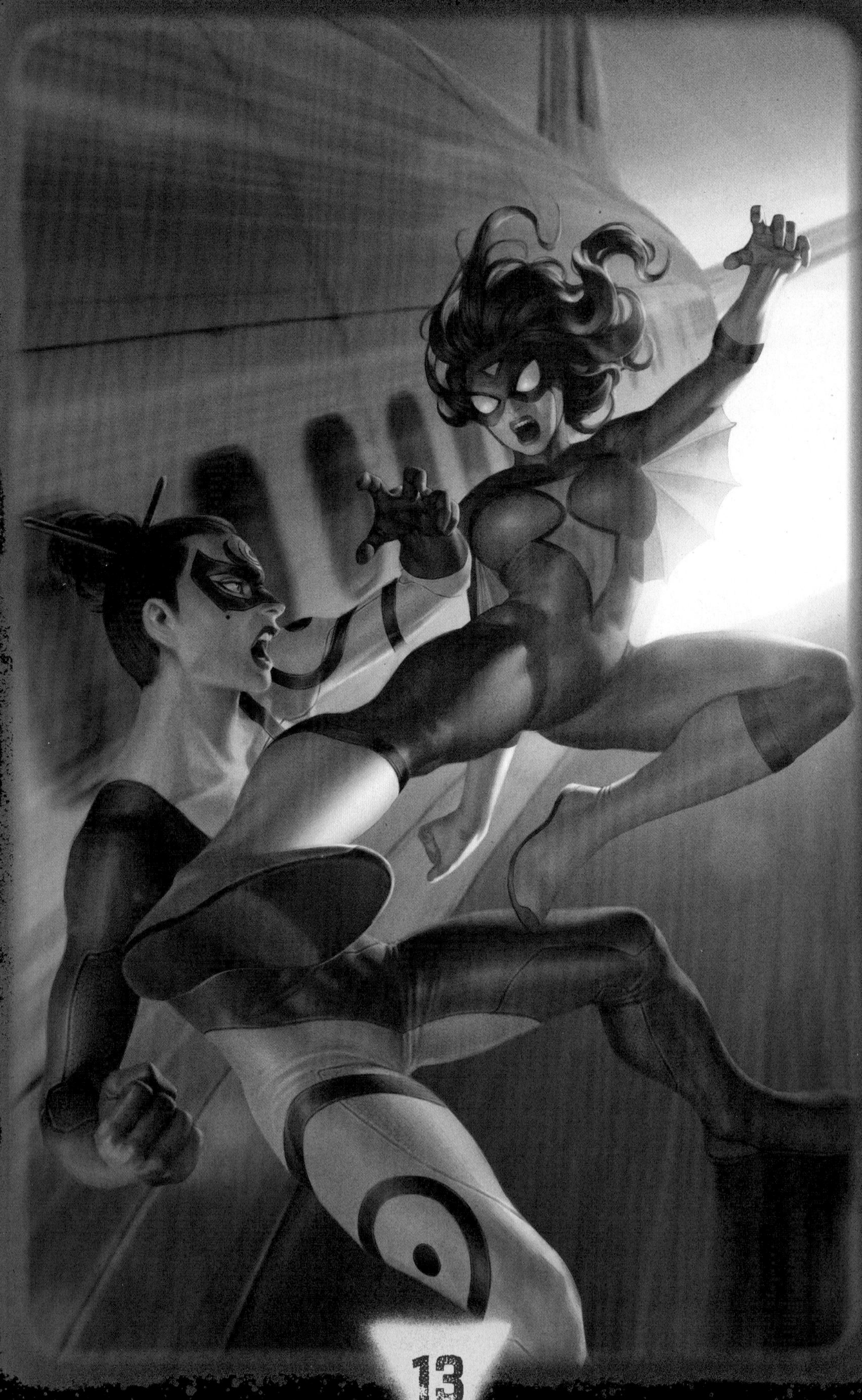

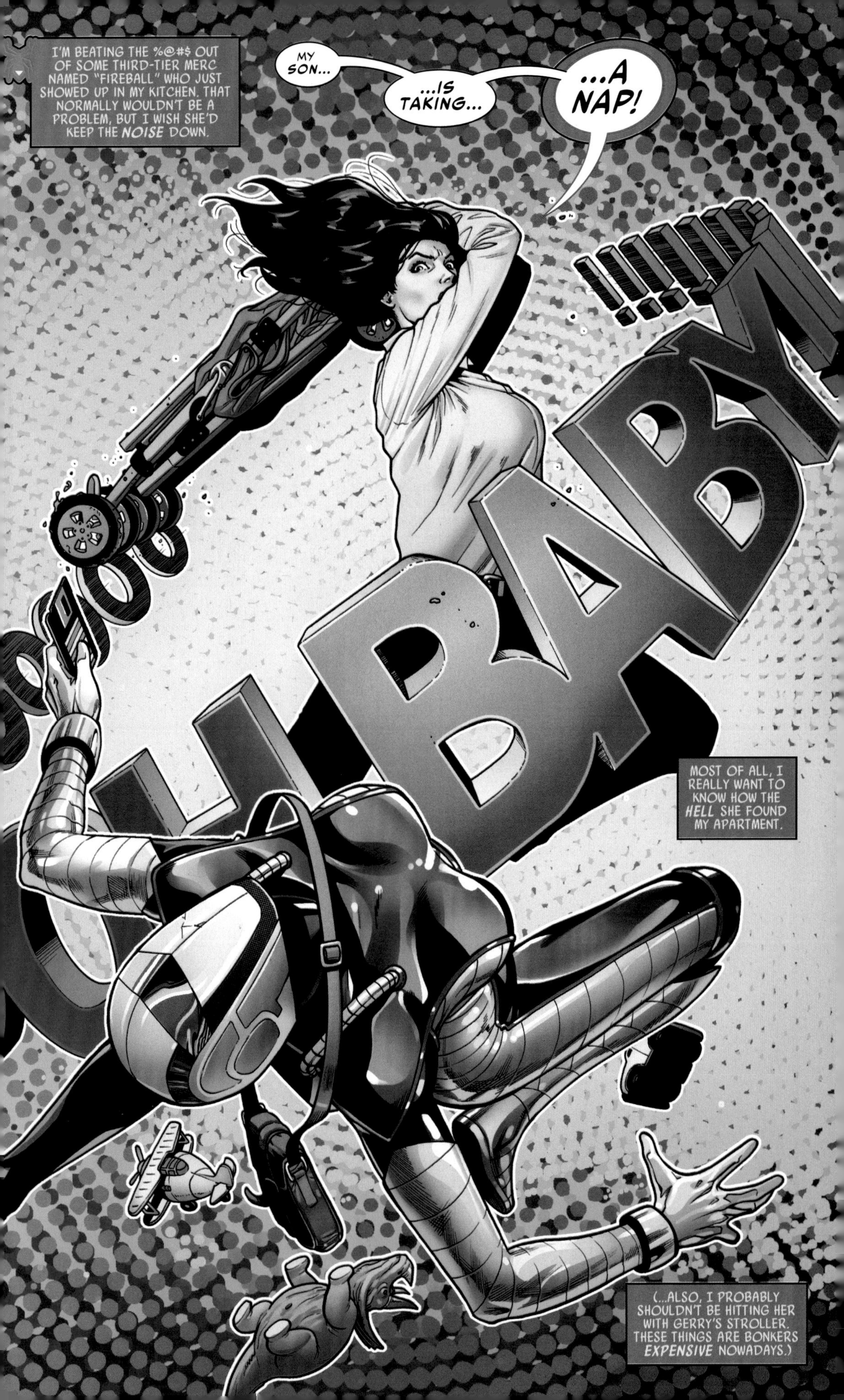

I'M BEATING THE %@#$ OUT OF SOME THIRD-TIER MERC NAMED "FIREBALL" WHO JUST SHOWED UP IN MY KITCHEN. THAT NORMALLY WOULDN'T BE A PROBLEM, BUT I WISH SHE'D KEEP THE NOISE DOWN.
MY SON...
...IS TAKING...
...A NAP!
BABY!!!!!!!!
MOST OF ALL, I REALLY WANT TO KNOW HOW THE HELL SHE FOUND MY APARTMENT.
(...ALSO, I PROBABLY SHOULDN'T BE HITTING HER WITH GERRY'S STROLLER. THESE THINGS ARE BONKERS EXPENSIVE NOWADAYS.)

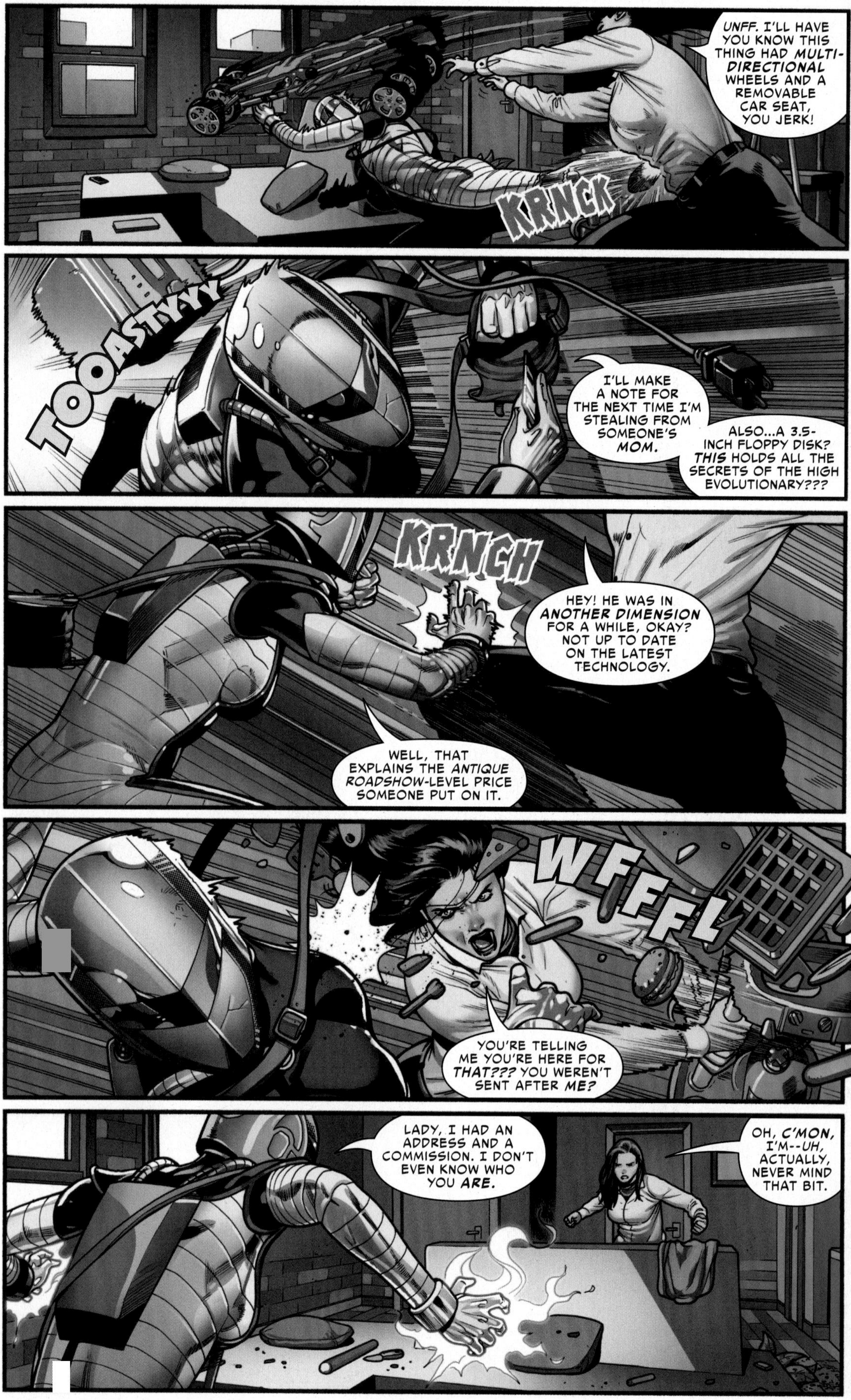

UNFF. I'LL HAVE YOU KNOW THIS THING HAD MULTI-DIRECTIONAL WHEELS AND A REMOVABLE CAR SEAT, YOU JERK!
KRNCK
TOOASTYYY
I'LL MAKE A NOTE FOR THE NEXT TIME I'M STEALING FROM SOMEONE'S MOM.
ALSO...A 3.5-INCH FLOPPY DISK? THIS HOLDS ALL THE SECRETS OF THE HIGH EVOLUTIONARY???
KRNCH
HEY! HE WAS IN ANOTHER DIMENSION FOR A WHILE, OKAY? NOT UP TO DATE ON THE LATEST TECHNOLOGY.
WELL, THAT EXPLAINS THE ANTIQUE ROADSHOW-LEVEL PRICE SOMEONE PUT ON IT.
WFFFL
YOU'RE TELLING ME YOU'RE HERE FOR THAT??? YOU WEREN'T SENT AFTER ME?
LADY, I HAD AN ADDRESS AND A COMMISSION. I DON'T EVEN KNOW WHO YOU ARE.
OH, C'MON, I'M--UH, ACTUALLY, NEVER MIND THAT BIT.

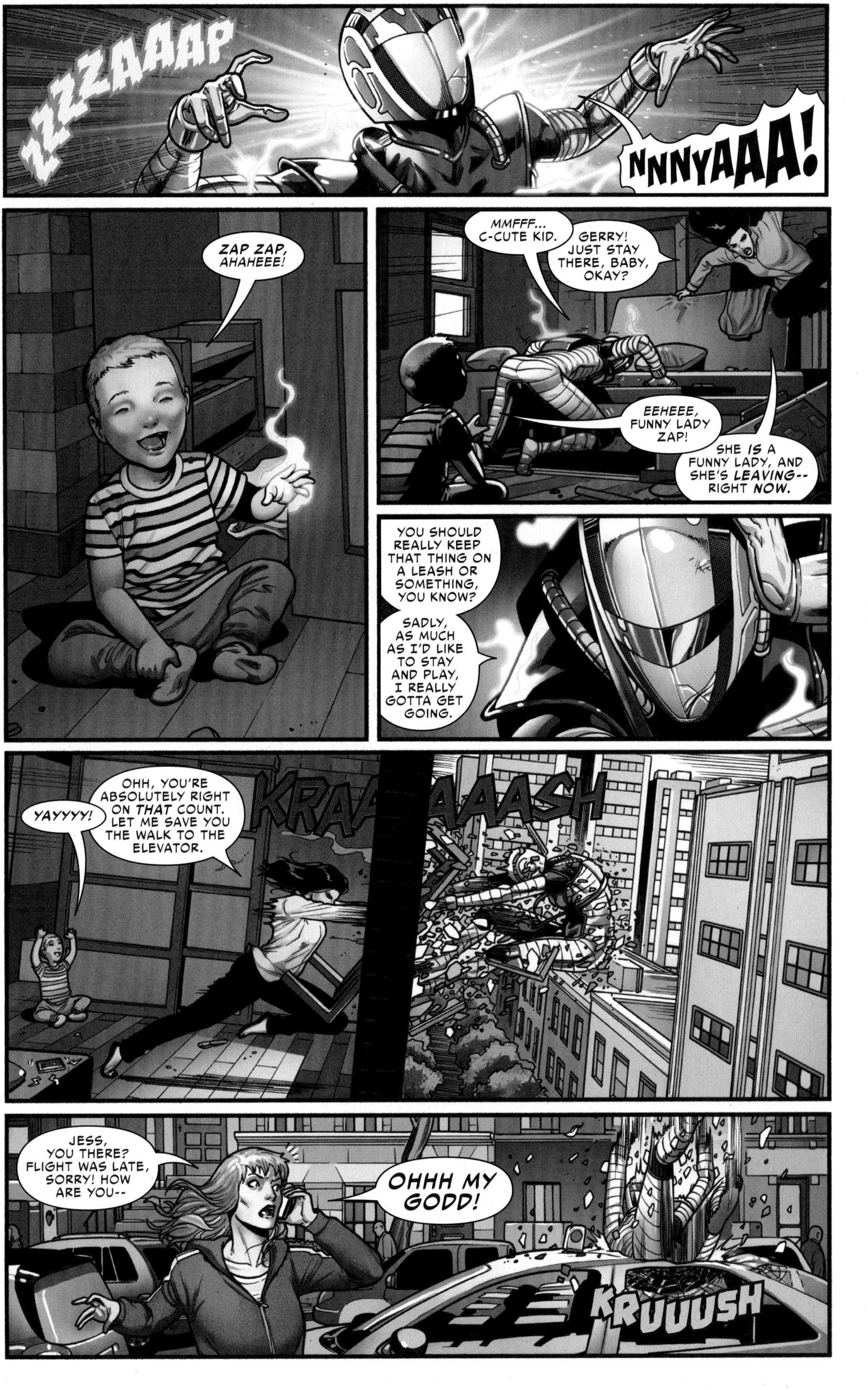
ZZZZAAAP
NNNYAAA!
ZAP ZAP, AHAHEEE!
MMFFF... C-CUTE KID.
GERRY! JUST STAY THERE, BABY, OKAY?
EEHEEE, FUNNY LADY ZAP!
SHE *IS* A FUNNY LADY, AND SHE'S *LEAVING*-- RIGHT *NOW*.
YOU SHOULD REALLY KEEP THAT THING ON A LEASH OR SOMETHING, YOU KNOW?
SADLY, AS MUCH AS I'D LIKE TO STAY AND PLAY, I REALLY GOTTA GET GOING.
YAYYYY!
OHH, YOU'RE ABSOLUTELY RIGHT ON *THAT* COUNT. LET ME SAVE YOU THE WALK TO THE ELEVATOR.
KRAAAAAAASH
JESS, YOU THERE? FLIGHT WAS LATE, SORRY! HOW ARE YOU--
OHHH MY GODD!
KRUUUSH

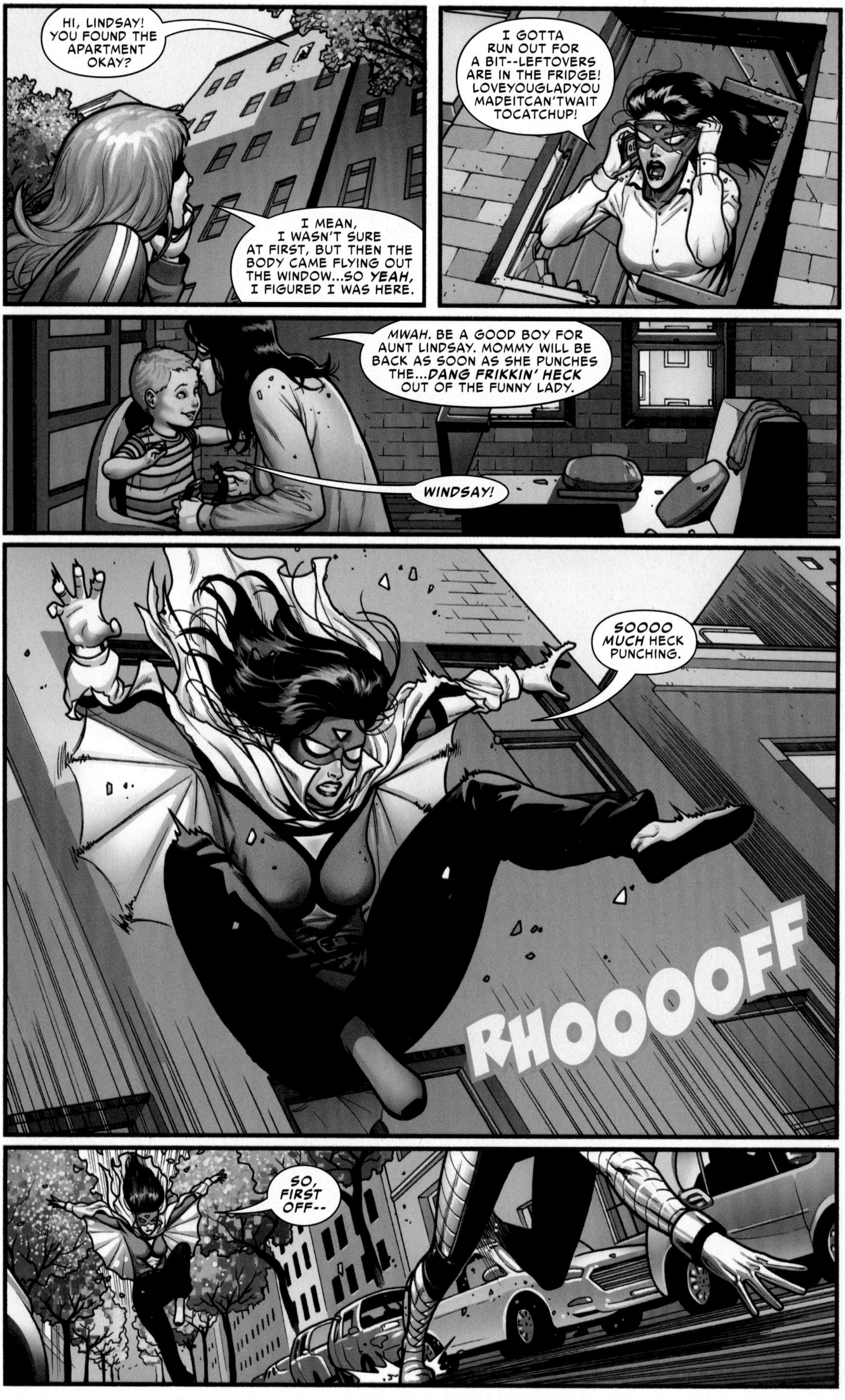
HI, LINDSAY! YOU FOUND THE APARTMENT OKAY?
I MEAN, I WASN'T SURE AT FIRST, BUT THEN THE BODY CAME FLYING OUT THE WINDOW...SO YEAH, I FIGURED I WAS HERE.
I GOTTA RUN OUT FOR A BIT--LEFTOVERS ARE IN THE FRIDGE! LOVEYOUGLADYOU MADEITCAN'TWAIT TOCATCHUP!
MWAH. BE A GOOD BOY FOR AUNT LINDSAY. MOMMY WILL BE BACK AS SOON AS SHE PUNCHES THE...DANG FRIKKIN' HECK OUT OF THE FUNNY LADY.
WINDSAY!
SOOOO MUCH HECK PUNCHING.
RHOOOOFF
SO, FIRST OFF--

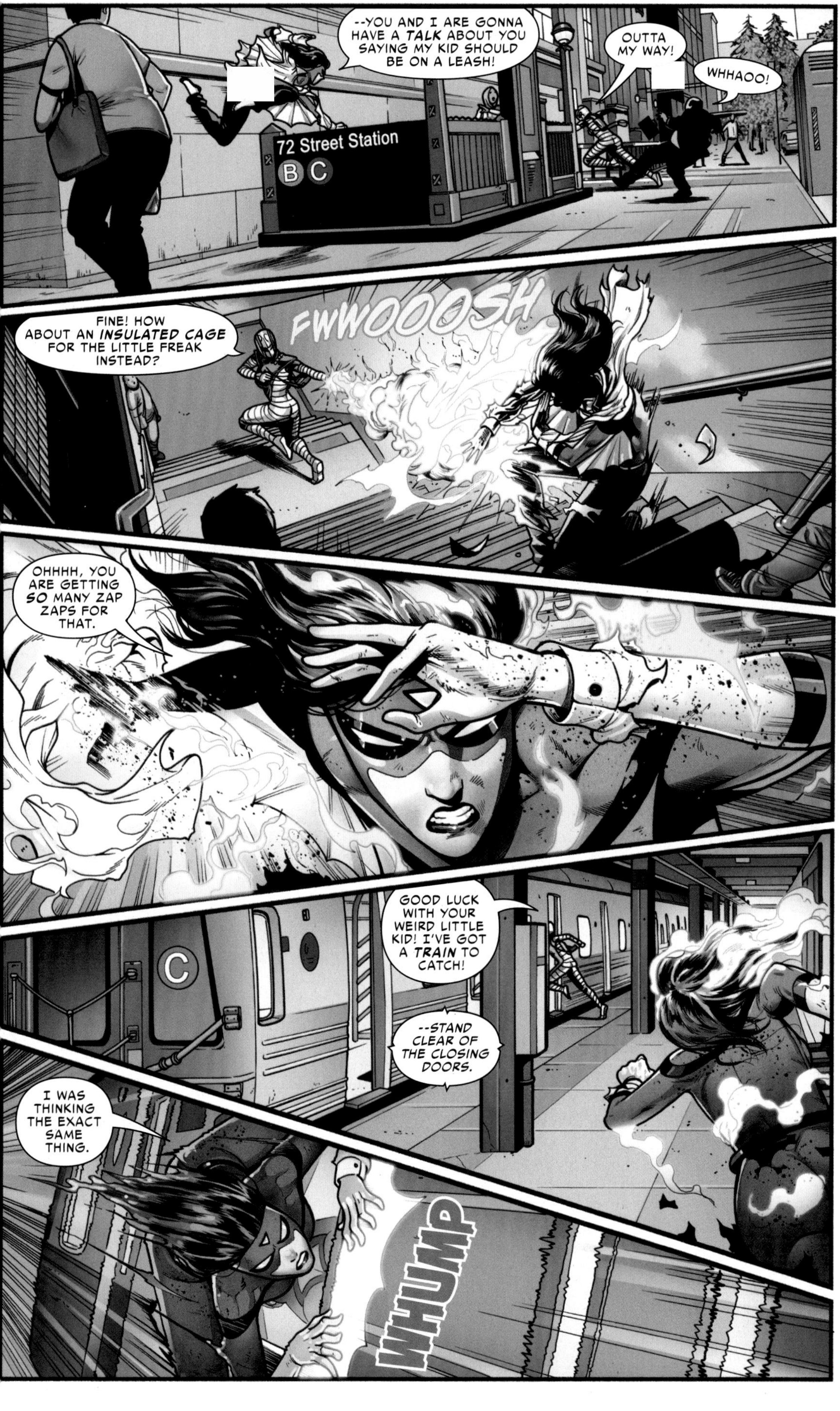
--YOU AND I ARE GONNA HAVE A *TALK* ABOUT YOU SAYING MY KID SHOULD BE ON A LEASH!
72 Street Station
B C
OUTTA MY WAY!
WHHAOO!
FINE! HOW ABOUT AN *INSULATED CAGE* FOR THE LITTLE FREAK INSTEAD?
FWWOOOSH
OHHHH, YOU ARE GETTING *SO* MANY ZAP ZAPS FOR THAT.
C
GOOD LUCK WITH YOUR WEIRD LITTLE KID! I'VE GOT A *TRAIN* TO CATCH!
--STAND CLEAR OF THE CLOSING DOORS.
I WAS THINKING THE EXACT SAME THING.
WHUMP

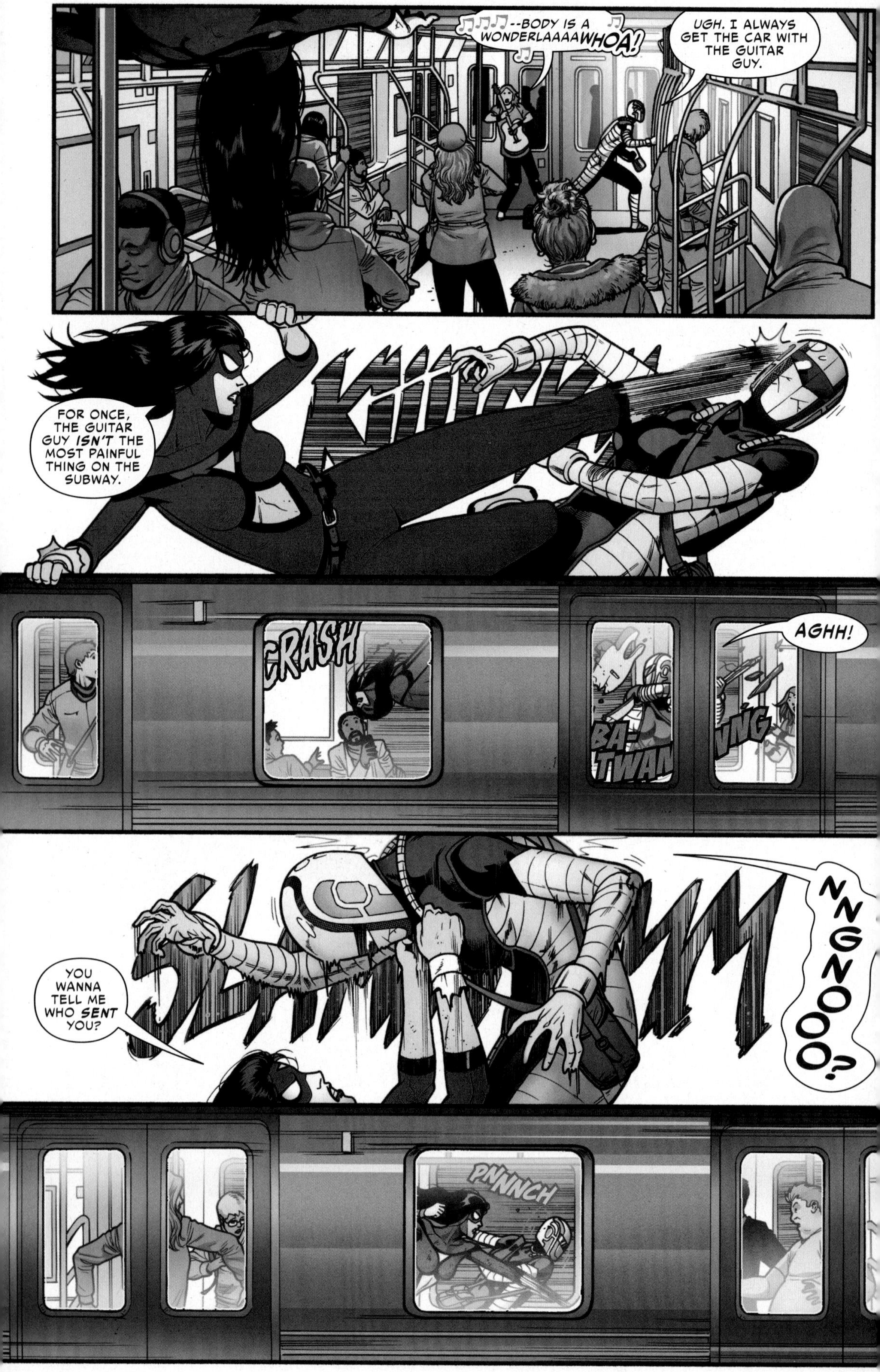

♫♫♫ --BODY IS A WONDERLAAAAWHOA! ♫ ♫
UGH. I ALWAYS GET THE CAR WITH THE GUITAR GUY.
KTHUNK
FOR ONCE, THE GUITAR GUY ISN'T THE MOST PAINFUL THING ON THE SUBWAY.
CRASH
AGHH!
BA-TWANNNG
NNGNOOO?
YOU WANNA TELL ME WHO SENT YOU?
PNNNCH

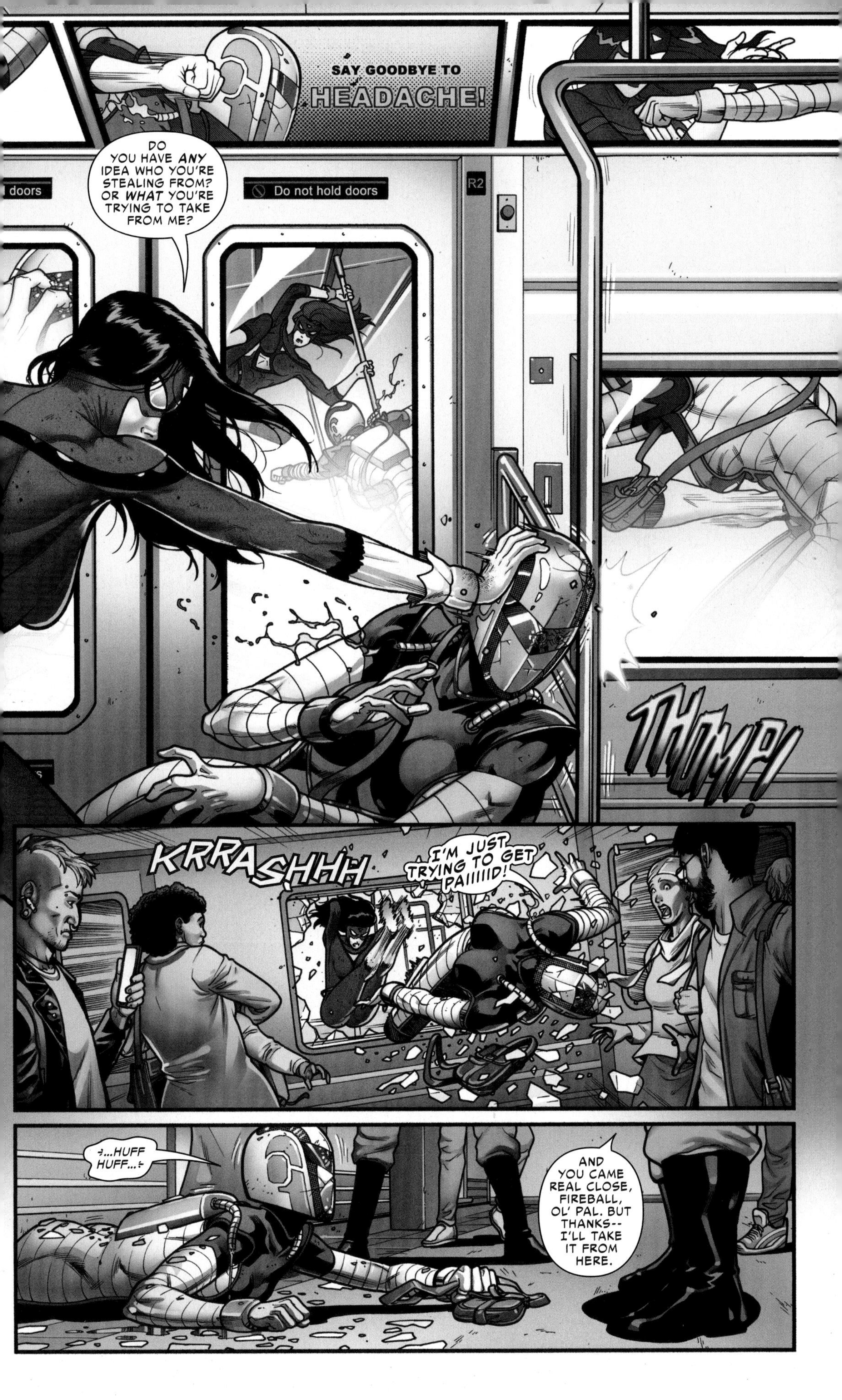

SAY GOODBYE TO
HEADACHE!
doors
Do not hold doors
R2
DO YOU HAVE ANY IDEA WHO YOU'RE STEALING FROM? OR WHAT YOU'RE TRYING TO TAKE FROM ME?
THMP!
KRRASHHH
I'M JUST TRYING TO GET PAIIIIID!
~...HUFF HUFF...~
AND YOU CAME REAL CLOSE, FIREBALL, OL' PAL. BUT THANKS-- I'LL TAKE IT FROM HERE.

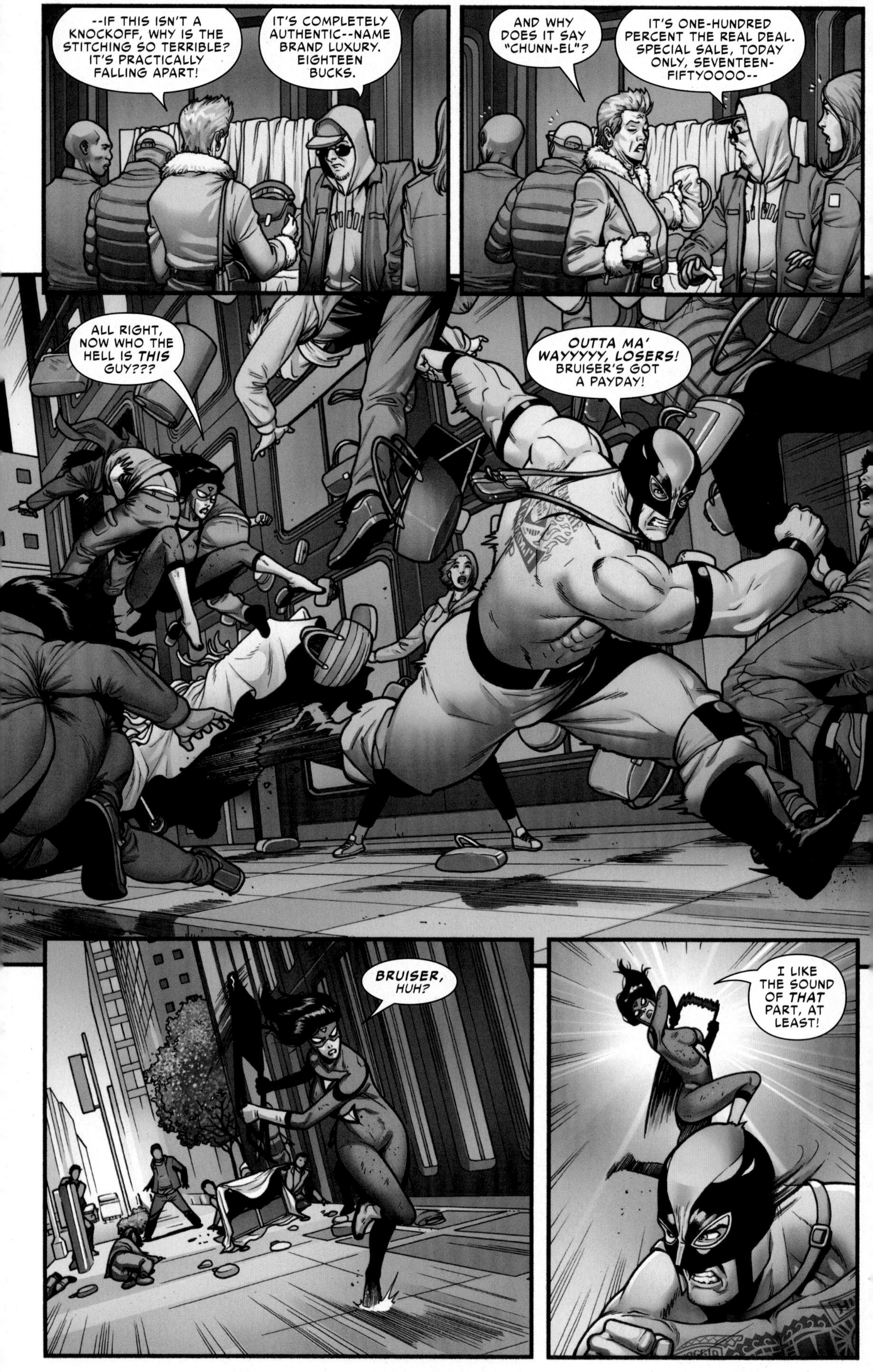
--IF THIS ISN'T A KNOCKOFF, WHY IS THE STITCHING SO TERRIBLE? IT'S PRACTICALLY FALLING APART!
IT'S COMPLETELY AUTHENTIC--NAME BRAND LUXURY. EIGHTEEN BUCKS.
AND WHY DOES IT SAY "CHUNN-EL"?
IT'S ONE-HUNDRED PERCENT THE REAL DEAL. SPECIAL SALE, TODAY ONLY, SEVENTEEN-FIFTYOOOO--
ALL RIGHT, NOW WHO THE HELL IS *THIS* GUY???
OUTTA MA' WAYYYYY, LOSERS! BRUISER'S GOT A PAYDAY!
BRUISER, HUH?
I LIKE THE SOUND OF *THAT* PART, AT LEAST!

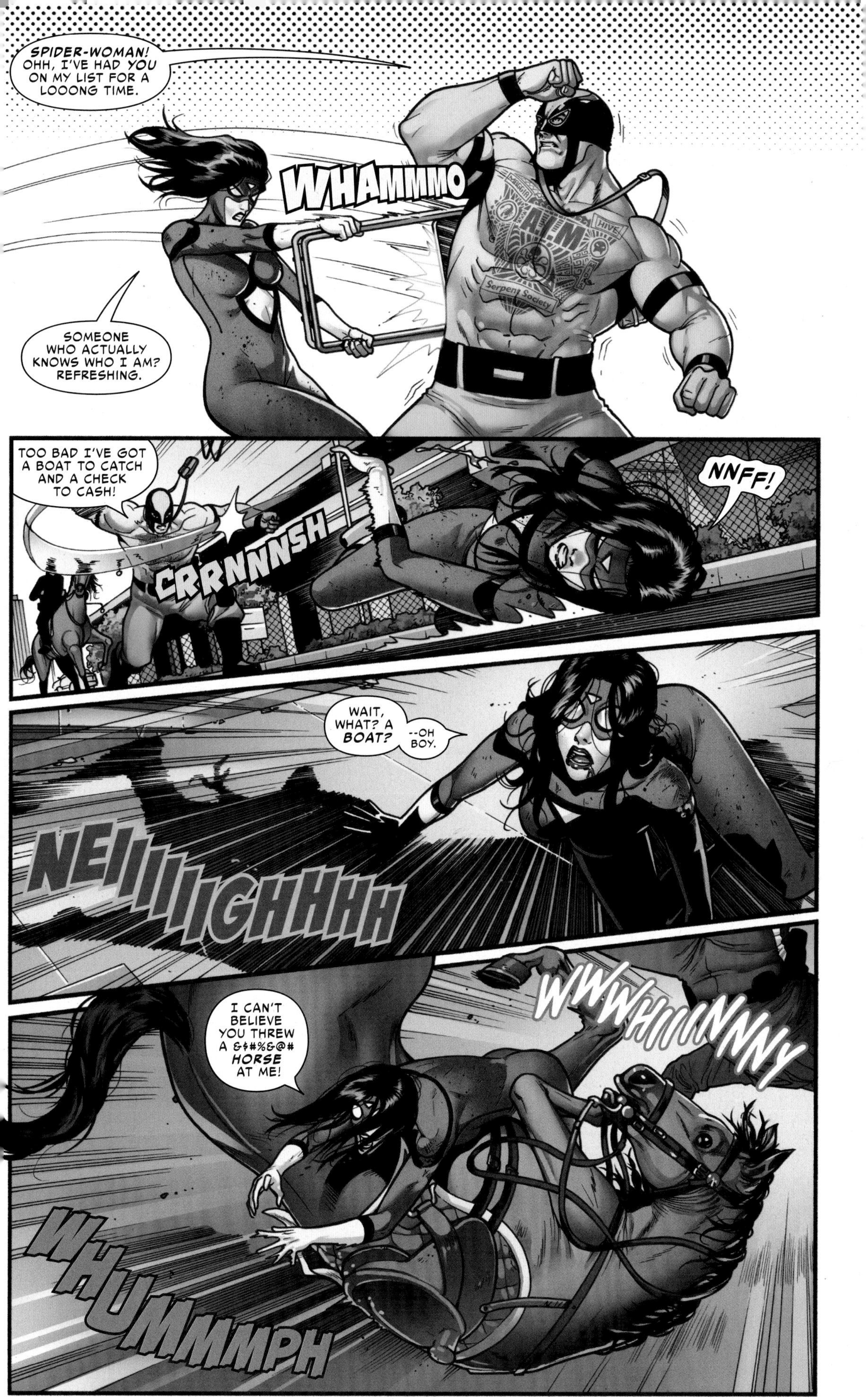

SPIDER-WOMAN! OHH, I'VE HAD YOU ON MY LIST FOR A LOOONG TIME.
WHAMMMO
SOMEONE WHO ACTUALLY KNOWS WHO I AM? REFRESHING.
A.I.M.
HIVE
Serpent Society
TOO BAD I'VE GOT A BOAT TO CATCH AND A CHECK TO CASH!
CRRNNNSH
NNFF!
WAIT, WHAT? A BOAT?
--OH BOY.
NEIIIIIGHHHH
I CAN'T BELIEVE YOU THREW A &$#%&@# HORSE AT ME!
WWWHIIINNNY
WHUMMMMPH

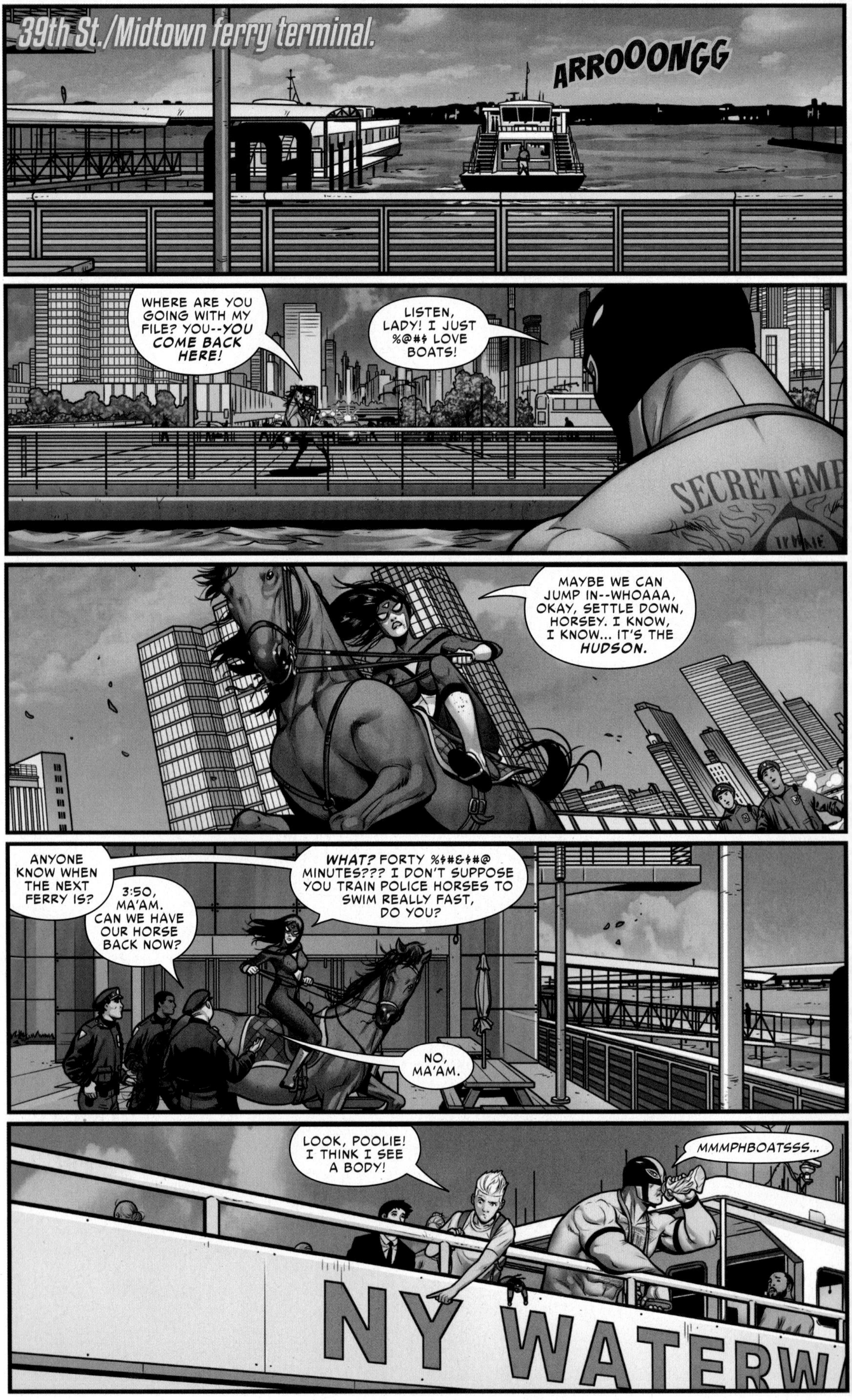
39th St./Midtown ferry terminal.
ARROOONGG
WHERE ARE YOU GOING WITH MY FILE? YOU--YOU COME BACK HERE!
LISTEN, LADY! I JUST %@#$ LOVE BOATS!
MAYBE WE CAN JUMP IN--WHOAAA, OKAY, SETTLE DOWN, HORSEY. I KNOW, I KNOW... IT'S THE HUDSON.
ANYONE KNOW WHEN THE NEXT FERRY IS?
3:50, MA'AM. CAN WE HAVE OUR HORSE BACK NOW?
WHAT? FORTY %$#&$#@ MINUTES??? I DON'T SUPPOSE YOU TRAIN POLICE HORSES TO SWIM REALLY FAST, DO YOU?
NO, MA'AM.
LOOK, POOLIE! I THINK I SEE A BODY!
MMMPHBOATSSS...
NY WATERW

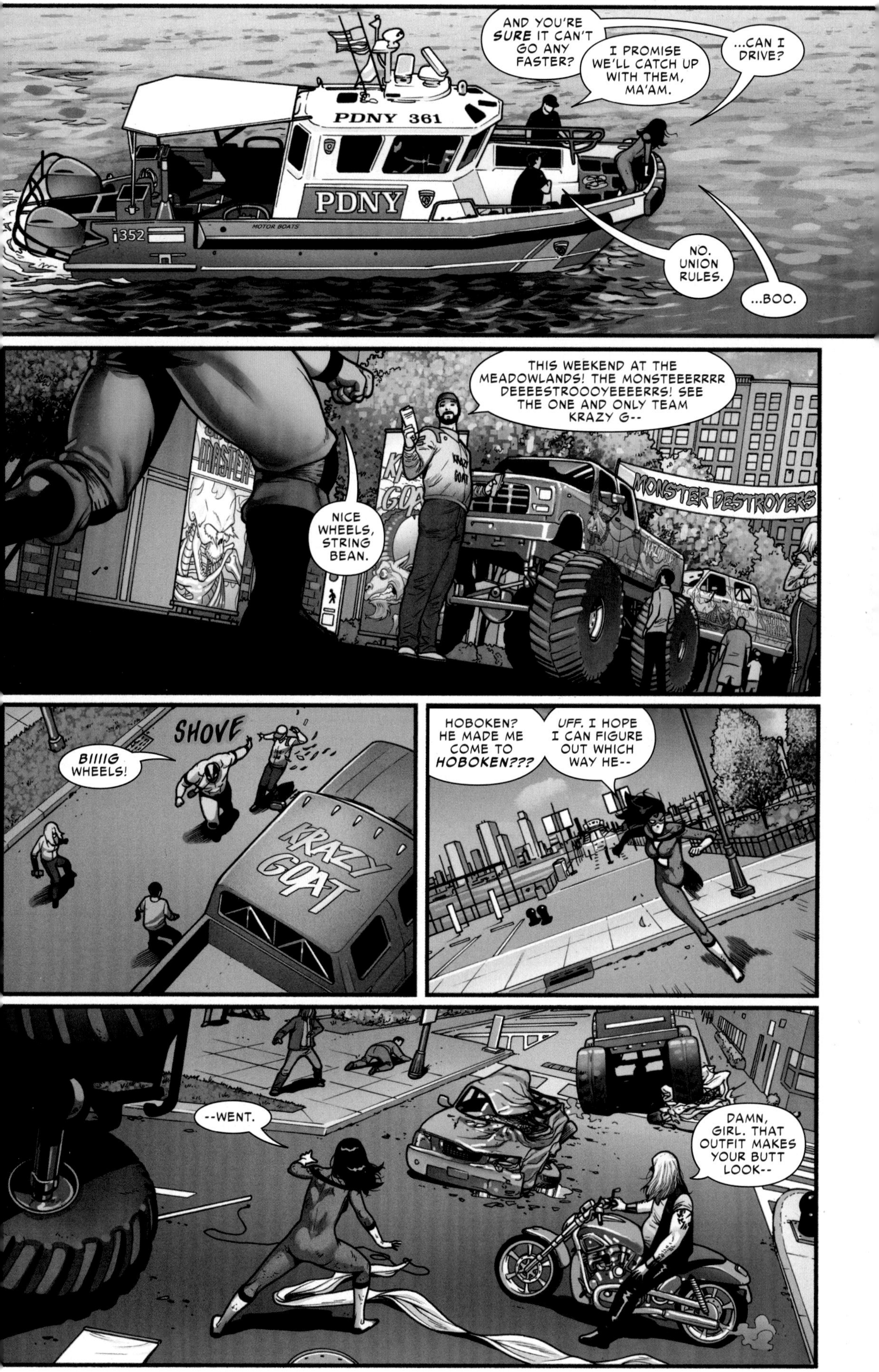

PDNY 361
PDNY
AND YOU'RE SURE IT CAN'T GO ANY FASTER?
I PROMISE WE'LL CATCH UP WITH THEM, MA'AM.
...CAN I DRIVE?
NO. UNION RULES.
...BOO.
THIS WEEKEND AT THE MEADOWLANDS! THE MONSTEEERRRR DEEEESTROOOYEEEERRS! SEE THE ONE AND ONLY TEAM KRAZY G--
NICE WHEELS, STRING BEAN.
MONSTER DESTROYERS
SHOVE
BIIIIG WHEELS!
KRAZY GOAT
HOBOKEN? HE MADE ME COME TO HOBOKEN???
UFF. I HOPE I CAN FIGURE OUT WHICH WAY HE--
--WENT.
DAMN, GIRL. THAT OUTFIT MAKES YOUR BUTT LOOK--

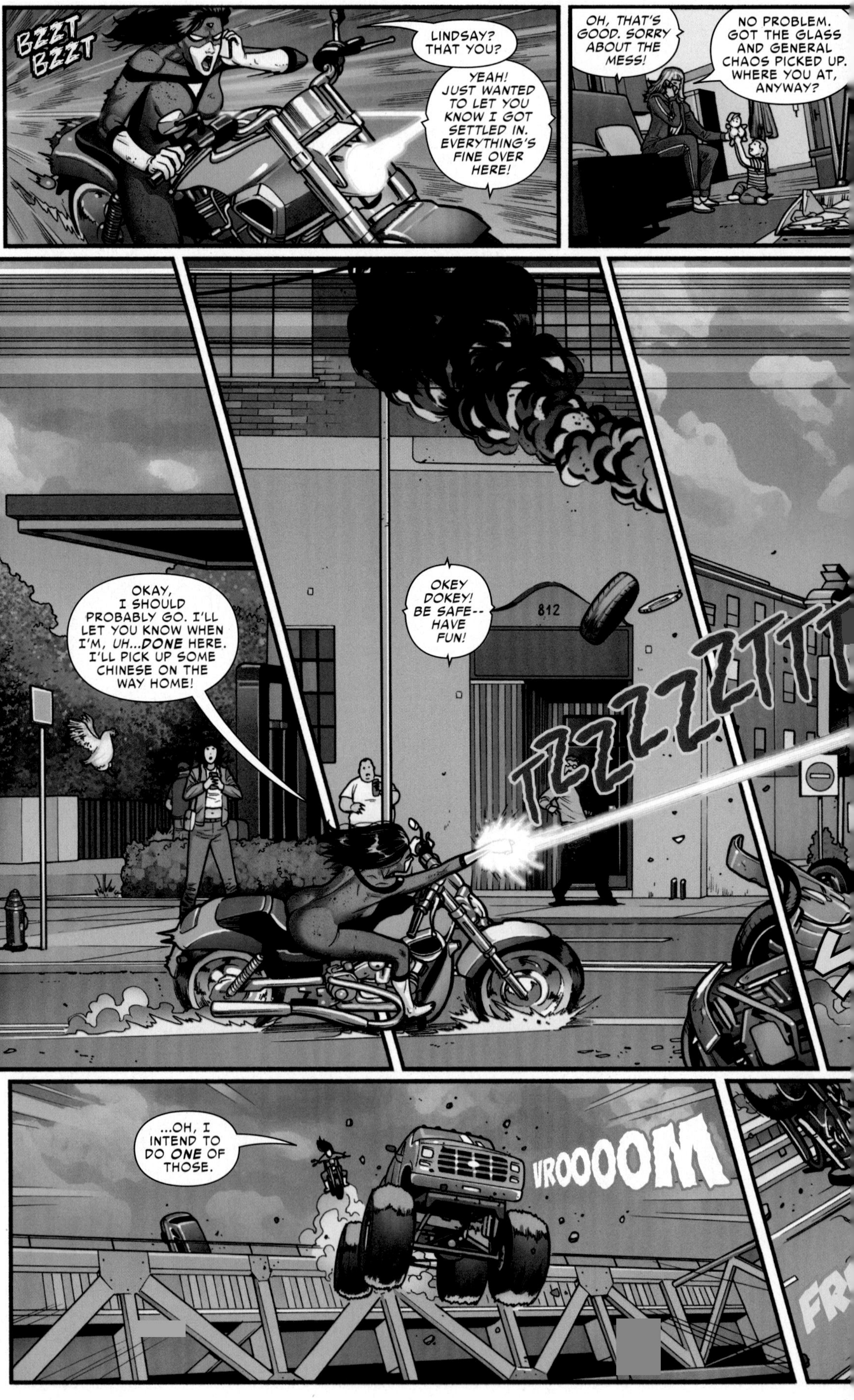
BZZZT BZZZT
LINDSAY? THAT YOU?
YEAH! JUST WANTED TO LET YOU KNOW I GOT SETTLED IN. EVERYTHING'S FINE OVER HERE!
OH, THAT'S GOOD. SORRY ABOUT THE MESS!
NO PROBLEM. GOT THE GLASS AND GENERAL CHAOS PICKED UP. WHERE YOU AT, ANYWAY?
OKAY, I SHOULD PROBABLY GO. I'LL LET YOU KNOW WHEN I'M, *UH*...***DONE*** HERE. I'LL PICK UP SOME CHINESE ON THE WAY HOME!
OKEY DOKEY! BE SAFE-- HAVE FUN!
812
...OH, I INTEND TO DO ***ONE*** OF THOSE.
VROOOOM

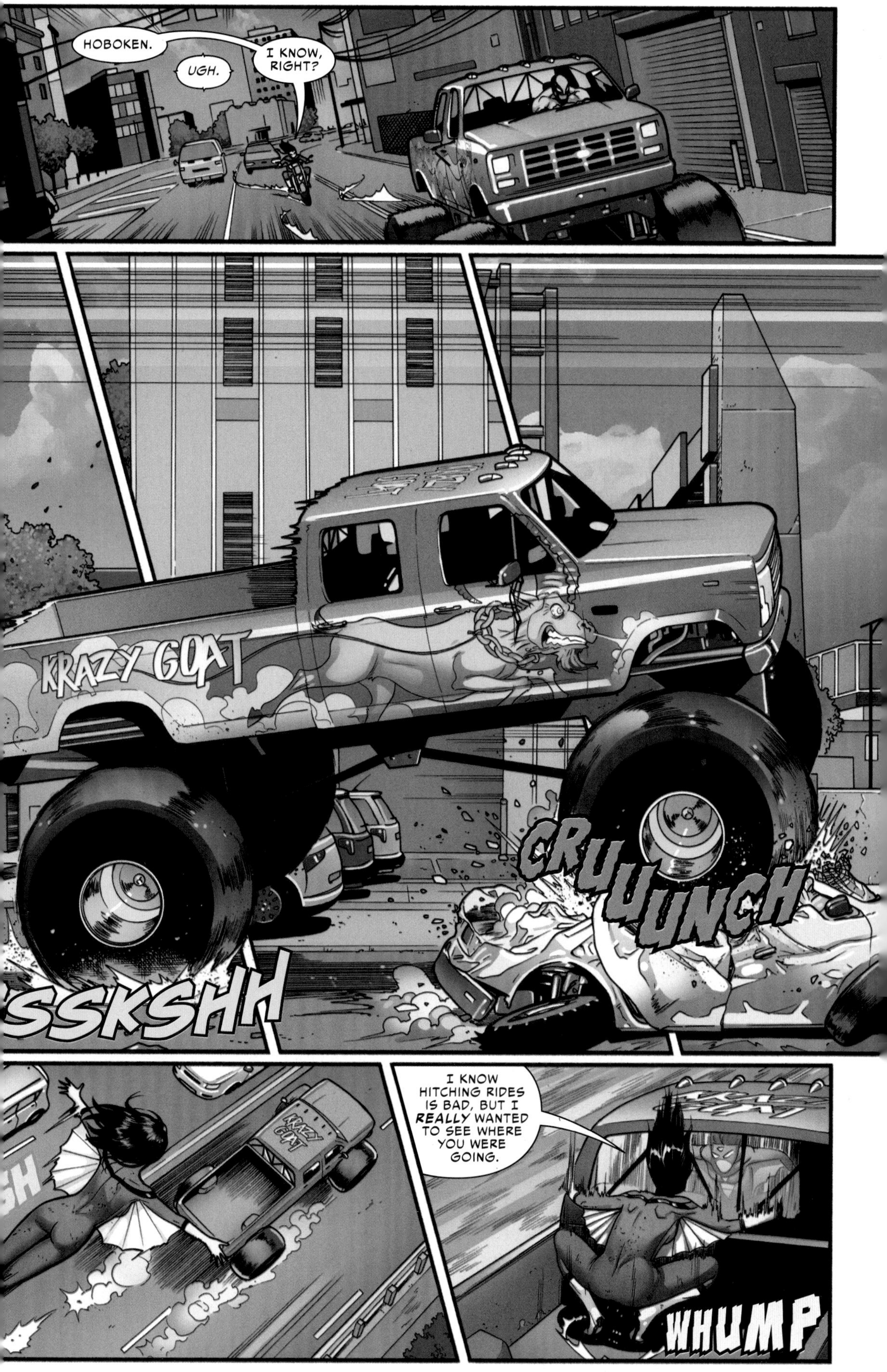
HOBOKEN.
UGH.
I KNOW, RIGHT?
KRAZY GOAT
CRUUUUNCH
SSKSHH
KRAZY GOAT
I KNOW HITCHING RIDES IS BAD, BUT I *REALLY* WANTED TO SEE WHERE YOU WERE GOING.
WHUMP

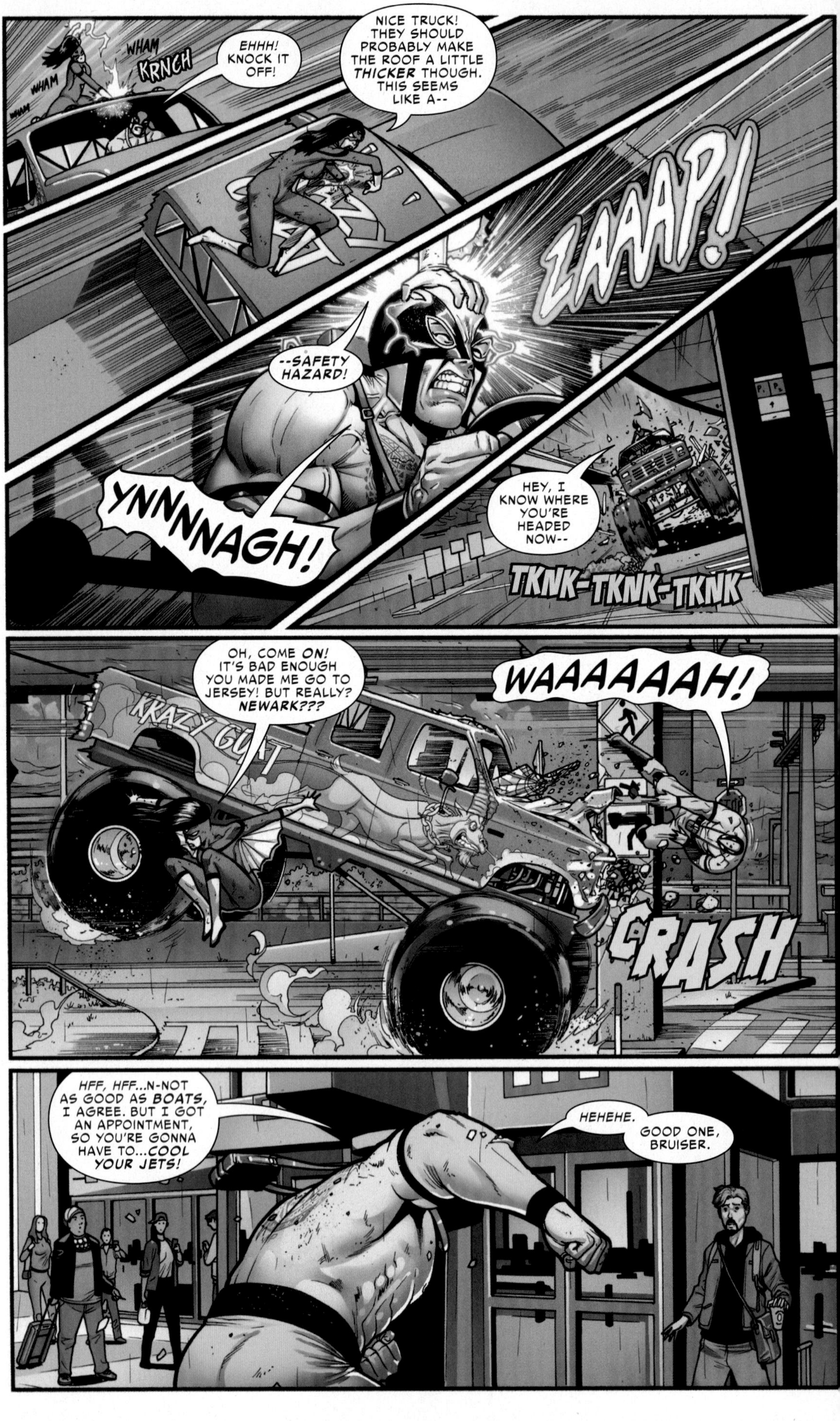
WHAM
KRNCH
WHAM
WHAM
EHHH! KNOCK IT OFF!
NICE TRUCK! THEY SHOULD PROBABLY MAKE THE ROOF A LITTLE THICKER THOUGH. THIS SEEMS LIKE A--
ZAAAP!
--SAFETY HAZARD!
YNNNNAGH!
HEY, I KNOW WHERE YOU'RE HEADED NOW--
TKNK-TKNK-TKNK
OH, COME ON! IT'S BAD ENOUGH YOU MADE ME GO TO JERSEY! BUT REALLY? NEWARK???
WAAAAAAH!
KRAZY GOAT
CRASH
HFF, HFF...N-NOT AS GOOD AS BOATS, I AGREE. BUT I GOT AN APPOINTMENT, SO YOU'RE GONNA HAVE TO...COOL YOUR JETS!
HEHEHE.
GOOD ONE, BRUISER.

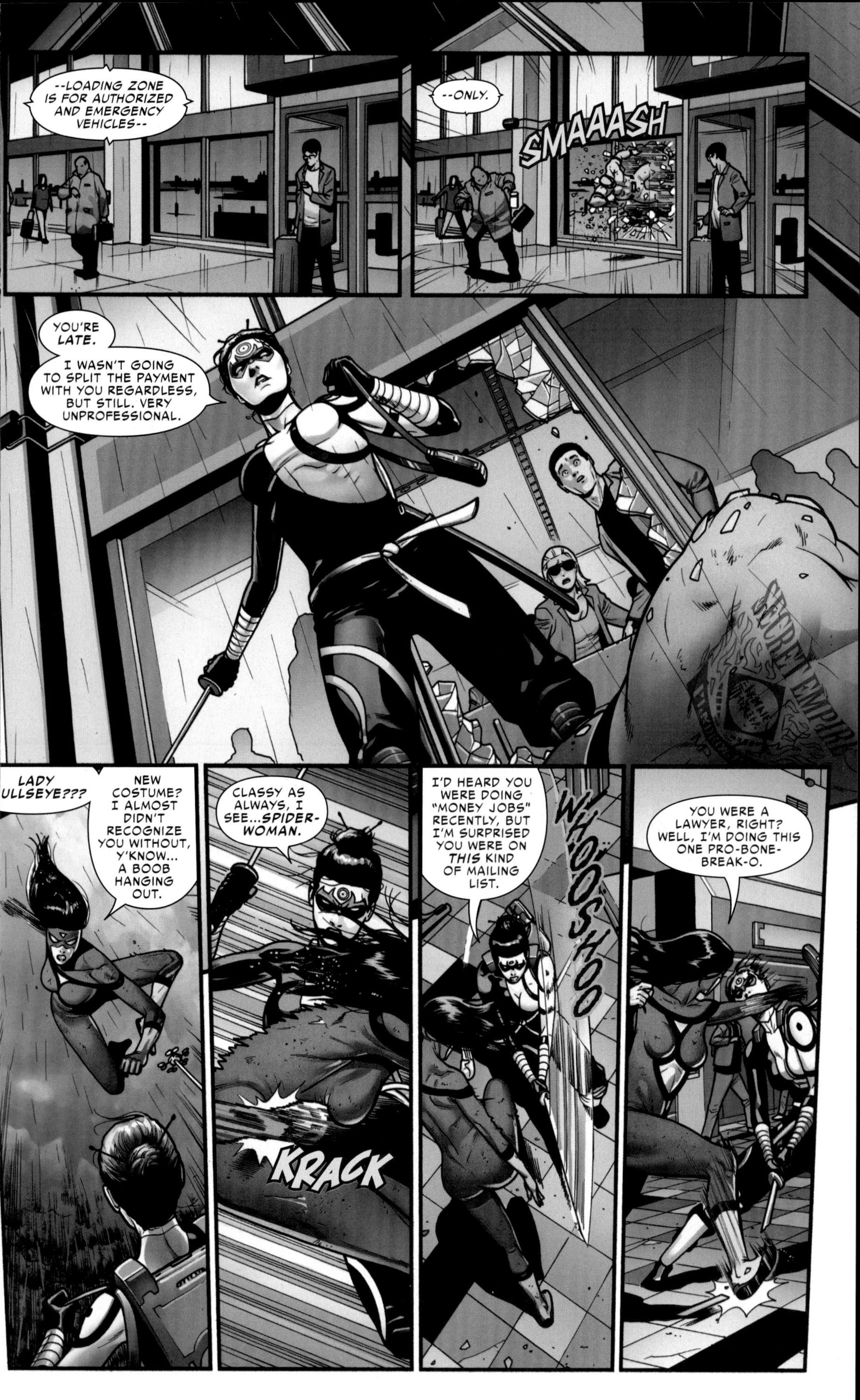
--LOADING ZONE IS FOR AUTHORIZED AND EMERGENCY VEHICLES--
--ONLY.
SMAAASH
YOU'RE LATE.
I WASN'T GOING TO SPLIT THE PAYMENT WITH YOU REGARDLESS, BUT STILL. VERY UNPROFESSIONAL.
SECRET EMPIRE
LADY ULLSEYE???
NEW COSTUME? I ALMOST DIDN'T RECOGNIZE YOU WITHOUT, Y'KNOW... A BOOB HANGING OUT.
CLASSY AS ALWAYS, I SEE...SPIDER-WOMAN.
KRACK
I'D HEARD YOU WERE DOING "MONEY JOBS" RECENTLY, BUT I'M SURPRISED YOU WERE ON THIS KIND OF MAILING LIST.
WHOOOSHOO
YOU WERE A LAWYER, RIGHT? WELL, I'M DOING THIS ONE PRO-BONE-BREAK-O.

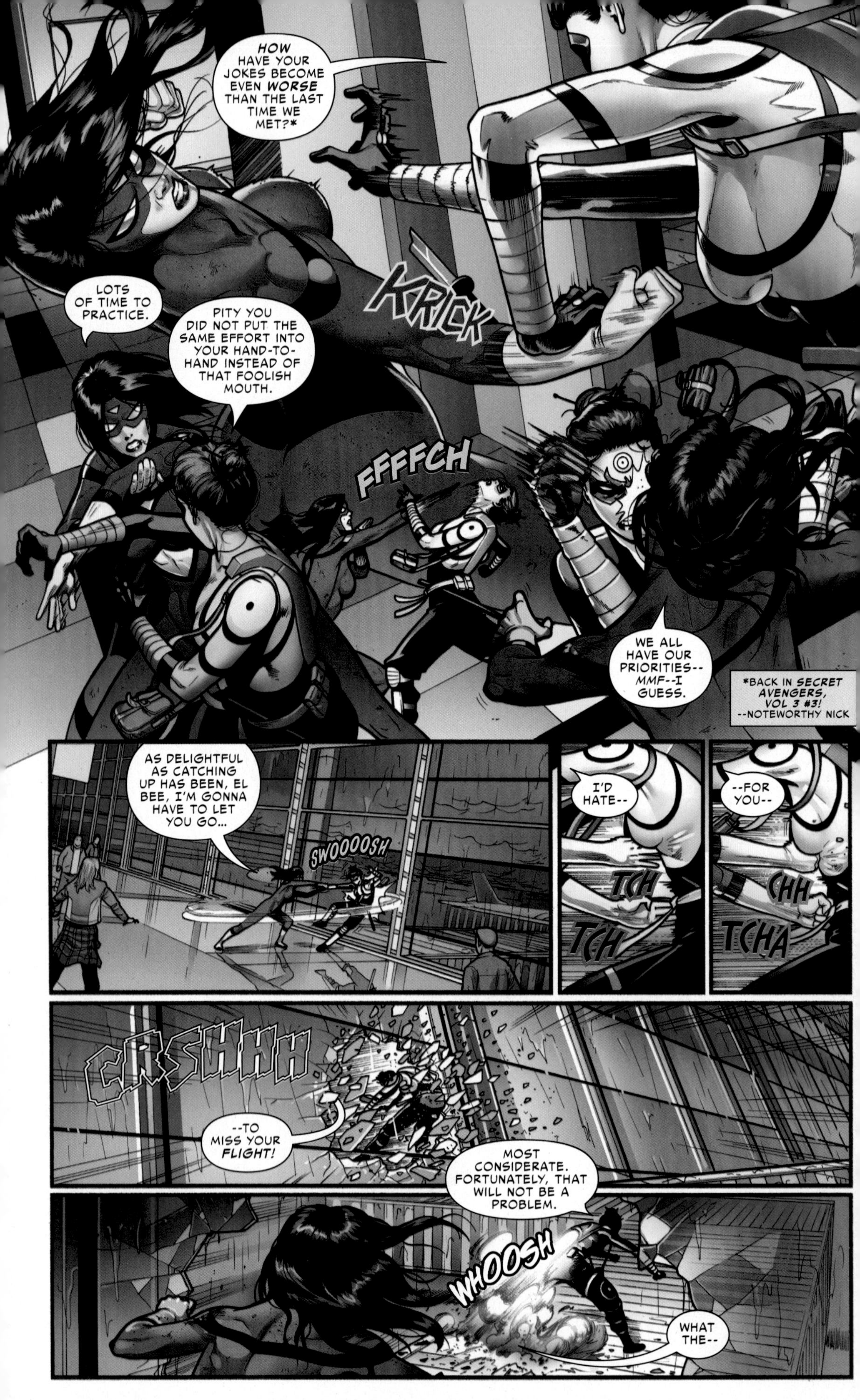
HOW HAVE YOUR JOKES BECOME EVEN WORSE THAN THE LAST TIME WE MET?*
KRICK
LOTS OF TIME TO PRACTICE.
PITY YOU DID NOT PUT THE SAME EFFORT INTO YOUR HAND-TO-HAND INSTEAD OF THAT FOOLISH MOUTH.
FFFFCH
WE ALL HAVE OUR PRIORITIES--MMF--I GUESS.
*BACK IN SECRET AVENGERS, VOL 3 #3! --NOTEWORTHY NICK
AS DELIGHTFUL AS CATCHING UP HAS BEEN, EL BEE, I'M GONNA HAVE TO LET YOU GO...
SWOOOOSH
I'D HATE--
TCH
TCH
--FOR YOU--
CHH
TCHA
CRSHHH
--TO MISS YOUR FLIGHT!
MOST CONSIDERATE. FORTUNATELY, THAT WILL NOT BE A PROBLEM.
WHOOSH
WHAT THE--

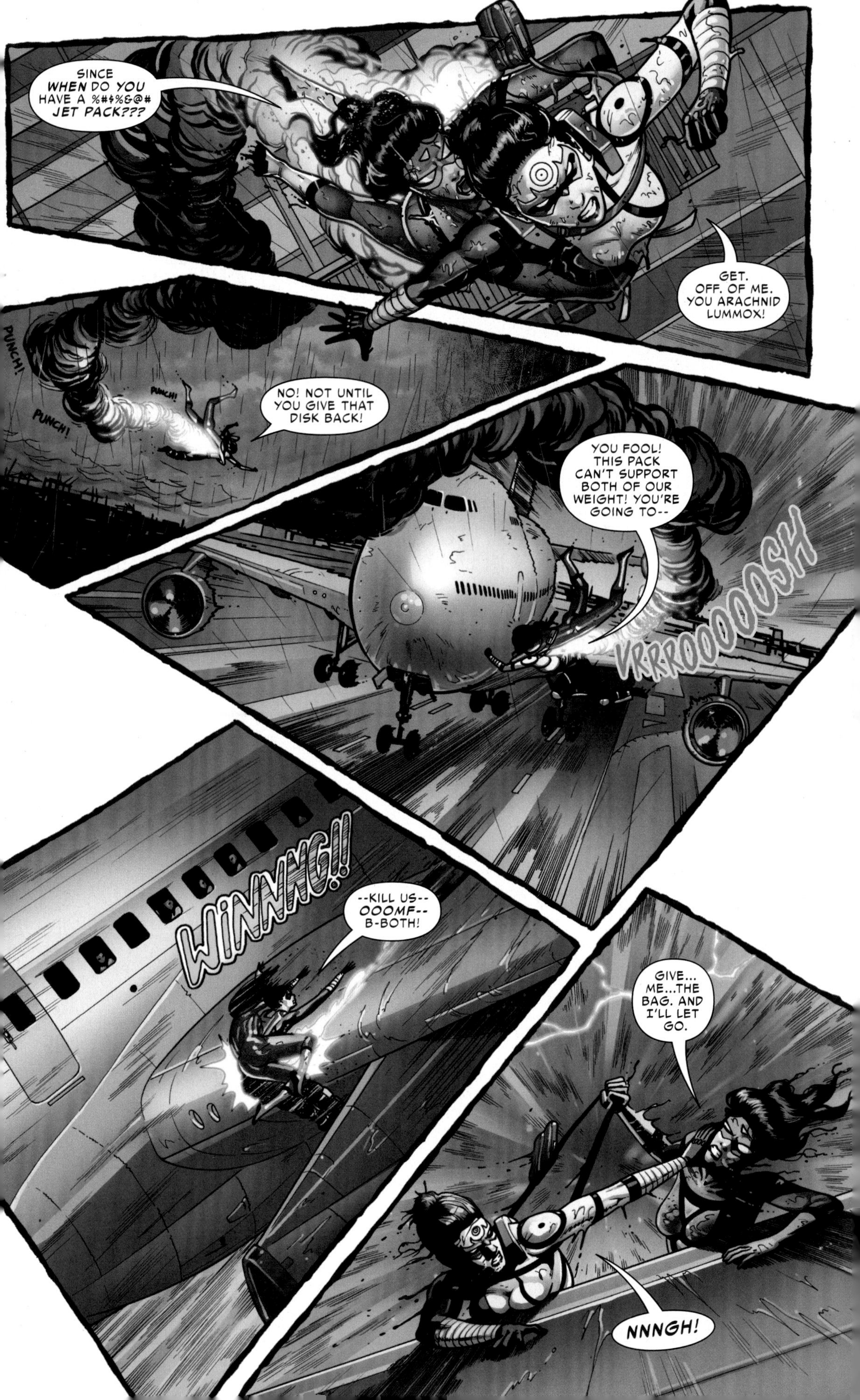
SINCE WHEN DO YOU HAVE A %#$%&@# JET PACK???
GET. OFF. OF ME. YOU ARACHNID LUMMOX!
PUNCH!
PUNCH!
PUNCH!
NO! NOT UNTIL YOU GIVE THAT DISK BACK!
YOU FOOL! THIS PACK CAN'T SUPPORT BOTH OF OUR WEIGHT! YOU'RE GOING TO--
VRRROOOOOSH
WINNNG!!
--KILL US-- OOOMF-- B-BOTH!
GIVE... ME...THE BAG. AND I'LL LET GO.
NNNGH!

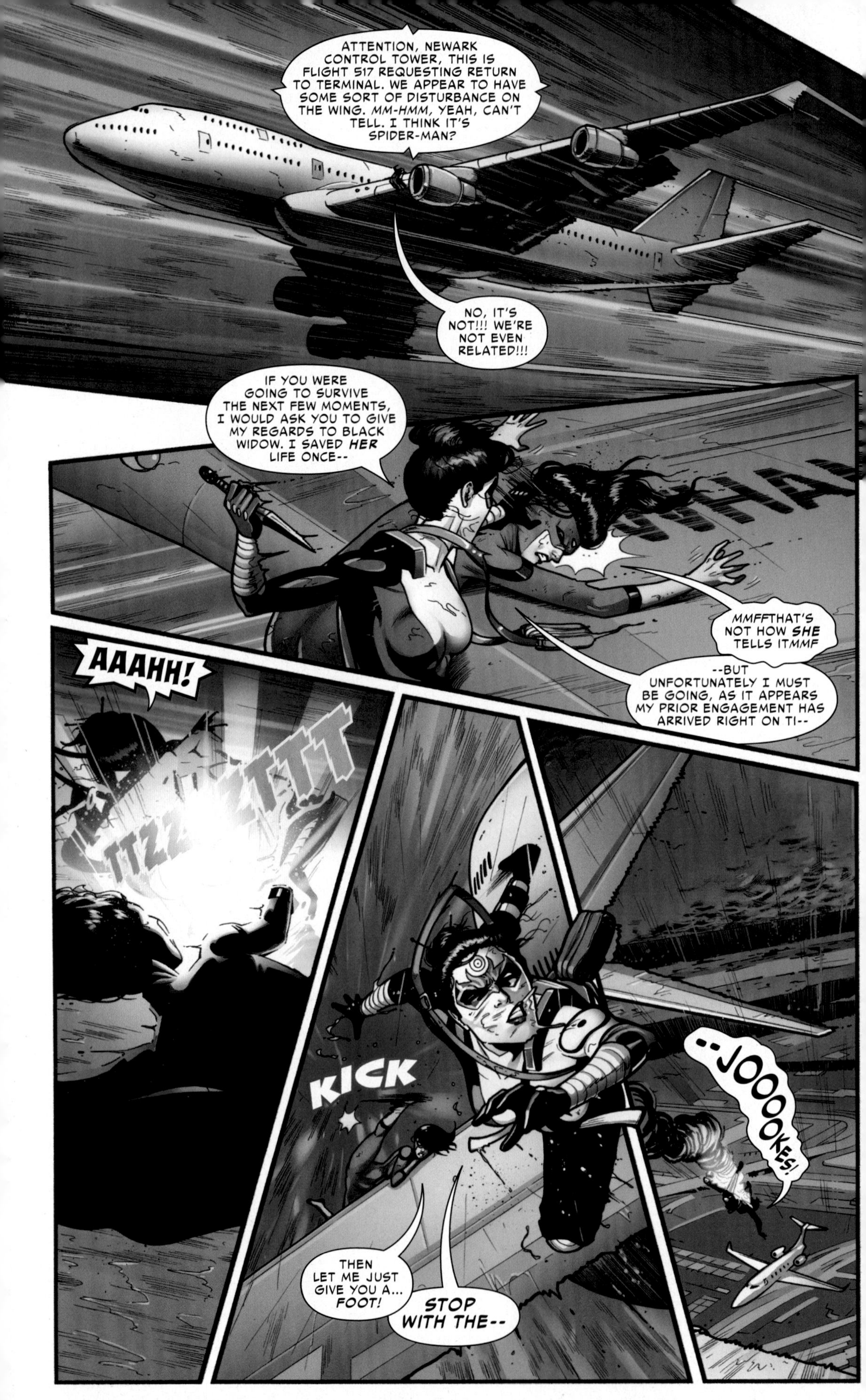
ATTENTION, NEWARK CONTROL TOWER, THIS IS FLIGHT 517 REQUESTING RETURN TO TERMINAL. WE APPEAR TO HAVE SOME SORT OF DISTURBANCE ON THE WING. MM-HMM, YEAH, CAN'T TELL. I THINK IT'S SPIDER-MAN?
NO, IT'S NOT!!! WE'RE NOT EVEN RELATED!!!
IF YOU WERE GOING TO SURVIVE THE NEXT FEW MOMENTS, I WOULD ASK YOU TO GIVE MY REGARDS TO BLACK WIDOW. I SAVED HER LIFE ONCE--
MMFFTHAT'S NOT HOW SHE TELLS ITMMF
--BUT UNFORTUNATELY I MUST BE GOING, AS IT APPEARS MY PRIOR ENGAGEMENT HAS ARRIVED RIGHT ON TI--
AAAHH!
KICK
THEN LET ME JUST GIVE YOU A... FOOT!
STOP WITH THE--
--JOOOOKES!

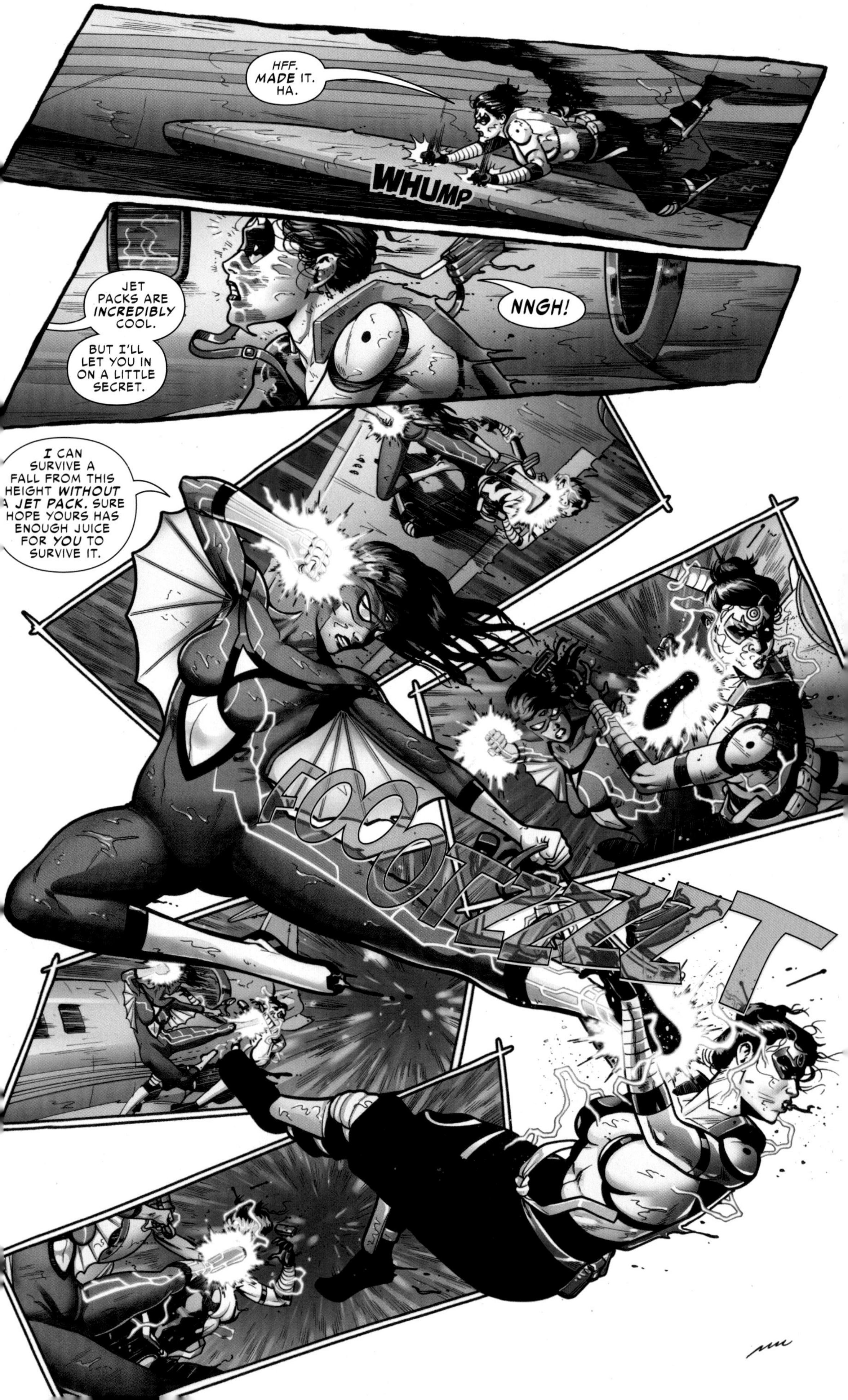
HFF. MADE IT. HA.
WHUMP
JET PACKS ARE INCREDIBLY COOL.
BUT I'LL LET YOU IN ON A LITTLE SECRET.
NNGH!
I CAN SURVIVE A FALL FROM THIS HEIGHT WITHOUT A JET PACK. SURE HOPE YOURS HAS ENOUGH JUICE FOR YOU TO SURVIVE IT.
FOOOTZZZT

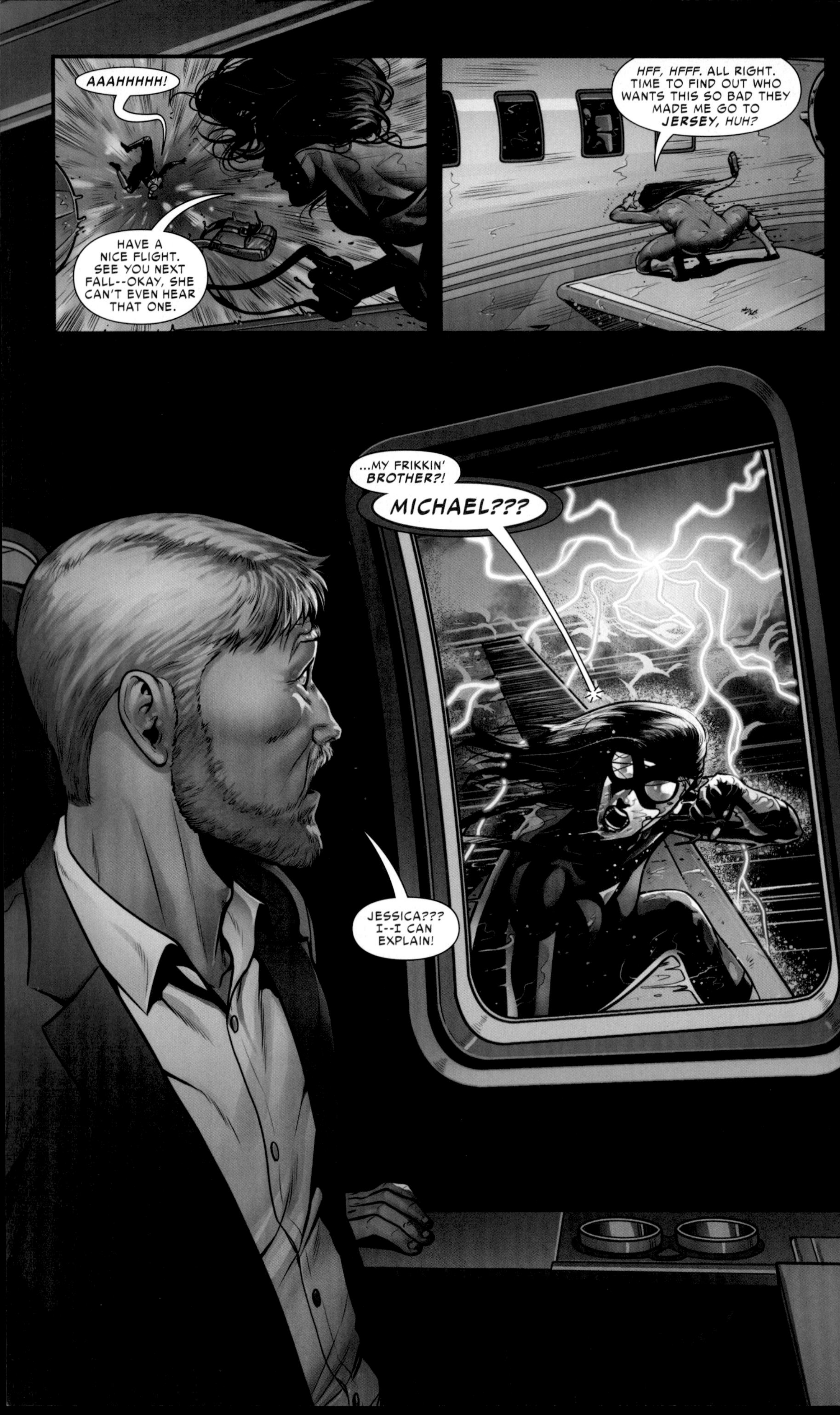
AAAHHHHH!
HAVE A NICE FLIGHT. SEE YOU NEXT FALL--OKAY, SHE CAN'T EVEN HEAR THAT ONE.
HFF, HFFF. ALL RIGHT. TIME TO FIND OUT WHO WANTS THIS SO BAD THEY MADE ME GO TO JERSEY, HUH?
...MY FRIKKIN' BROTHER?!
MICHAEL???
JESSICA??? I--I CAN EXPLAIN!

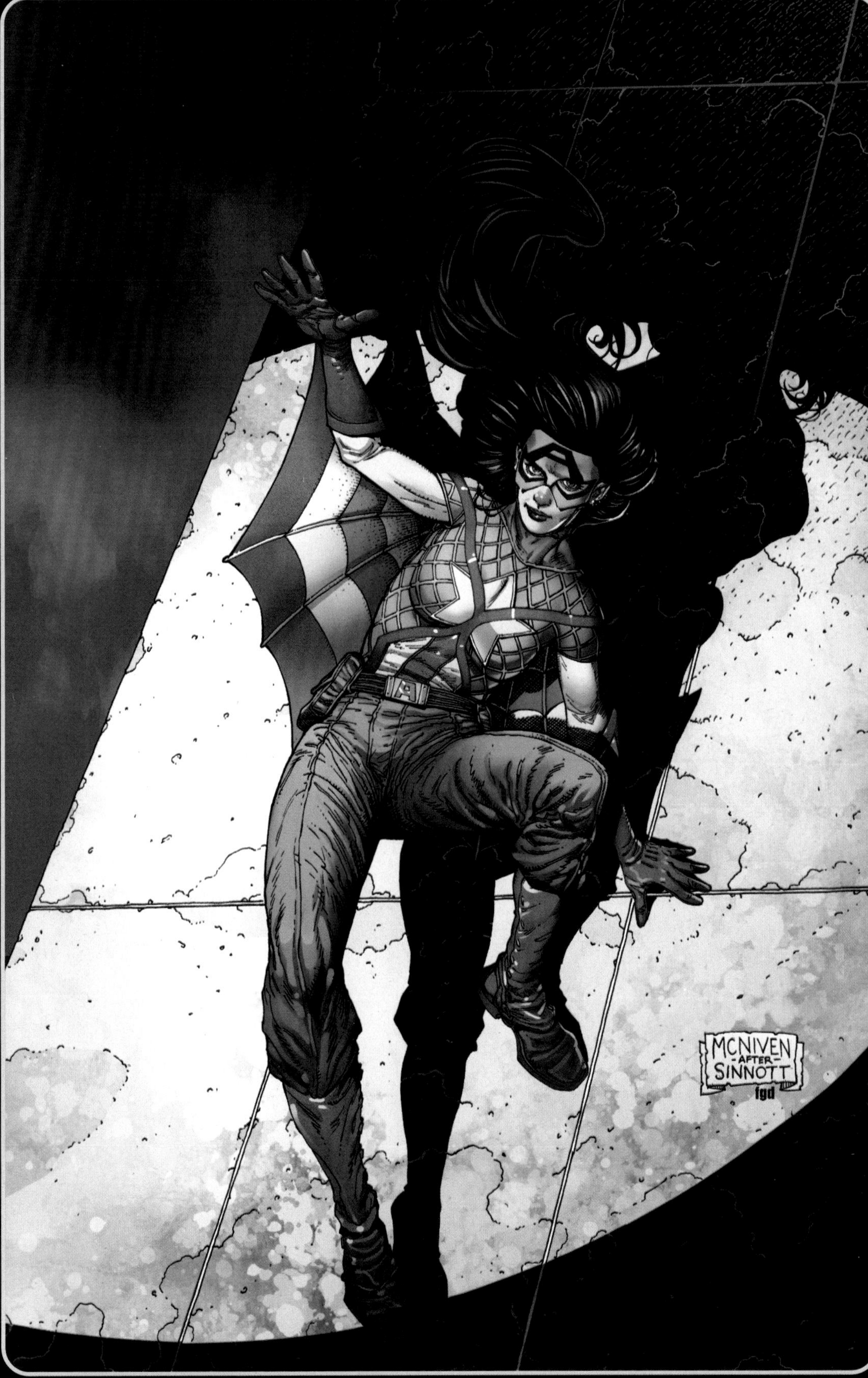
MCNIVEN
-AFTER-
SINNOTT
fgd

#13 CAPTAIN AMERICA 80TH ANNIVERSARY VARIANT BY
STEVE McNIVEN & FRANK D'ARMATA

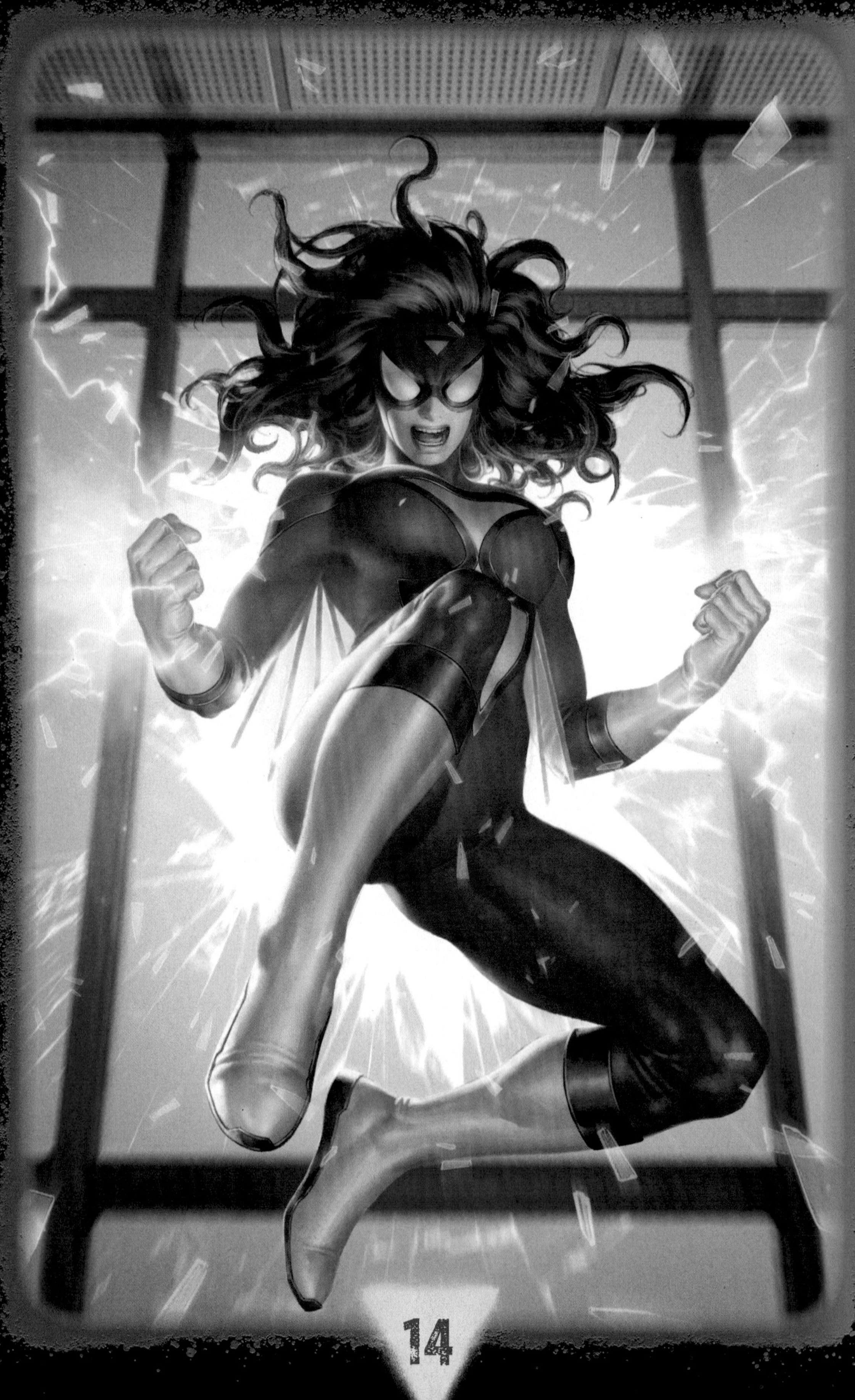

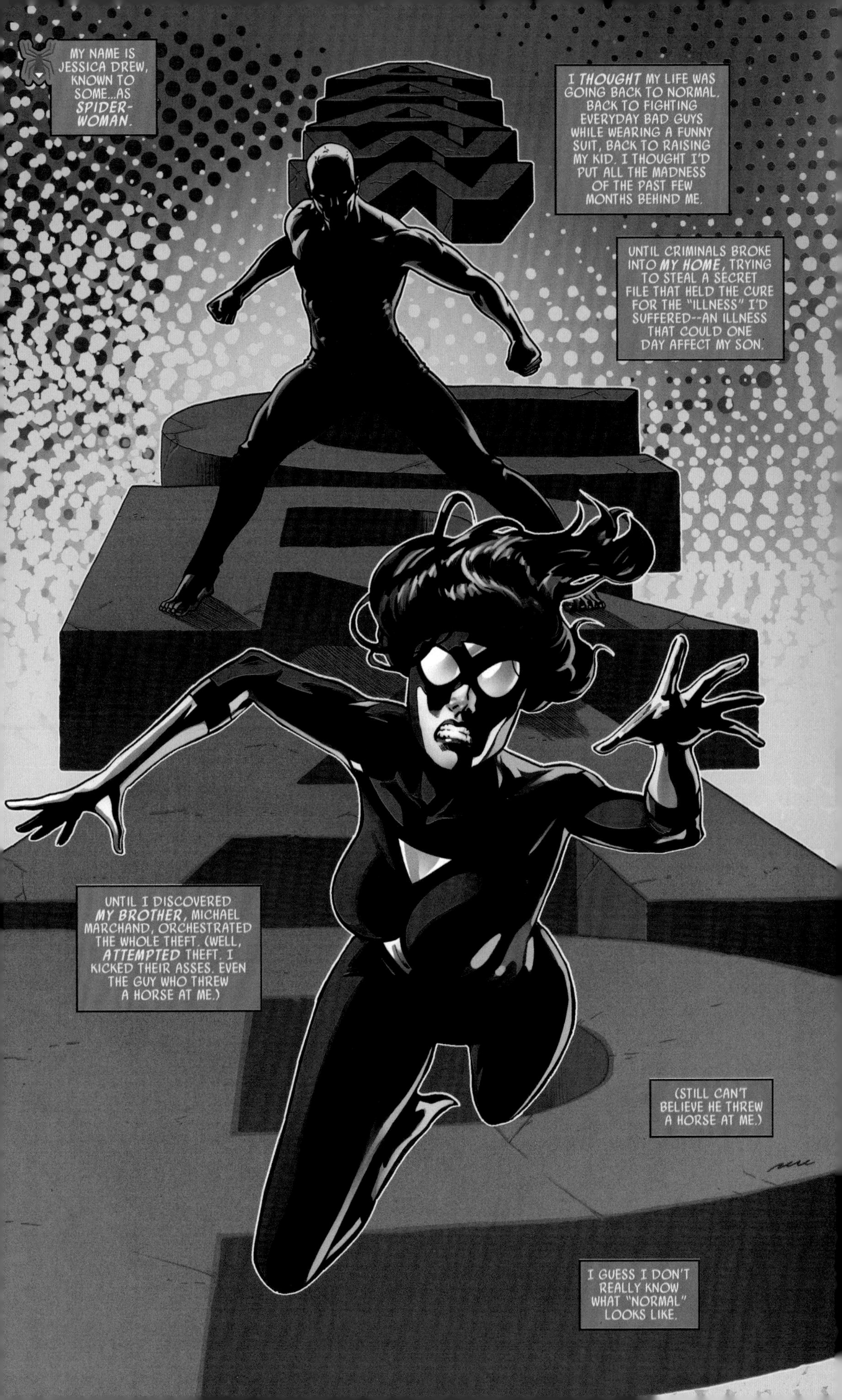
MY NAME IS JESSICA DREW, KNOWN TO SOME...AS *SPIDER-WOMAN*.
I *THOUGHT* MY LIFE WAS GOING BACK TO NORMAL. BACK TO FIGHTING EVERYDAY BAD GUYS WHILE WEARING A FUNNY SUIT, BACK TO RAISING MY KID. I THOUGHT I'D PUT ALL THE MADNESS OF THE PAST FEW MONTHS BEHIND ME.
UNTIL CRIMINALS BROKE INTO *MY HOME*, TRYING TO STEAL A SECRET FILE THAT HELD THE CURE FOR THE "ILLNESS" I'D SUFFERED--AN ILLNESS THAT COULD ONE DAY AFFECT MY SON.
UNTIL I DISCOVERED *MY BROTHER*, MICHAEL MARCHAND, ORCHESTRATED THE WHOLE THEFT. (WELL, *ATTEMPTED* THEFT. I KICKED THEIR ASSES. EVEN THE GUY WHO THREW A HORSE AT ME.)
(STILL CAN'T BELIEVE HE THREW A HORSE AT ME.)
I GUESS I DON'T REALLY KNOW WHAT "NORMAL" LOOKS LIKE.

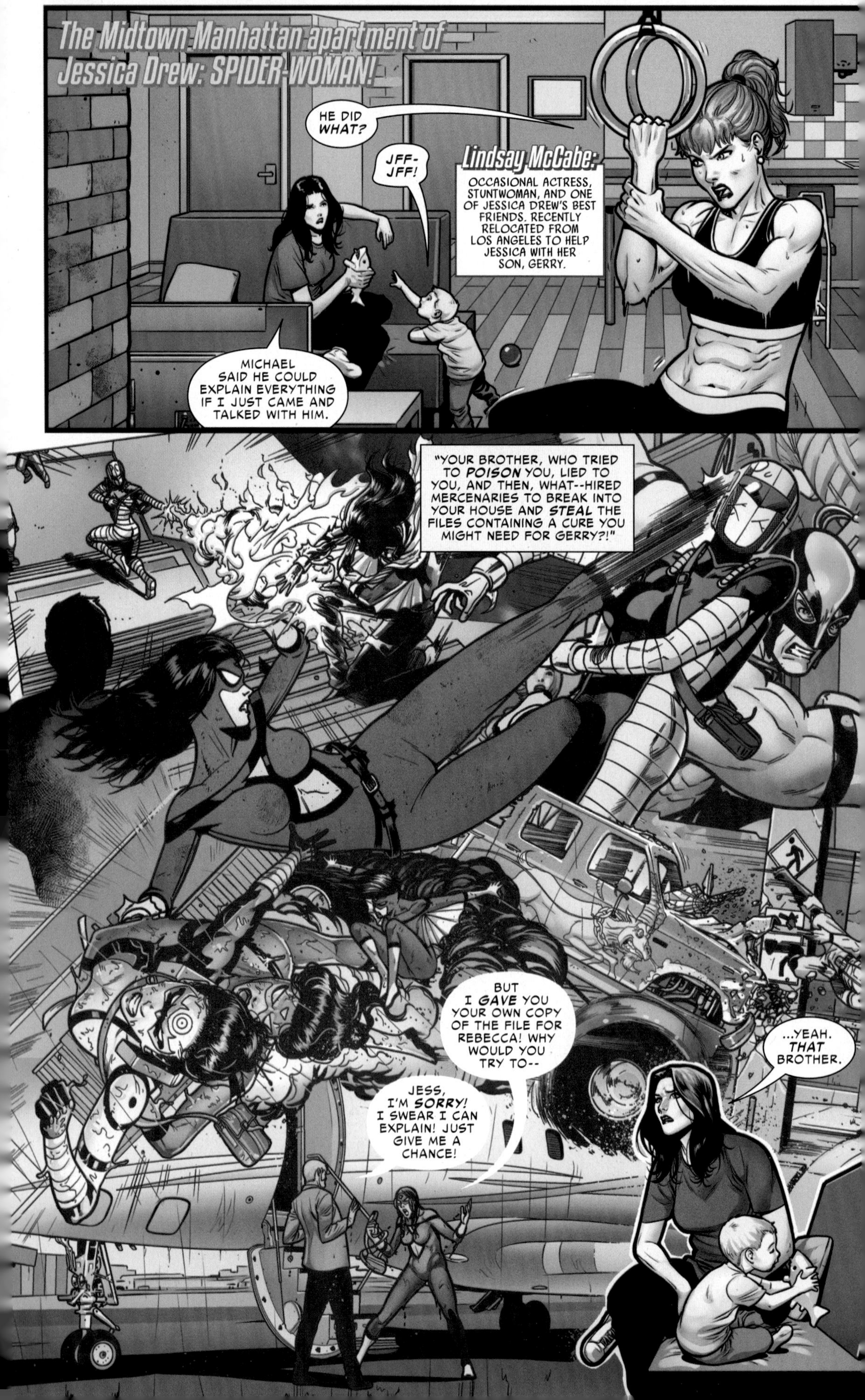
The Midtown Manhattan apartment of Jessica Drew: SPIDER-WOMAN!
HE DID WHAT?
JFF-JFF!
Lindsay McCabe:
OCCASIONAL ACTRESS, STUNTWOMAN, AND ONE OF JESSICA DREW'S BEST FRIENDS. RECENTLY RELOCATED FROM LOS ANGELES TO HELP JESSICA WITH HER SON, GERRY.
MICHAEL SAID HE COULD EXPLAIN EVERYTHING IF I JUST CAME AND TALKED WITH HIM.
"YOUR BROTHER, WHO TRIED TO POISON YOU, LIED TO YOU, AND THEN, WHAT--HIRED MERCENARIES TO BREAK INTO YOUR HOUSE AND STEAL THE FILES CONTAINING A CURE YOU MIGHT NEED FOR GERRY?!"
BUT I GAVE YOU YOUR OWN COPY OF THE FILE FOR REBECCA! WHY WOULD YOU TRY TO--
JESS, I'M SORRY! I SWEAR I CAN EXPLAIN! JUST GIVE ME A CHANCE!
...YEAH. THAT BROTHER.

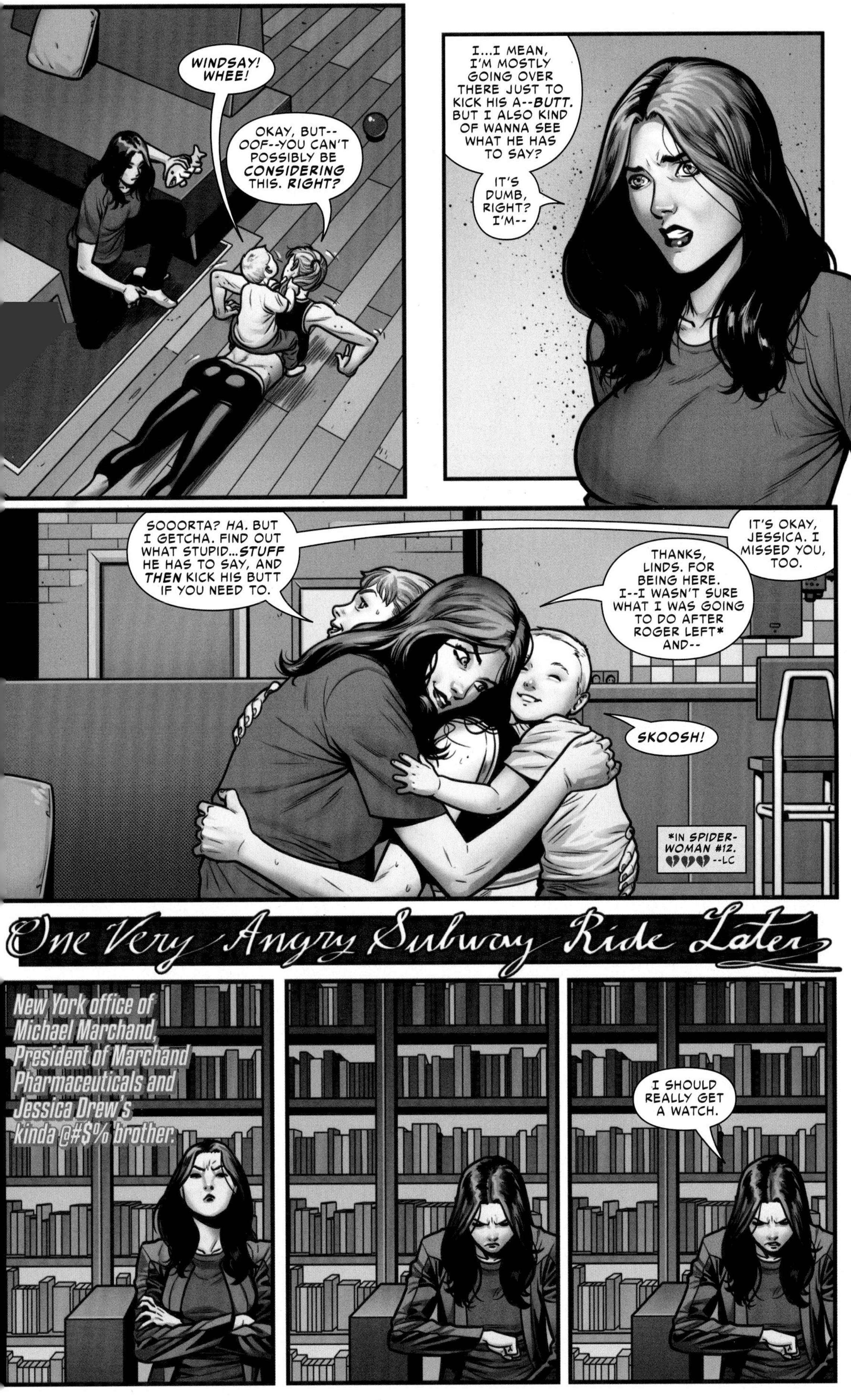
WINDSAY! WHEE!
OKAY, BUT-- OOF--YOU CAN'T POSSIBLY BE CONSIDERING THIS. RIGHT?
I...I MEAN, I'M MOSTLY GOING OVER THERE JUST TO KICK HIS A--BUTT. BUT I ALSO KIND OF WANNA SEE WHAT HE HAS TO SAY?
IT'S DUMB, RIGHT? I'M--
SOOORTA? HA. BUT I GETCHA. FIND OUT WHAT STUPID...STUFF HE HAS TO SAY, AND THEN KICK HIS BUTT IF YOU NEED TO.
THANKS, LINDS. FOR BEING HERE. I--I WASN'T SURE WHAT I WAS GOING TO DO AFTER ROGER LEFT* AND--
IT'S OKAY, JESSICA. I MISSED YOU, TOO.
SKOOSH!
*IN SPIDER-WOMAN #12. --LC
One Very Angry Subway Ride Later
New York office of Michael Marchand, President of Marchand Pharmaceuticals and Jessica Drew's kinda @#$% brother.
I SHOULD REALLY GET A WATCH.

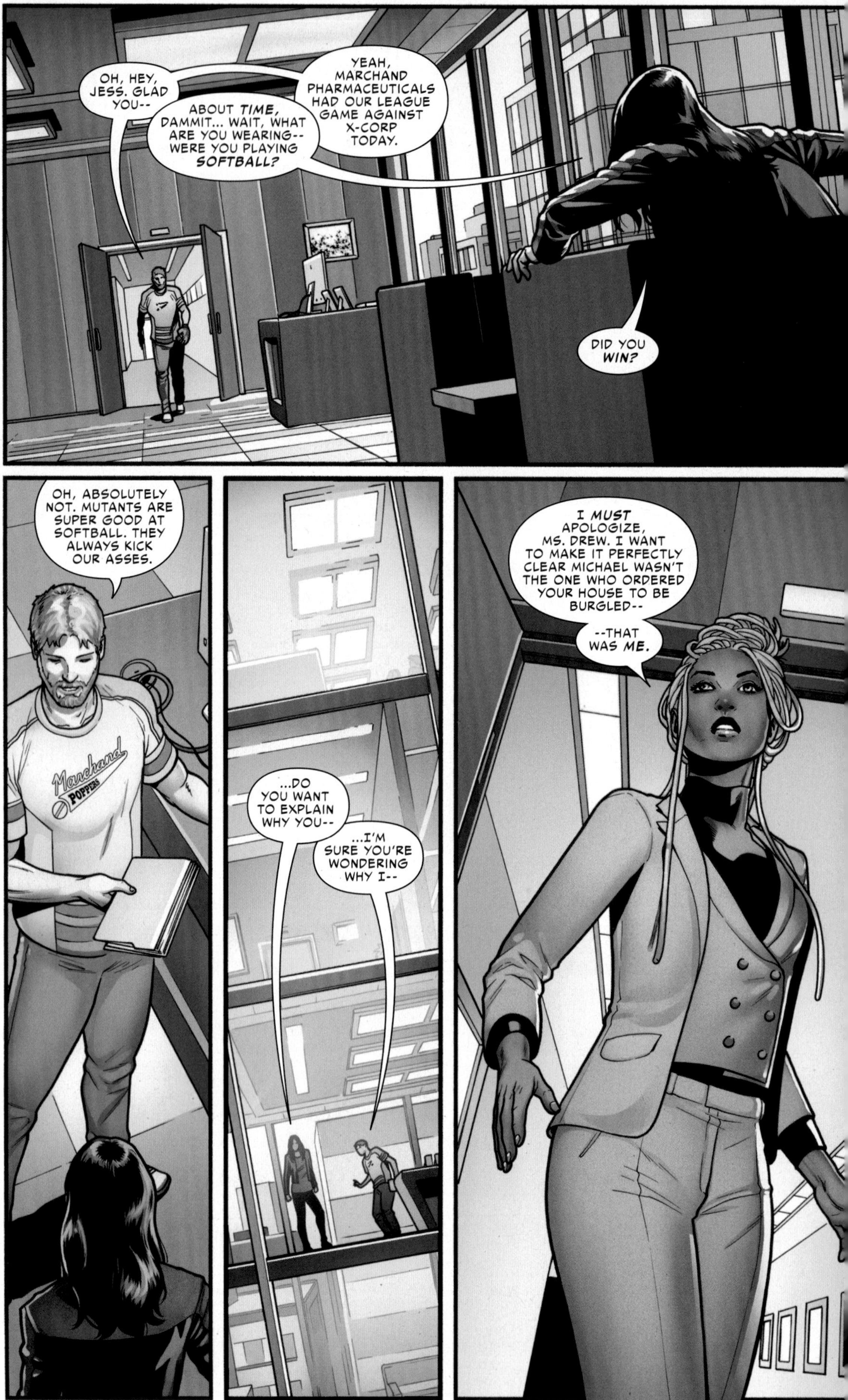
OH, HEY, JESS. GLAD YOU--
ABOUT TIME, DAMMIT... WAIT, WHAT ARE YOU WEARING-- WERE YOU PLAYING SOFTBALL?
YEAH, MARCHAND PHARMACEUTICALS HAD OUR LEAGUE GAME AGAINST X-CORP TODAY.
DID YOU WIN?
OH, ABSOLUTELY NOT. MUTANTS ARE SUPER GOOD AT SOFTBALL. THEY ALWAYS KICK OUR ASSES.
Marchand
POPPERS
...DO YOU WANT TO EXPLAIN WHY YOU--
...I'M SURE YOU'RE WONDERING WHY I--
I MUST APOLOGIZE, MS. DREW. I WANT TO MAKE IT PERFECTLY CLEAR MICHAEL WASN'T THE ONE WHO ORDERED YOUR HOUSE TO BE BURGLED--
--THAT WAS ME.

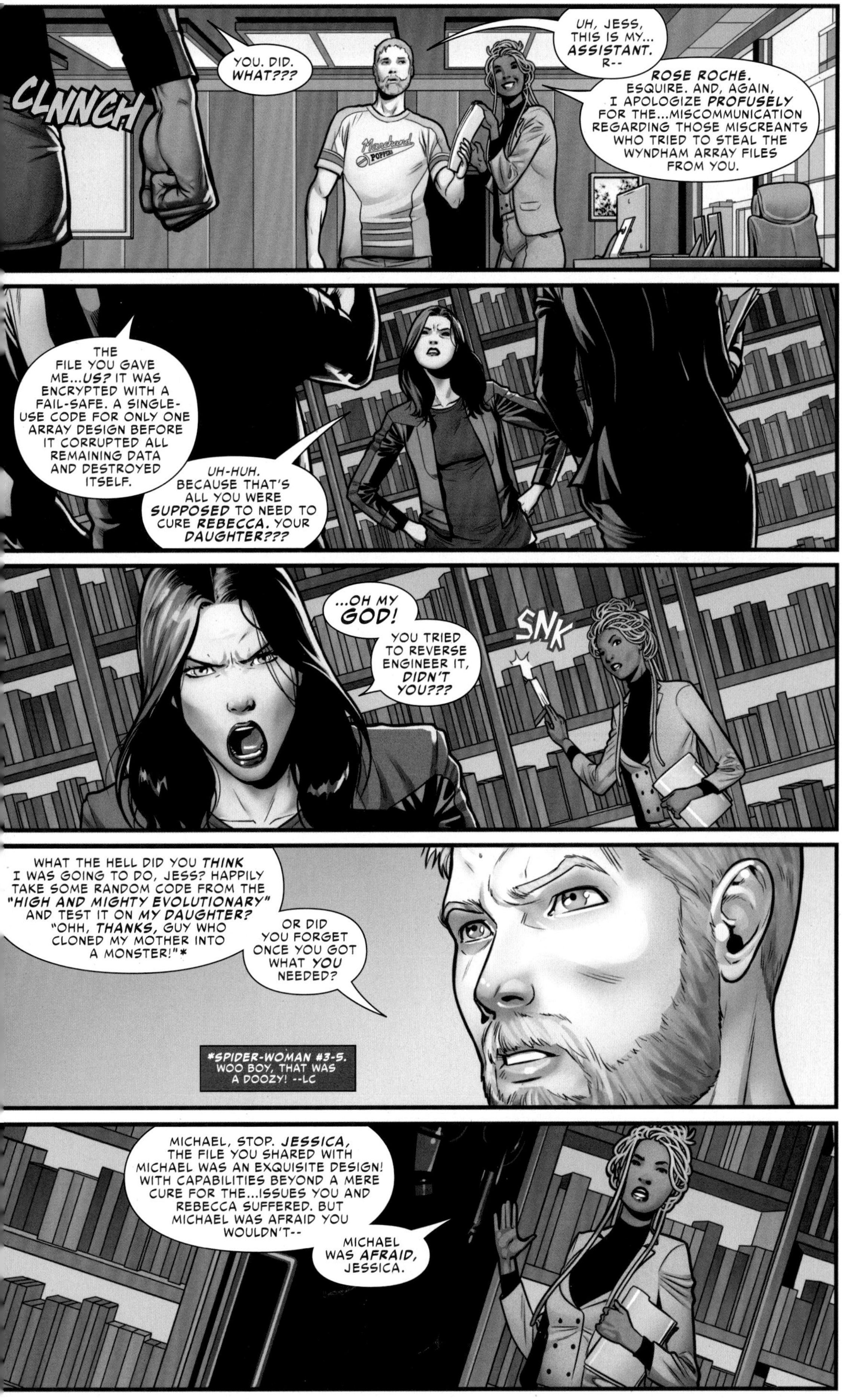
CLNNCH
YOU. DID. WHAT???
UH, JESS, THIS IS MY... ASSISTANT. R--
ROSE ROCHE. ESQUIRE. AND, AGAIN, I APOLOGIZE PROFUSELY FOR THE...MISCOMMUNICATION REGARDING THOSE MISCREANTS WHO TRIED TO STEAL THE WYNDHAM ARRAY FILES FROM YOU.
THE FILE YOU GAVE ME...US? IT WAS ENCRYPTED WITH A FAIL-SAFE. A SINGLE-USE CODE FOR ONLY ONE ARRAY DESIGN BEFORE IT CORRUPTED ALL REMAINING DATA AND DESTROYED ITSELF.
UH-HUH. BECAUSE THAT'S ALL YOU WERE SUPPOSED TO NEED TO CURE REBECCA. YOUR DAUGHTER???
...OH MY GOD!
YOU TRIED TO REVERSE ENGINEER IT, DIDN'T YOU???
SNK
WHAT THE HELL DID YOU THINK I WAS GOING TO DO, JESS? HAPPILY TAKE SOME RANDOM CODE FROM THE "HIGH AND MIGHTY EVOLUTIONARY" AND TEST IT ON MY DAUGHTER? "OHH, THANKS, GUY WHO CLONED MY MOTHER INTO A MONSTER!"*
OR DID YOU FORGET ONCE YOU GOT WHAT YOU NEEDED?
*SPIDER-WOMAN #3-5. WOO BOY, THAT WAS A DOOZY! --LC
MICHAEL, STOP. JESSICA, THE FILE YOU SHARED WITH MICHAEL WAS AN EXQUISITE DESIGN! WITH CAPABILITIES BEYOND A MERE CURE FOR THE...ISSUES YOU AND REBECCA SUFFERED. BUT MICHAEL WAS AFRAID YOU WOULDN'T--
MICHAEL WAS AFRAID, JESSICA.

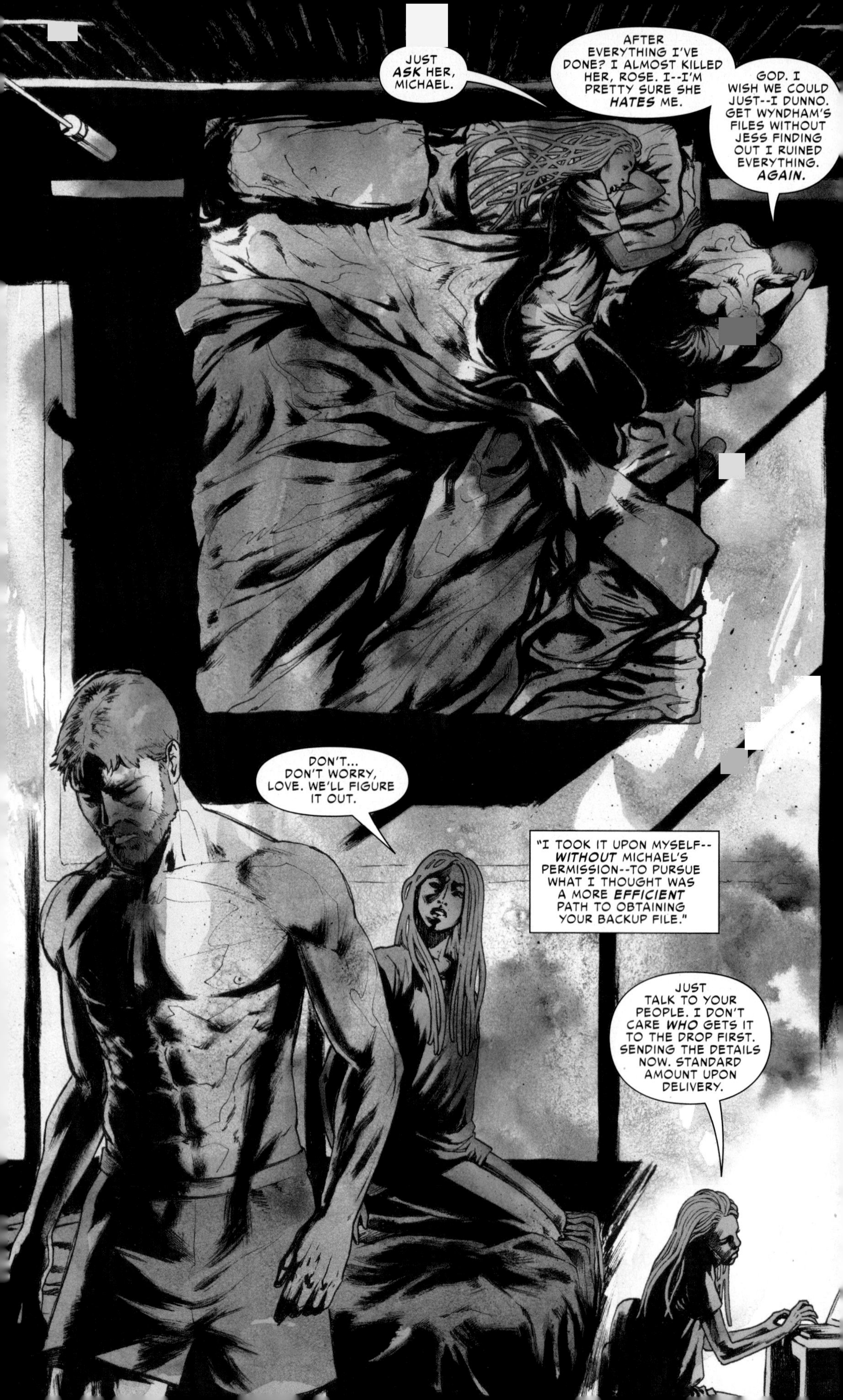
JUST ASK HER, MICHAEL.
AFTER EVERYTHING I'VE DONE? I ALMOST KILLED HER, ROSE. I--I'M PRETTY SURE SHE HATES ME.
GOD. I WISH WE COULD JUST--I DUNNO. GET WYNDHAM'S FILES WITHOUT JESS FINDING OUT I RUINED EVERYTHING. AGAIN.
DON'T... DON'T WORRY, LOVE. WE'LL FIGURE IT OUT.
"I TOOK IT UPON MYSELF--WITHOUT MICHAEL'S PERMISSION--TO PURSUE WHAT I THOUGHT WAS A MORE EFFICIENT PATH TO OBTAINING YOUR BACKUP FILE."
JUST TALK TO YOUR PEOPLE. I DON'T CARE WHO GETS IT TO THE DROP FIRST. SENDING THE DETAILS NOW. STANDARD AMOUNT UPON DELIVERY.

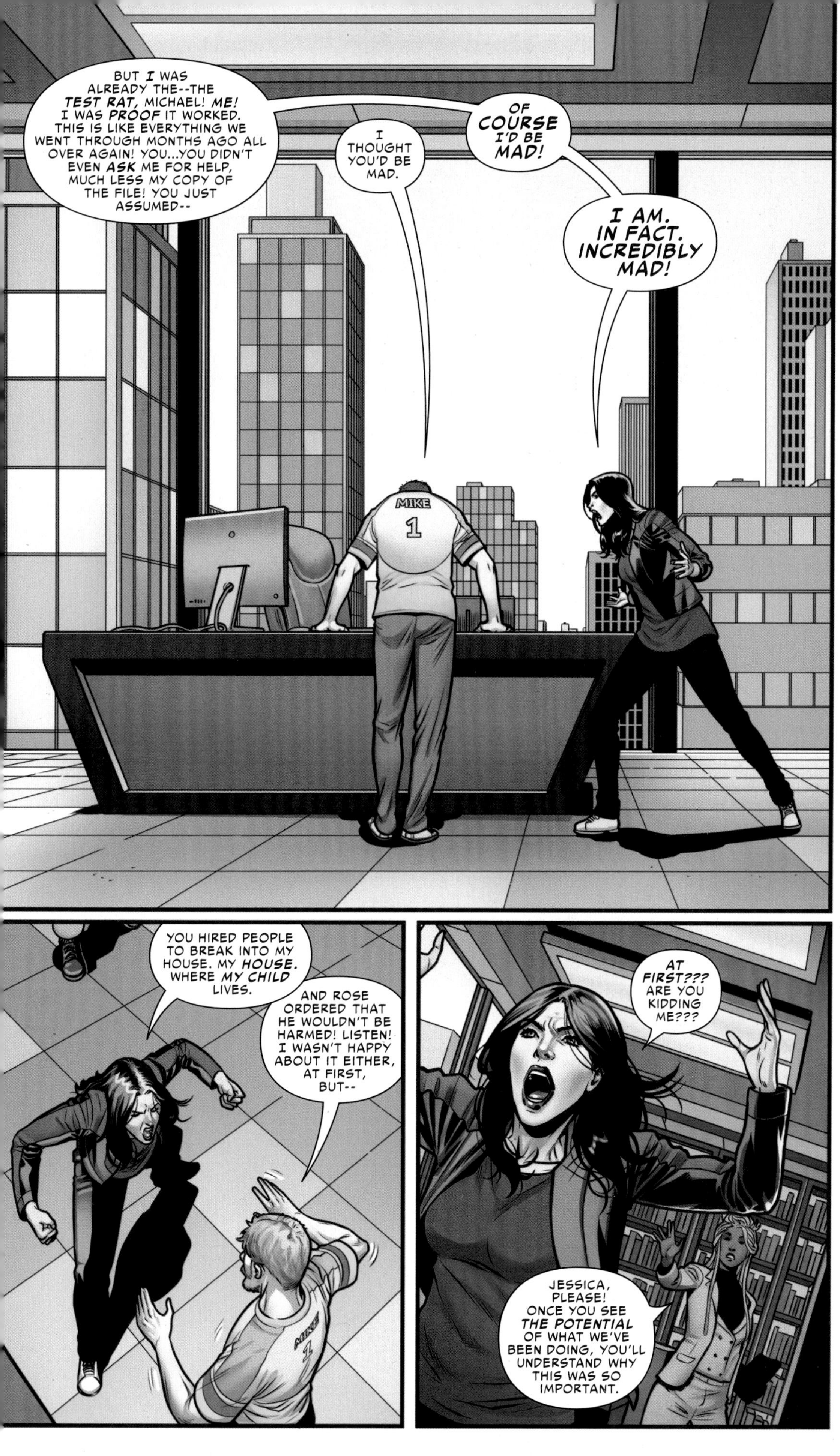

BUT I WAS ALREADY THE--THE TEST RAT, MICHAEL! ME! I WAS PROOF IT WORKED. THIS IS LIKE EVERYTHING WE WENT THROUGH MONTHS AGO ALL OVER AGAIN! YOU...YOU DIDN'T EVEN ASK ME FOR HELP, MUCH LESS MY COPY OF THE FILE! YOU JUST ASSUMED--
I THOUGHT YOU'D BE MAD.
OF COURSE I'D BE MAD!
I AM. IN FACT. INCREDIBLY MAD!
MIKE
1
YOU HIRED PEOPLE TO BREAK INTO MY HOUSE. MY HOUSE. WHERE MY CHILD LIVES.
AND ROSE ORDERED THAT HE WOULDN'T BE HARMED! LISTEN! I WASN'T HAPPY ABOUT IT EITHER, AT FIRST, BUT--
AT FIRST??? ARE YOU KIDDING ME???
JESSICA, PLEASE! ONCE YOU SEE THE POTENTIAL OF WHAT WE'VE BEEN DOING, YOU'LL UNDERSTAND WHY THIS WAS SO IMPORTANT.

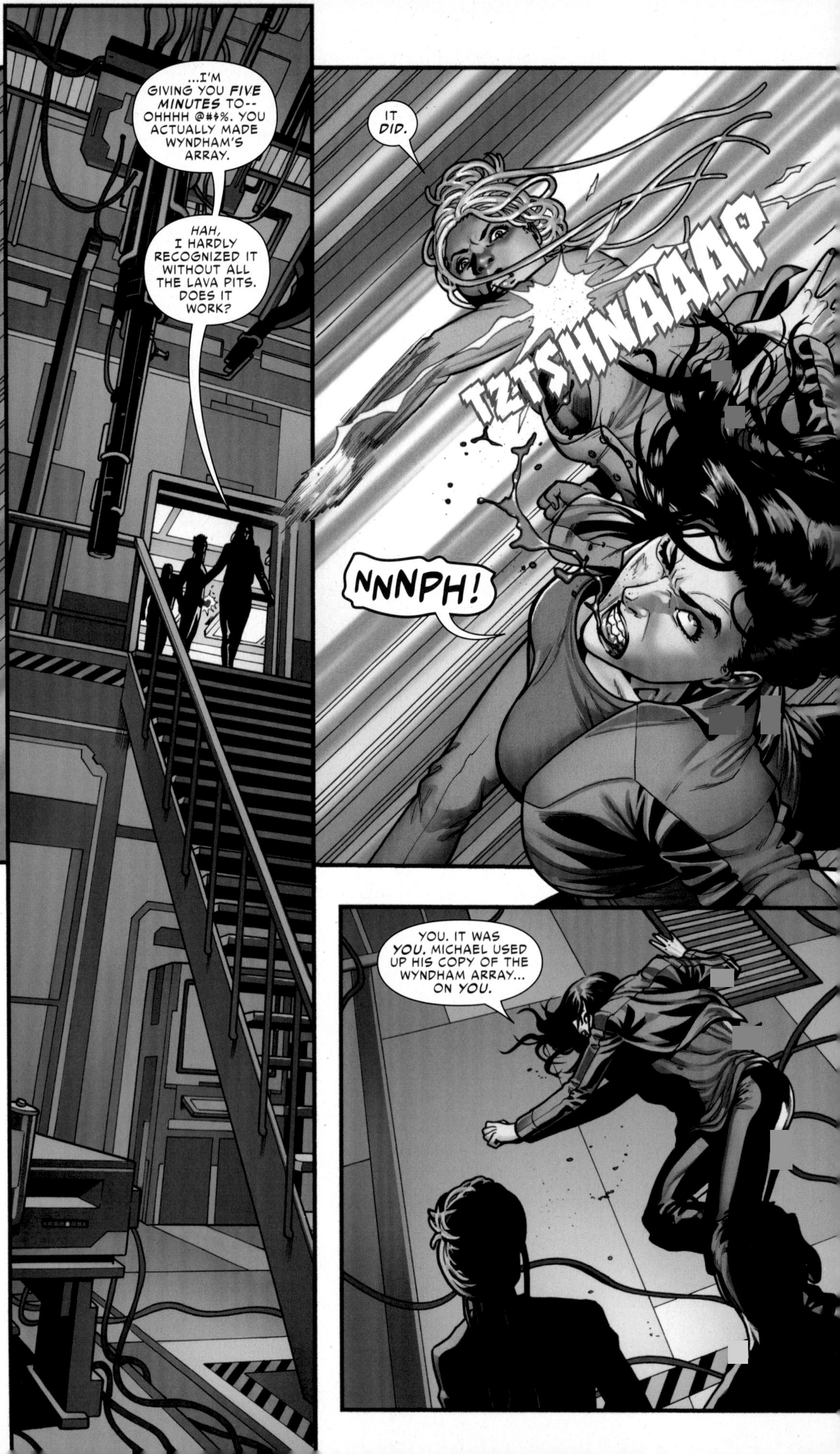
...I'M GIVING YOU FIVE MINUTES TO-- OHHHH @#$%. YOU ACTUALLY MADE WYNDHAM'S ARRAY.
HAH, I HARDLY RECOGNIZED IT WITHOUT ALL THE LAVA PITS. DOES IT WORK?
IT DID.
TZTSHNAAAP
NNNPH!
YOU. IT WAS YOU. MICHAEL USED UP HIS COPY OF THE WYNDHAM ARRAY... ON YOU.

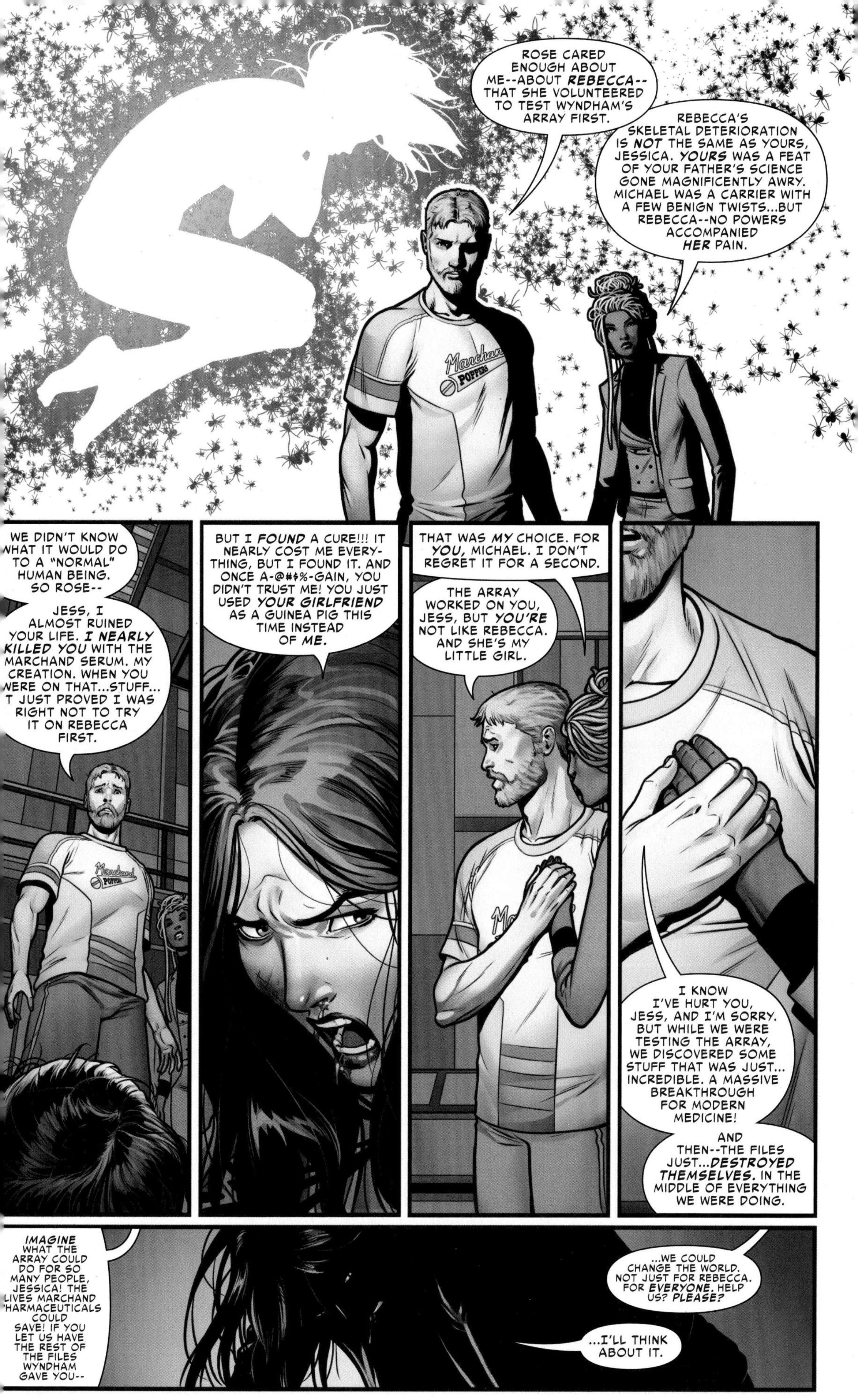
ROSE CARED ENOUGH ABOUT ME--ABOUT REBECCA--THAT SHE VOLUNTEERED TO TEST WYNDHAM'S ARRAY FIRST.
REBECCA'S SKELETAL DETERIORATION IS NOT THE SAME AS YOURS, JESSICA. YOURS WAS A FEAT OF YOUR FATHER'S SCIENCE GONE MAGNIFICENTLY AWRY. MICHAEL WAS A CARRIER WITH A FEW BENIGN TWISTS...BUT REBECCA--NO POWERS ACCOMPANIED HER PAIN.
Marchand POPPERS
WE DIDN'T KNOW WHAT IT WOULD DO TO A "NORMAL" HUMAN BEING. SO ROSE--
JESS, I ALMOST RUINED YOUR LIFE. I NEARLY KILLED YOU WITH THE MARCHAND SERUM. MY CREATION. WHEN YOU WERE ON THAT...STUFF... IT JUST PROVED I WAS RIGHT NOT TO TRY IT ON REBECCA FIRST.
BUT I FOUND A CURE!!! IT NEARLY COST ME EVERYTHING, BUT I FOUND IT. AND ONCE A-@#$%-GAIN, YOU DIDN'T TRUST ME! YOU JUST USED YOUR GIRLFRIEND AS A GUINEA PIG THIS TIME INSTEAD OF ME.
THAT WAS MY CHOICE. FOR YOU, MICHAEL. I DON'T REGRET IT FOR A SECOND.
THE ARRAY WORKED ON YOU, JESS, BUT YOU'RE NOT LIKE REBECCA. AND SHE'S MY LITTLE GIRL.
I KNOW I'VE HURT YOU, JESS, AND I'M SORRY. BUT WHILE WE WERE TESTING THE ARRAY, WE DISCOVERED SOME STUFF THAT WAS JUST... INCREDIBLE. A MASSIVE BREAKTHROUGH FOR MODERN MEDICINE!
AND THEN--THE FILES JUST...DESTROYED THEMSELVES. IN THE MIDDLE OF EVERYTHING WE WERE DOING.
IMAGINE WHAT THE ARRAY COULD DO FOR SO MANY PEOPLE, JESSICA! THE LIVES MARCHAND PHARMACEUTICALS COULD SAVE! IF YOU LET US HAVE THE REST OF THE FILES WYNDHAM GAVE YOU--
...WE COULD CHANGE THE WORLD. NOT JUST FOR REBECCA. FOR EVERYONE. HELP US? PLEASE?
...I'LL THINK ABOUT IT.

JESS, YOU'RE NOT ACTUALLY GOING TO THINK ABOUT IT, ARE YOU?

OH, GOD, NO. ARE YOU KIDDING?

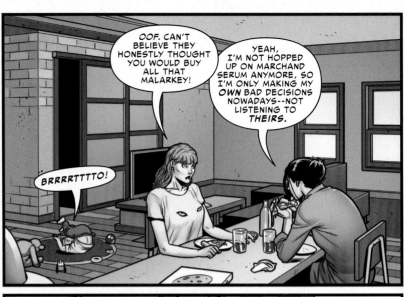

OOF. CAN'T BELIEVE THEY HONESTLY THOUGHT YOU WOULD BUY ALL THAT MALARKEY!

YEAH, I'M NOT HOPPED UP ON MARCHAND SERUM ANYMORE, SO I'M ONLY MAKING MY *OWN* BAD DECISIONS NOWADAYS--NOT LISTENING TO *THEIRS.*

BRRRRTTTTO!

OKAY, BUT WHAT *ARE* YOU GOING TO DO, FOR REAL?

I DUNNO, PROBABLY SOME OVERLY ELABORATE SCHEME WHERE I BREAK INTO MARCHAND PHARMACEUTICALS AND STEAL BACK WHAT'S LEFT OF THE HIGH EVOLUTIONARY'S TECHNOLOGY FROM MICHAEL BECAUSE HE CAN'T BE TRUSTED, I GUESS.

FUN. CAN I HELP?

WHO'S GONNA WATCH GERRY?

WE'LL TAKE HIM WITH US!

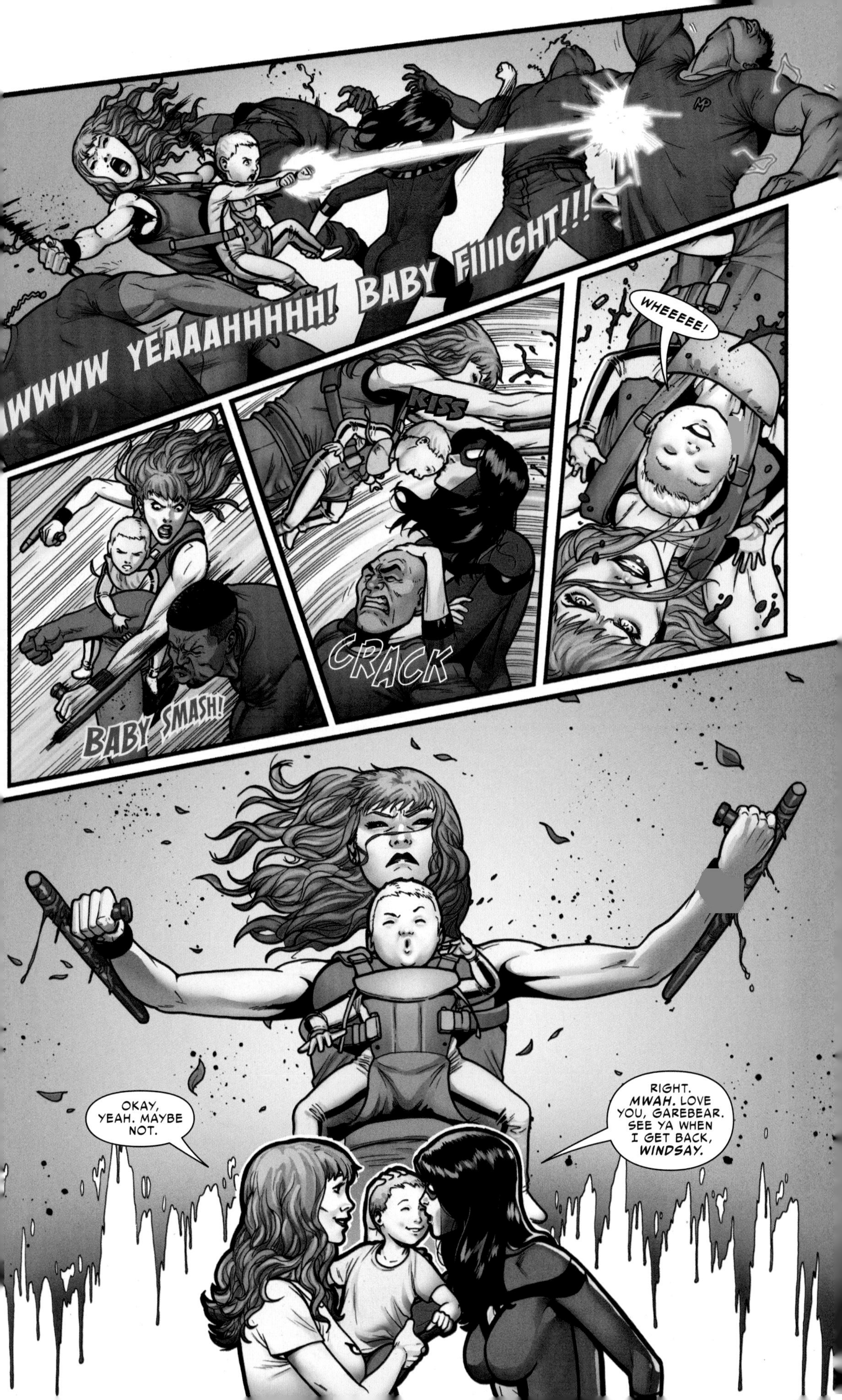

WWWWW YEAAAHHHHH! BABY FIIIIGHT!!!
WHEEEEE!
KISS
BABY SMASH!
CRACK
OKAY, YEAH. MAYBE NOT.
RIGHT. MWAH. LOVE YOU, GAREBEAR. SEE YA WHEN I GET BACK, WINDSAY.

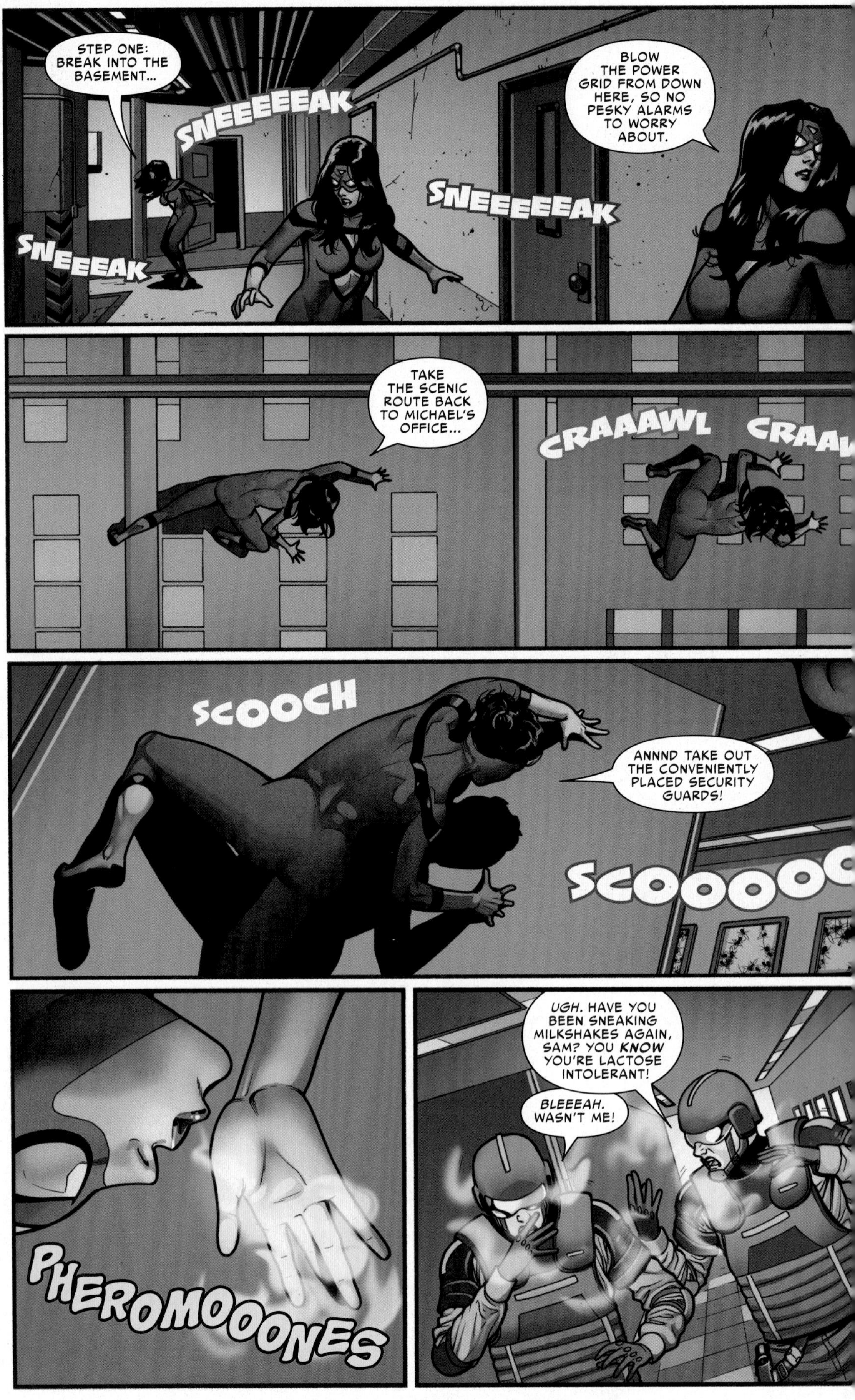

STEP ONE: BREAK INTO THE BASEMENT...
SNEEEEEEAK
SNEEEEAK
SNEEEEEEAK
BLOW THE POWER GRID FROM DOWN HERE, SO NO PESKY ALARMS TO WORRY ABOUT.
TAKE THE SCENIC ROUTE BACK TO MICHAEL'S OFFICE...
CRAAAWL
SCOOCH
ANNND TAKE OUT THE CONVENIENTLY PLACED SECURITY GUARDS!
PHEROMOOONES
UGH. HAVE YOU BEEN SNEAKING MILKSHAKES AGAIN, SAM? YOU KNOW YOU'RE LACTOSE INTOLERANT!
BLEEEAH. WASN'T ME!

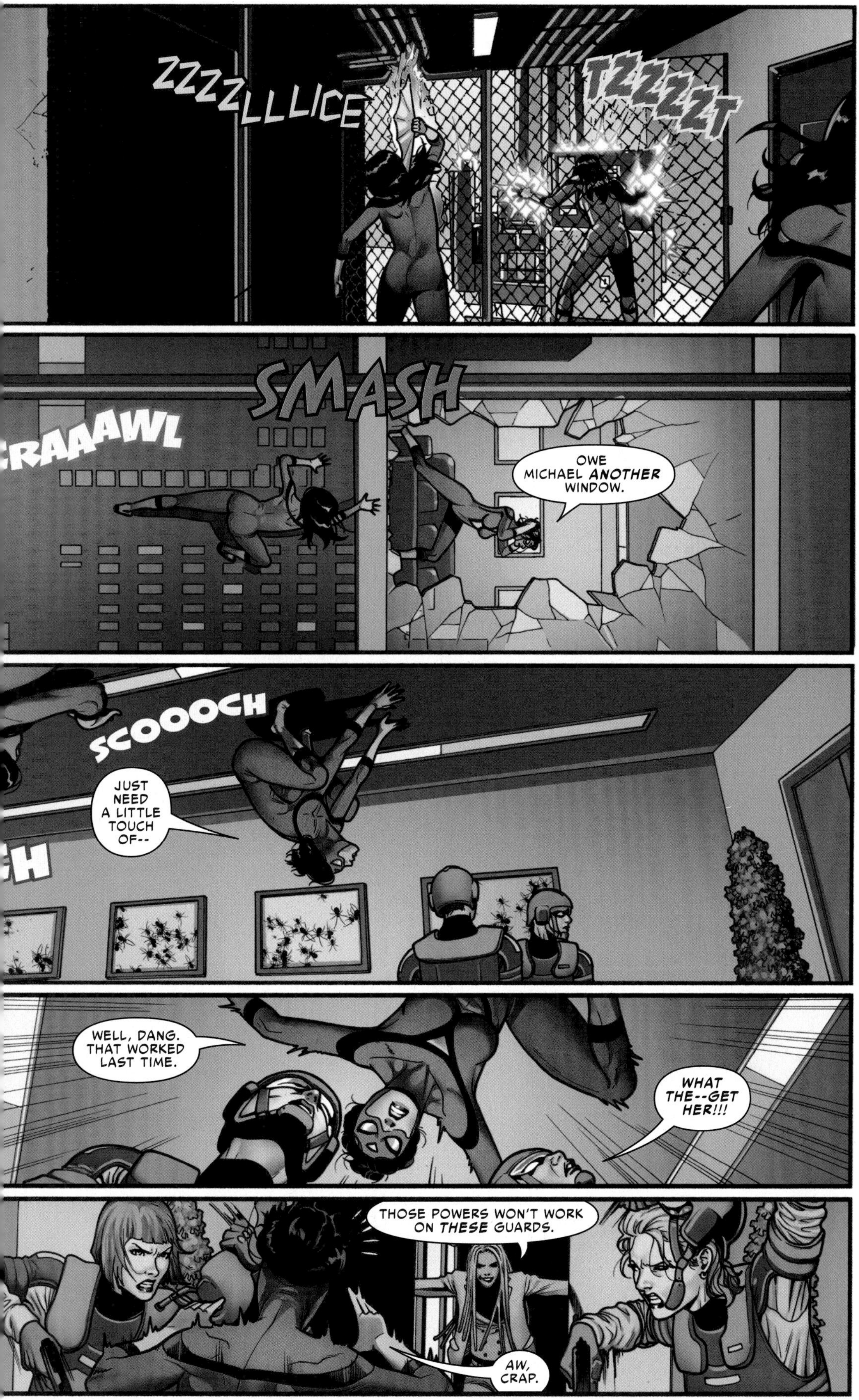
ZZZZLLLICE
TZZZZZT
SMASH
CRAAAWL
OWE MICHAEL ANOTHER WINDOW.
SCOOOCH
JUST NEED A LITTLE TOUCH OF--
WELL, DANG. THAT WORKED LAST TIME.
WHAT THE--GET HER!!!
THOSE POWERS WON'T WORK ON THESE GUARDS.
AW, CRAP.

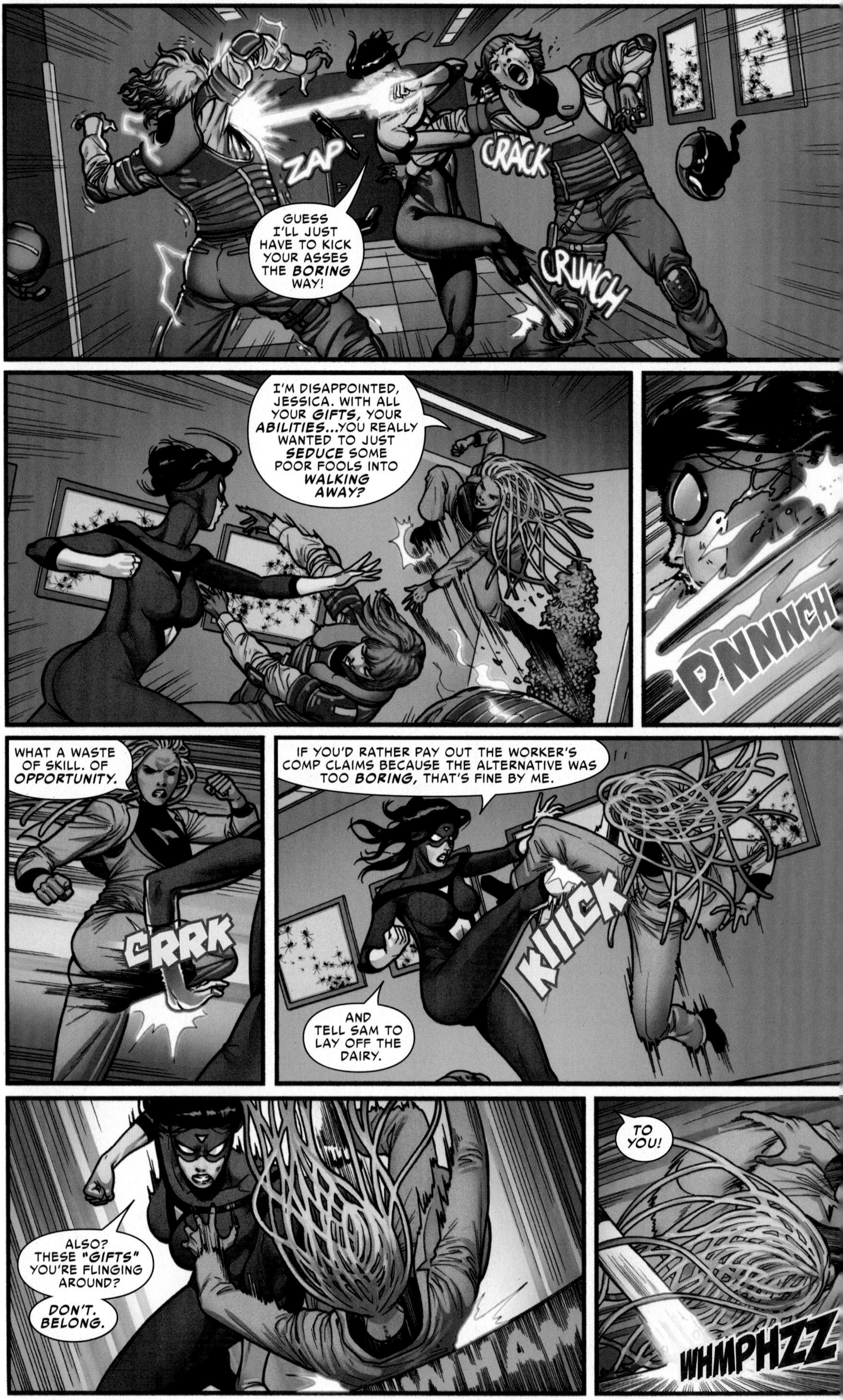
ZAP
GUESS I'LL JUST HAVE TO KICK YOUR ASSES THE BORING WAY!
CRACK
CRUNCH
I'M DISAPPOINTED, JESSICA. WITH ALL YOUR GIFTS, YOUR ABILITIES...YOU REALLY WANTED TO JUST SEDUCE SOME POOR FOOLS INTO WALKING AWAY?
PNNNCH
WHAT A WASTE OF SKILL. OF OPPORTUNITY.
CRRK
IF YOU'D RATHER PAY OUT THE WORKER'S COMP CLAIMS BECAUSE THE ALTERNATIVE WAS TOO BORING, THAT'S FINE BY ME.
KIIICK
AND TELL SAM TO LAY OFF THE DAIRY.
ALSO? THESE "GIFTS" YOU'RE FLINGING AROUND?
DON'T. BELONG.
TO YOU!
WHMPHZZ

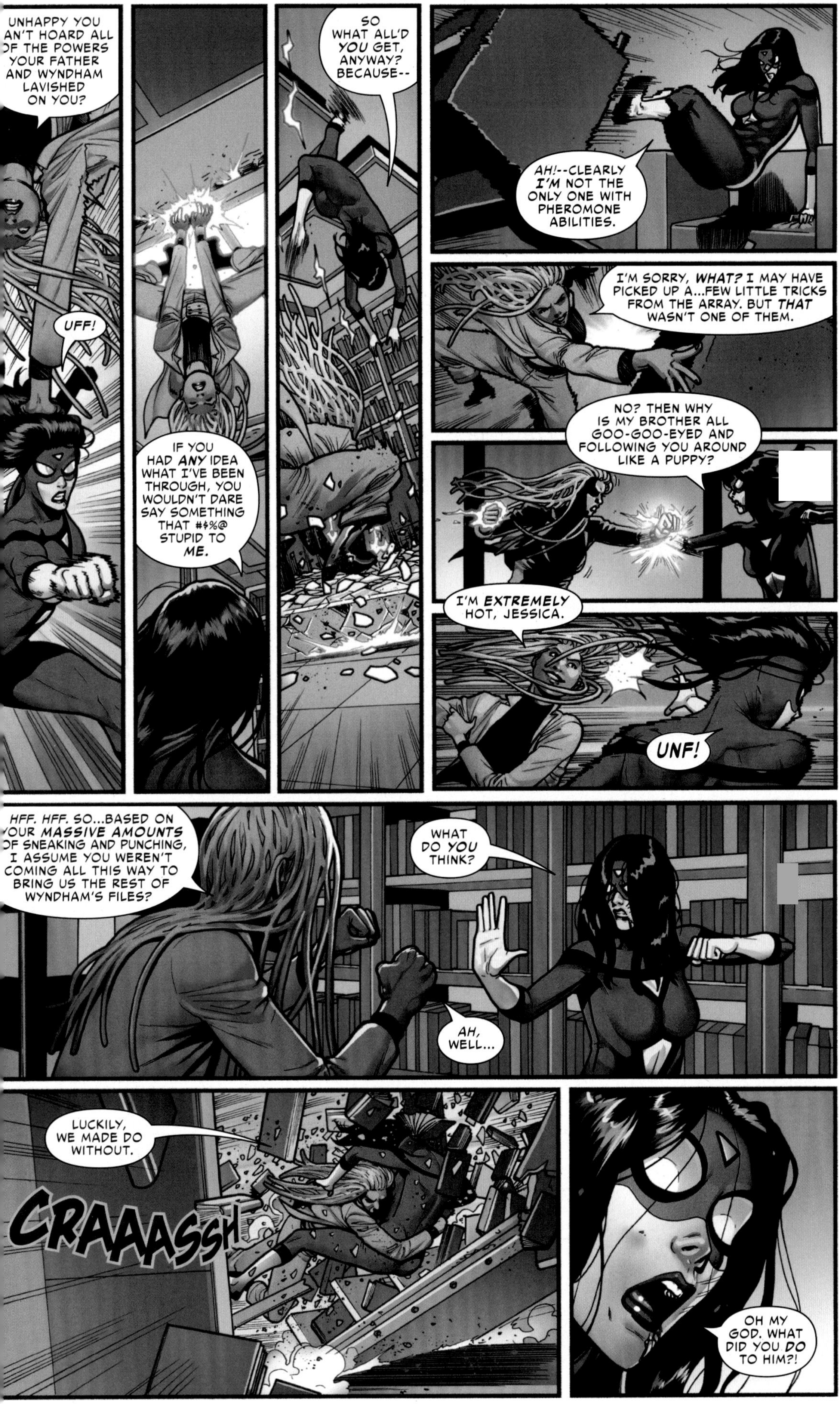

UNHAPPY YOU AN'T HOARD ALL OF THE POWERS YOUR FATHER AND WYNDHAM LAVISHED ON YOU?
UFF!
IF YOU HAD ANY IDEA WHAT I'VE BEEN THROUGH, YOU WOULDN'T DARE SAY SOMETHING THAT #$%@ STUPID TO ME.
SO WHAT ALL'D YOU GET, ANYWAY? BECAUSE--
AH!--CLEARLY I'M NOT THE ONLY ONE WITH PHEROMONE ABILITIES.
I'M SORRY, WHAT? I MAY HAVE PICKED UP A...FEW LITTLE TRICKS FROM THE ARRAY. BUT THAT WASN'T ONE OF THEM.
NO? THEN WHY IS MY BROTHER ALL GOO-GOO-EYED AND FOLLOWING YOU AROUND LIKE A PUPPY?
I'M EXTREMELY HOT, JESSICA.
UNF!
HFF. HFF. SO...BASED ON YOUR MASSIVE AMOUNTS OF SNEAKING AND PUNCHING, I ASSUME YOU WEREN'T COMING ALL THIS WAY TO BRING US THE REST OF WYNDHAM'S FILES?
WHAT DO YOU THINK?
AH, WELL...
LUCKILY, WE MADE DO WITHOUT.
CRAAAASSH
OH MY GOD. WHAT DID YOU DO TO HIM?!

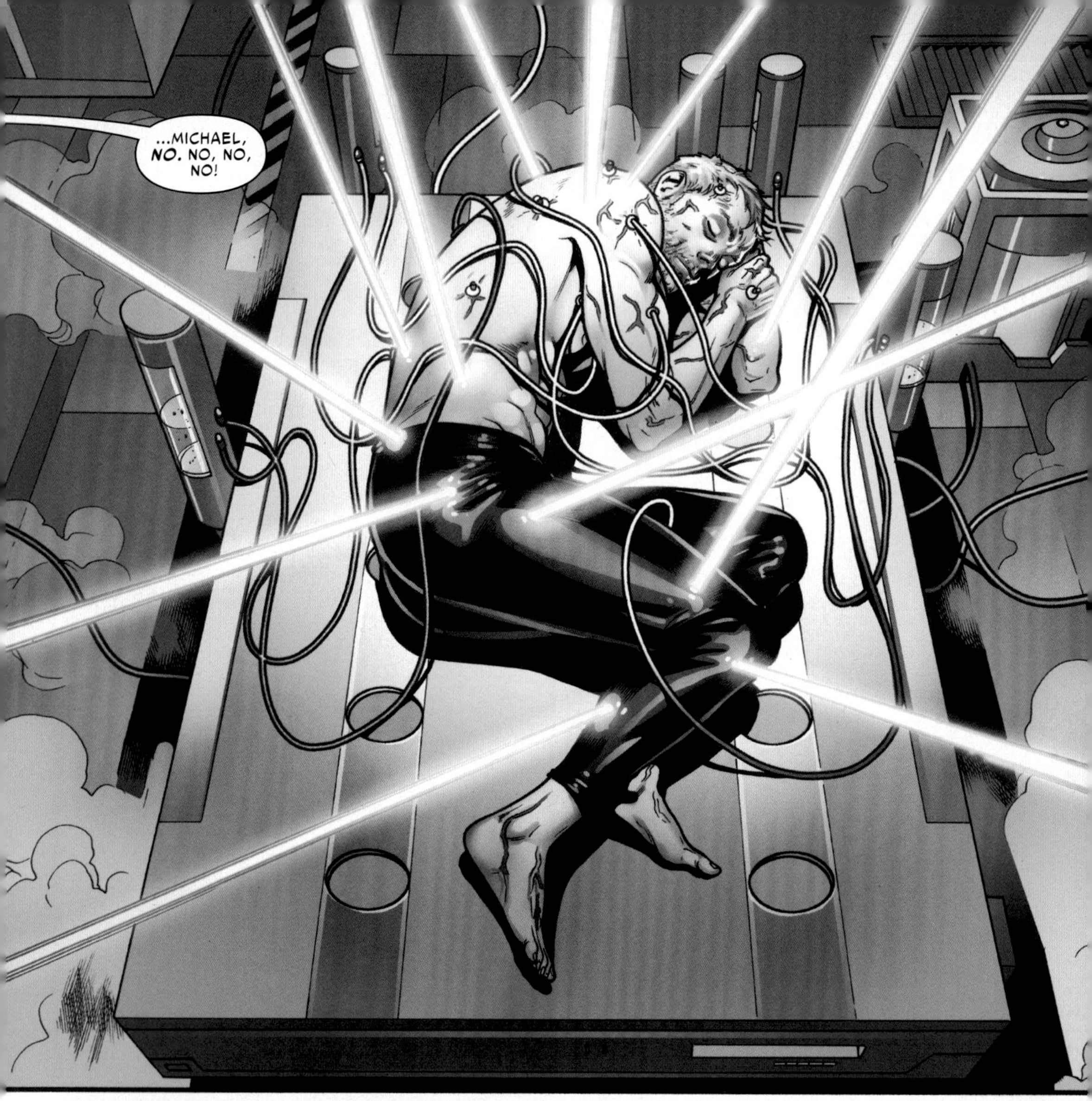
...MICHAEL, NO. NO, NO, NO!

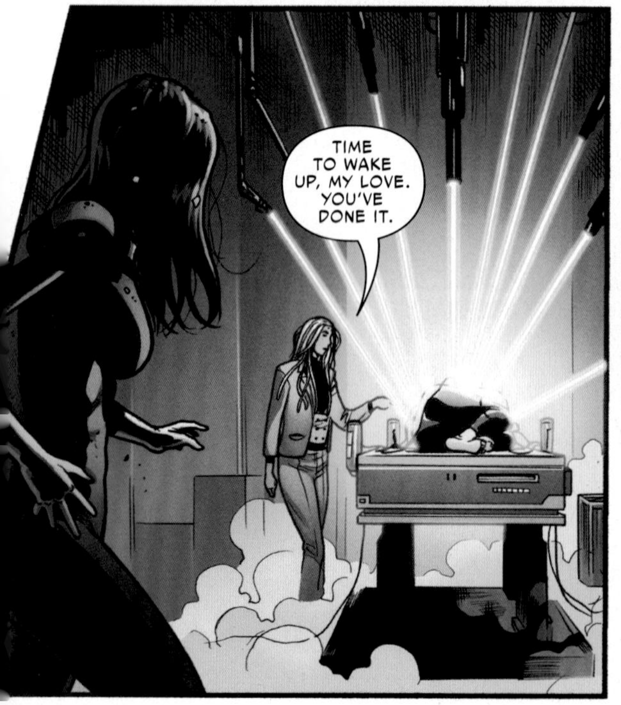
TIME TO WAKE UP, MY LOVE. YOU'VE DONE IT.

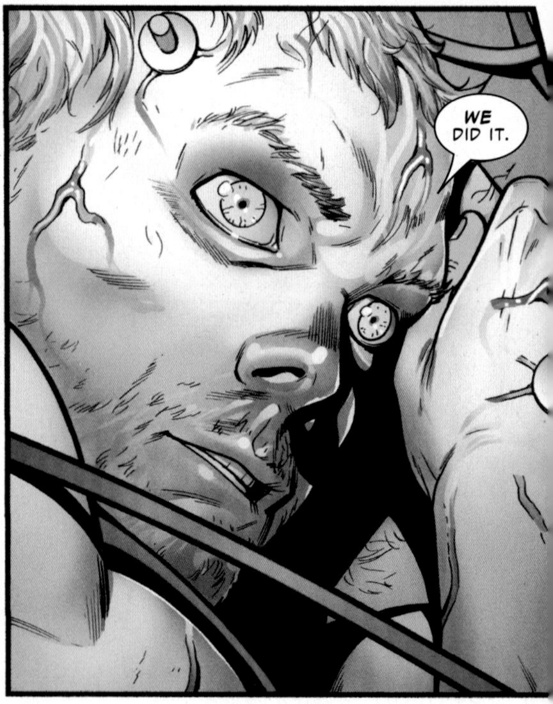
WE DID IT.

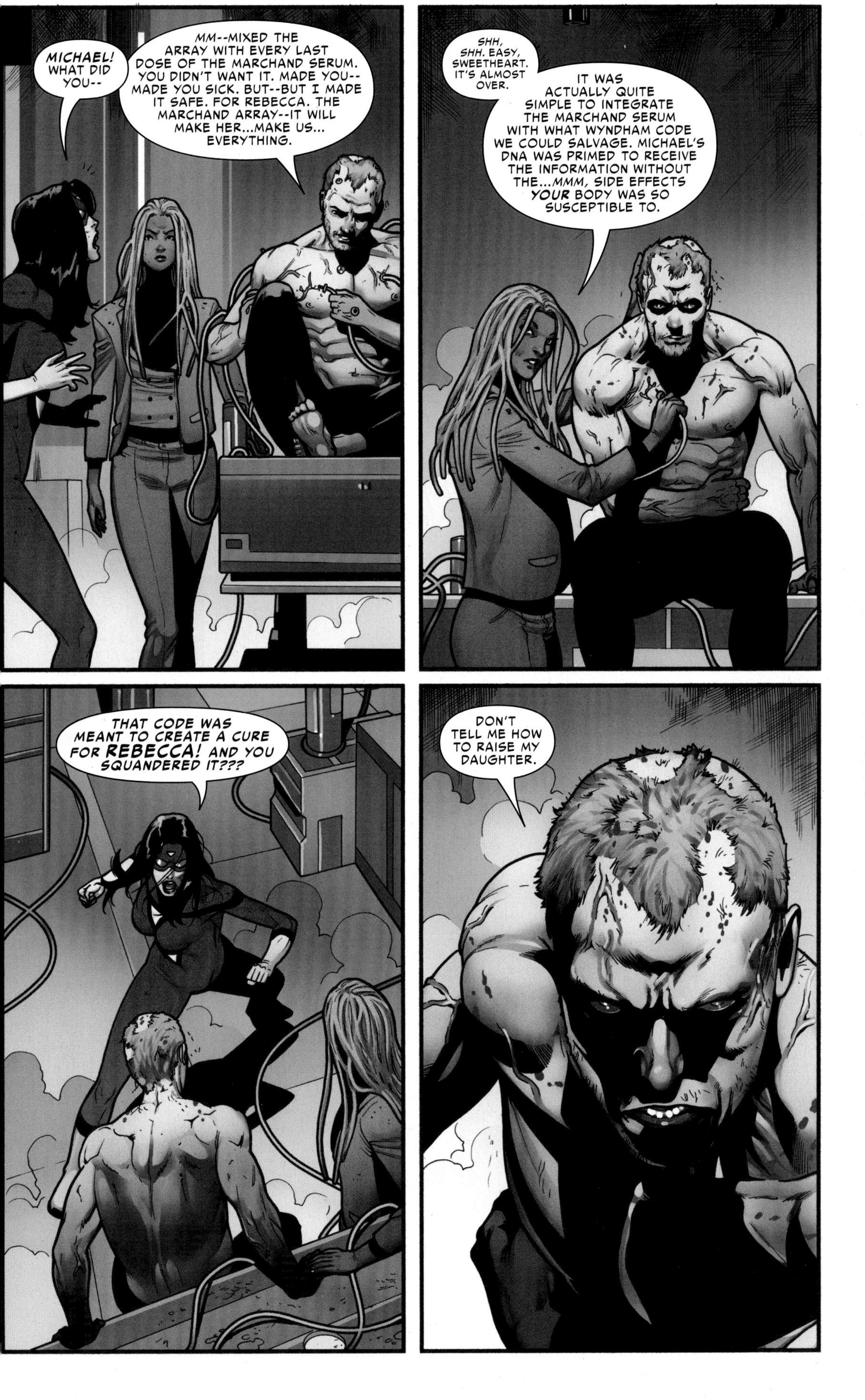
MICHAEL! WHAT DID YOU--
MM--MIXED THE ARRAY WITH EVERY LAST DOSE OF THE MARCHAND SERUM. YOU DIDN'T WANT IT. MADE YOU-- MADE YOU SICK. BUT--BUT I MADE IT SAFE. FOR REBECCA. THE MARCHAND ARRAY--IT WILL MAKE HER...MAKE US... EVERYTHING.
SHH, SHH. EASY, SWEETHEART. IT'S ALMOST OVER.
IT WAS ACTUALLY QUITE SIMPLE TO INTEGRATE THE MARCHAND SERUM WITH WHAT WYNDHAM CODE WE COULD SALVAGE. MICHAEL'S DNA WAS PRIMED TO RECEIVE THE INFORMATION WITHOUT THE...MMM, SIDE EFFECTS YOUR BODY WAS SO SUSCEPTIBLE TO.
THAT CODE WAS MEANT TO CREATE A CURE FOR REBECCA! AND YOU SQUANDERED IT???
DON'T TELL ME HOW TO RAISE MY DAUGHTER.

NNGYAAA!!!

I WANTED THIS TO BE *DIFFERENT*, JESSICA. I WANTED US TO BE A *FAMILY.* BUT I DIDN'T *EXIST* FOR YOU, DID I?

SLAAASH

THAT WASN'T *MY* FAULT! I DIDN'T *KNOW* YOU @#$% EXISTED!

GRRRSH

I KNOW!

AND I CAN'T STOP HATING YOU FOR IT.

WHMPH

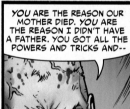

YOU ARE THE REASON OUR MOTHER DIED. YOU ARE THE REASON I DIDN'T HAVE A FATHER. YOU GOT ALL THE POWERS AND TRICKS AND--

SCHFFF

OH MY GOD, WANTING TO KILL ME REALLY DOES RUN IN THE FAMILY, DOESN'T IT?

MICHAEL, *STOP!* THINK OF REBECCA!

I AM *ALWAYS* THINKING OF REBECCA!

...DAD?

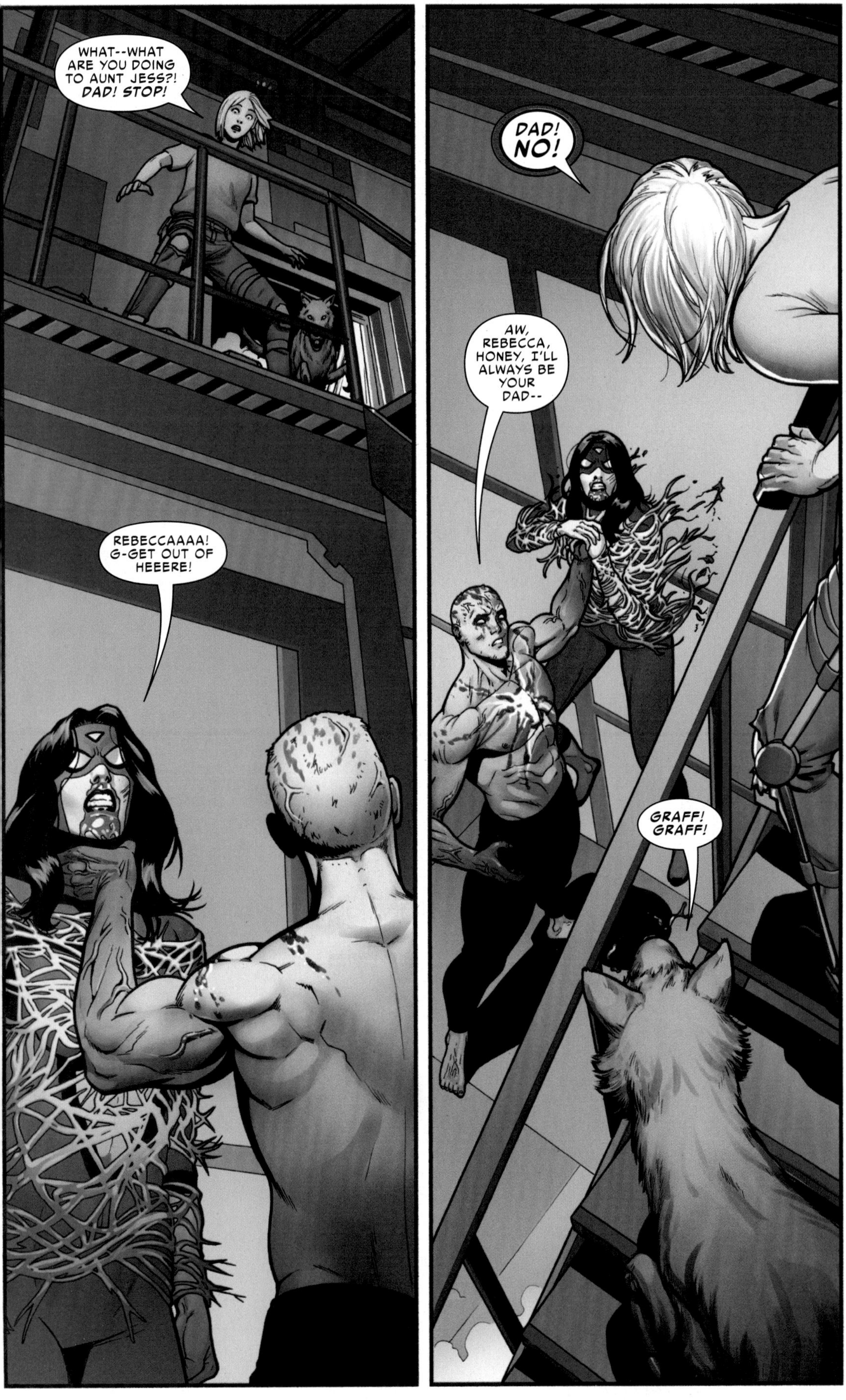

WHAT--WHAT ARE YOU DOING TO AUNT JESS?! DAD! STOP!
REBECCAAAA! G-GET OUT OF HEEERE!
DAD! NO!
AW, REBECCA, HONEY, I'LL ALWAYS BE YOUR DAD--
GRAFF! GRAFF!

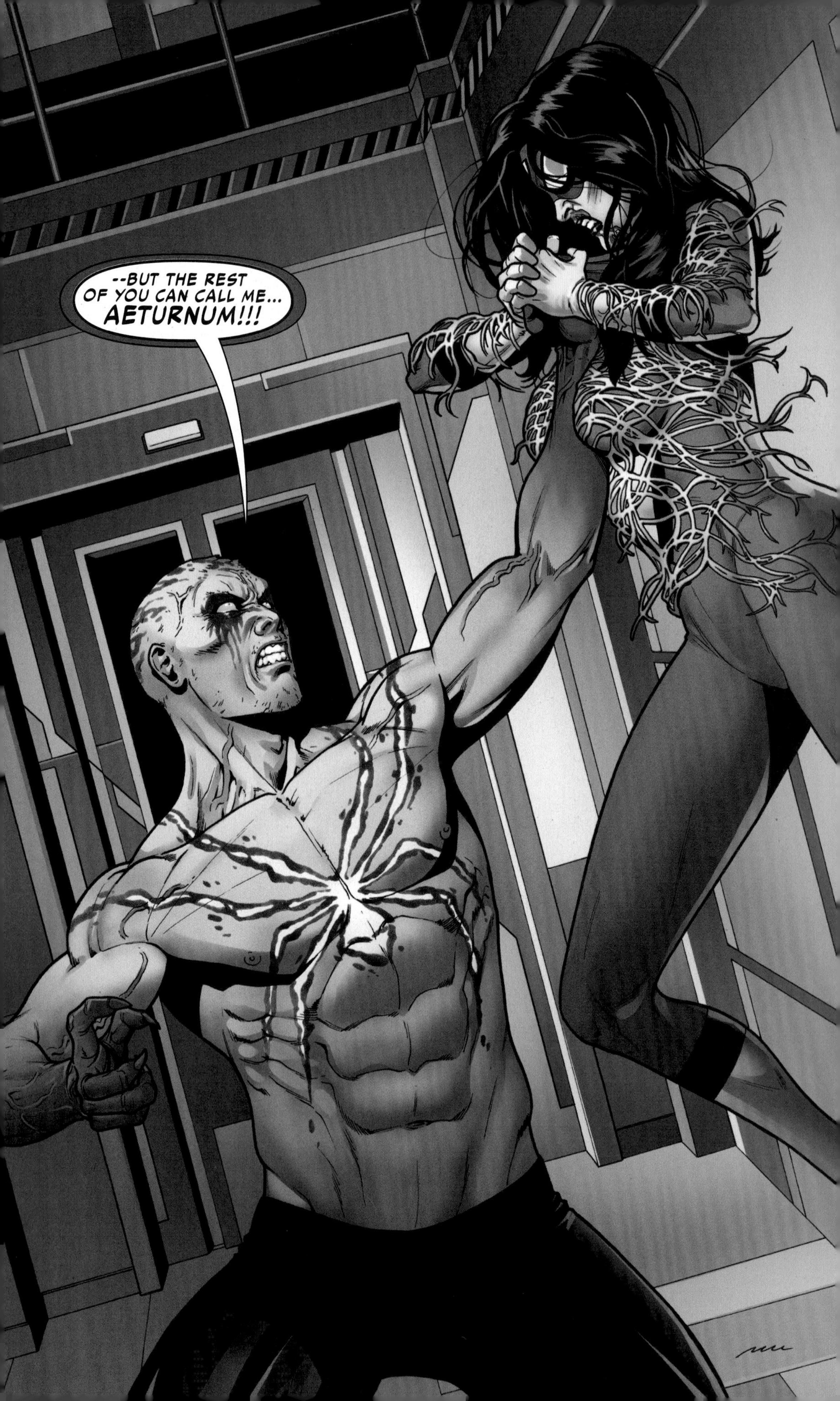
--BUT THE REST OF YOU CAN CALL ME... AETURNUM!!!

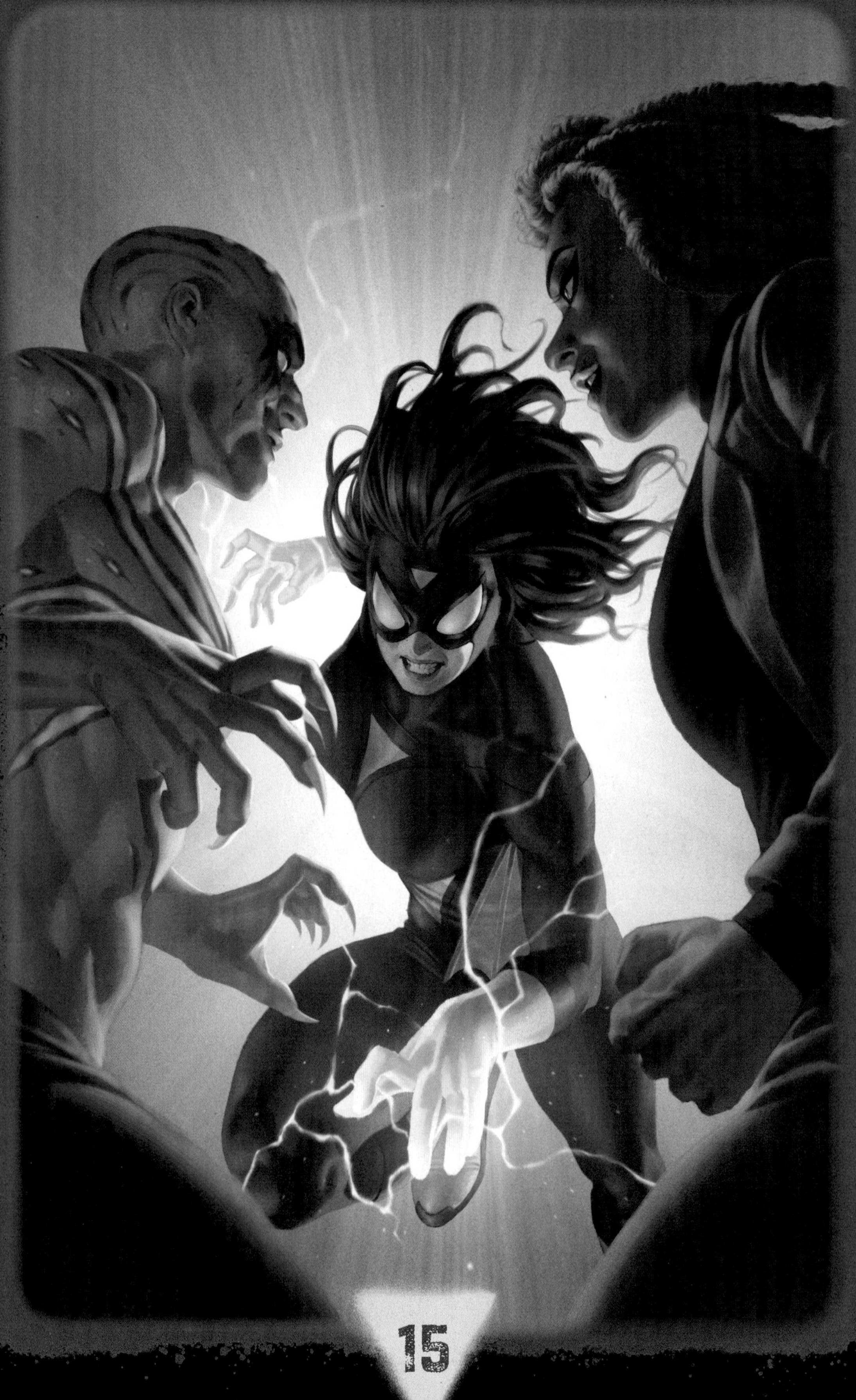

15

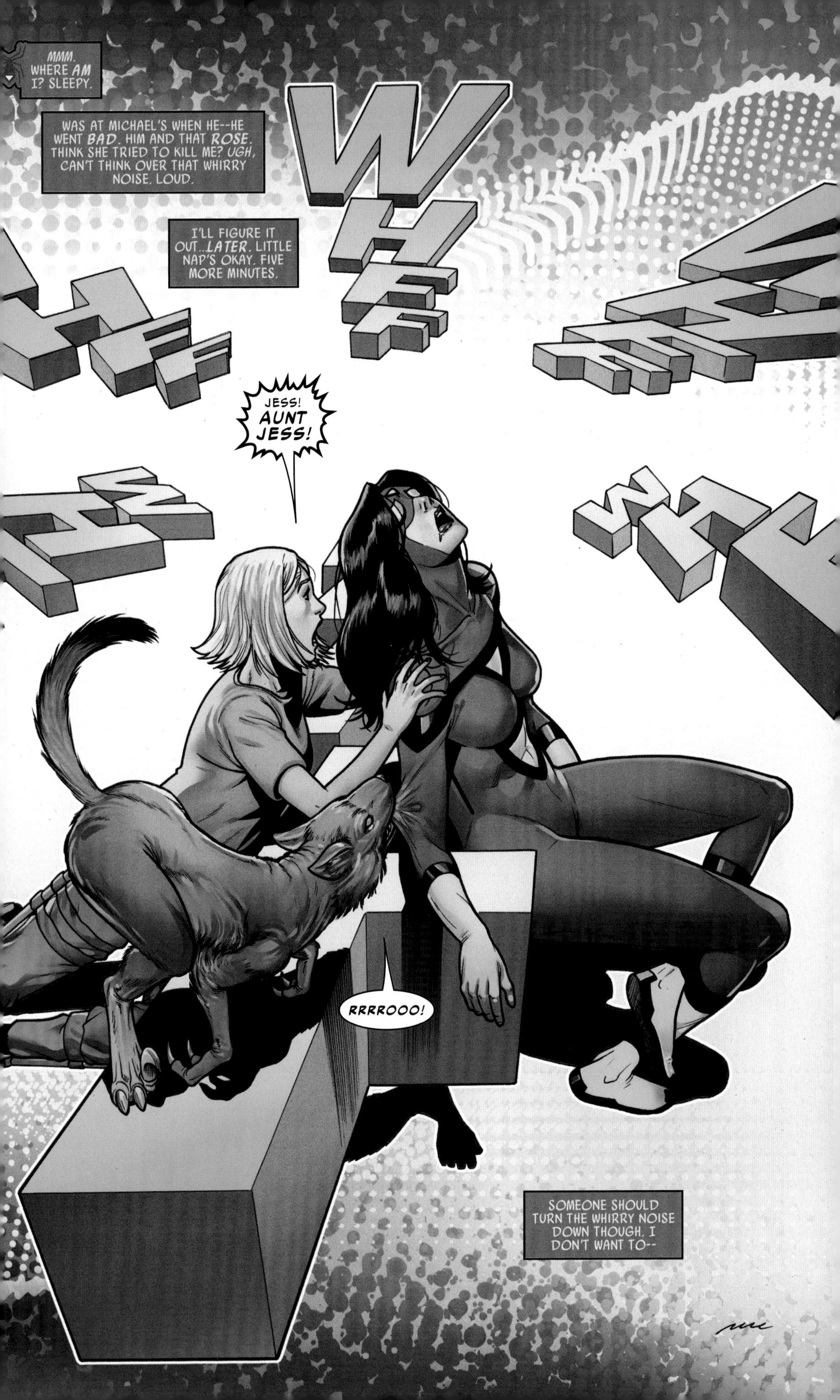

MMM. WHERE AM I? SLEEPY.
WAS AT MICHAEL'S WHEN HE--HE WENT BAD. HIM AND THAT ROSE. THINK SHE TRIED TO KILL ME? UGH, CAN'T THINK OVER THAT WHIRRY NOISE. LOUD.
I'LL FIGURE IT OUT...LATER. LITTLE NAP'S OKAY. FIVE MORE MINUTES.
JESS! AUNT JESS!
RRRROOO!
SOMEONE SHOULD TURN THE WHIRRY NOISE DOWN THOUGH. I DON'T WANT TO--

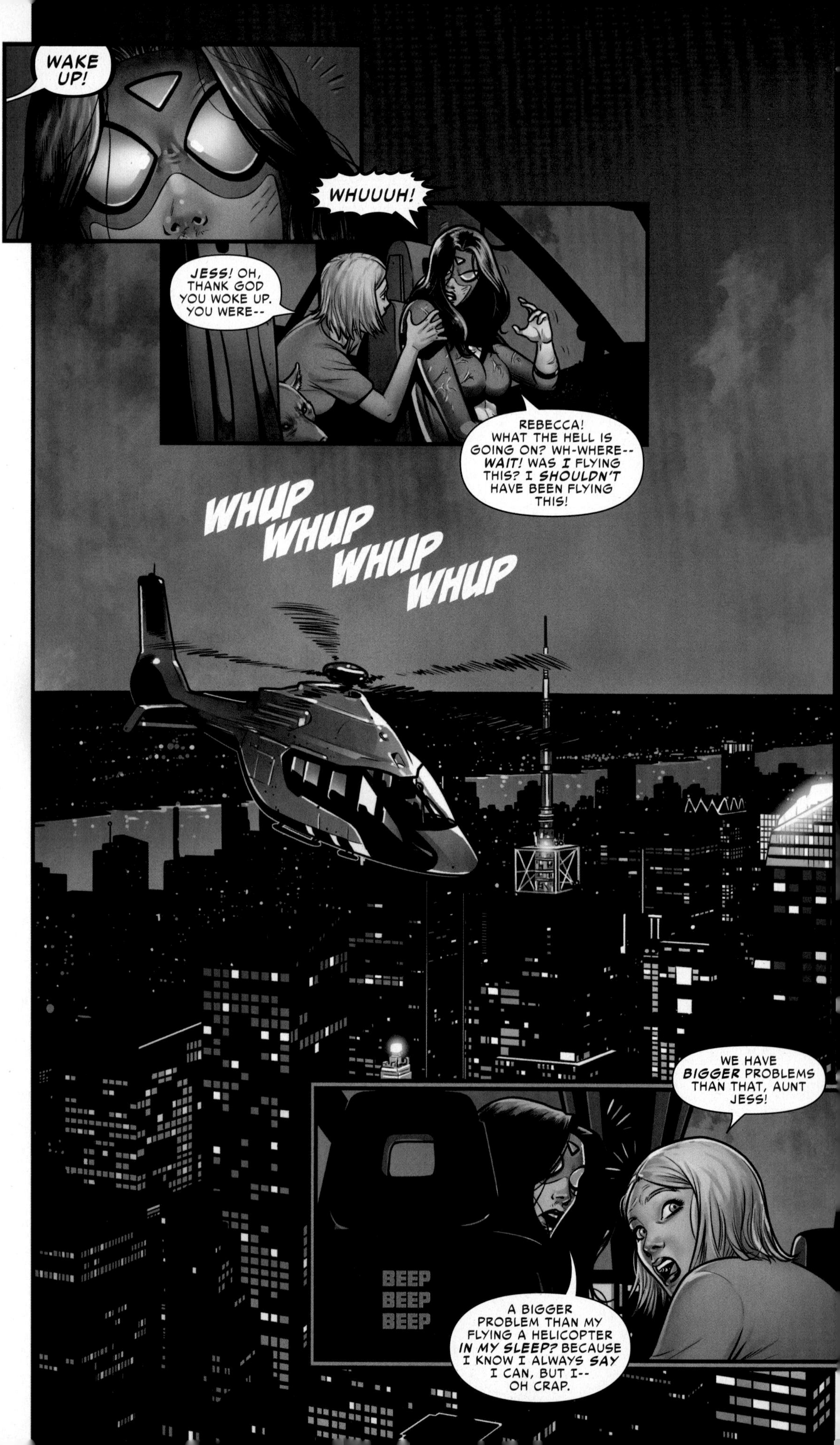
WAKE UP!
WHUUUH!
JESS! OH, THANK GOD YOU WOKE UP. YOU WERE--
REBECCA! WHAT THE HELL IS GOING ON? WH-WHERE-- WAIT! WAS I FLYING THIS? I SHOULDN'T HAVE BEEN FLYING THIS!
WHUP WHUP WHUP WHUP
WE HAVE BIGGER PROBLEMS THAN THAT, AUNT JESS!
BEEP BEEP BEEP
A BIGGER PROBLEM THAN MY FLYING A HELICOPTER IN MY SLEEP? BECAUSE I KNOW I ALWAYS SAY I CAN, BUT I-- OH CRAP.

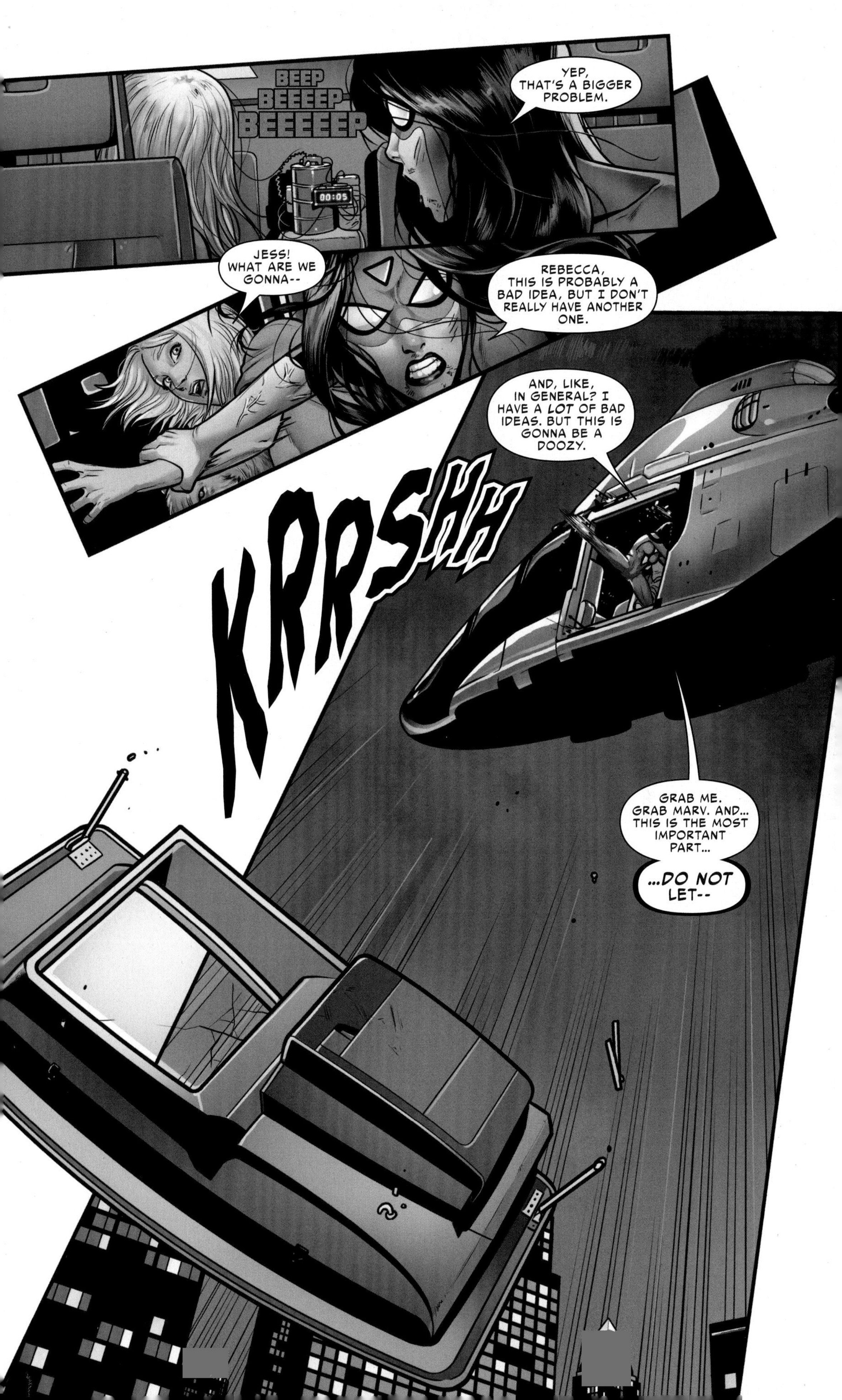

BEEP
BEEEEP
BEEEEEP
00:05
YEP, THAT'S A BIGGER PROBLEM.
JESS! WHAT ARE WE GONNA--
REBECCA, THIS IS PROBABLY A BAD IDEA, BUT I DON'T REALLY HAVE ANOTHER ONE.
AND, LIKE, IN GENERAL? I HAVE A *LOT* OF BAD IDEAS. BUT THIS IS GONNA BE A DOOZY.
KRRSHH
GRAB ME. GRAB MARV. AND... THIS IS THE MOST IMPORTANT PART...
...DO NOT LET--

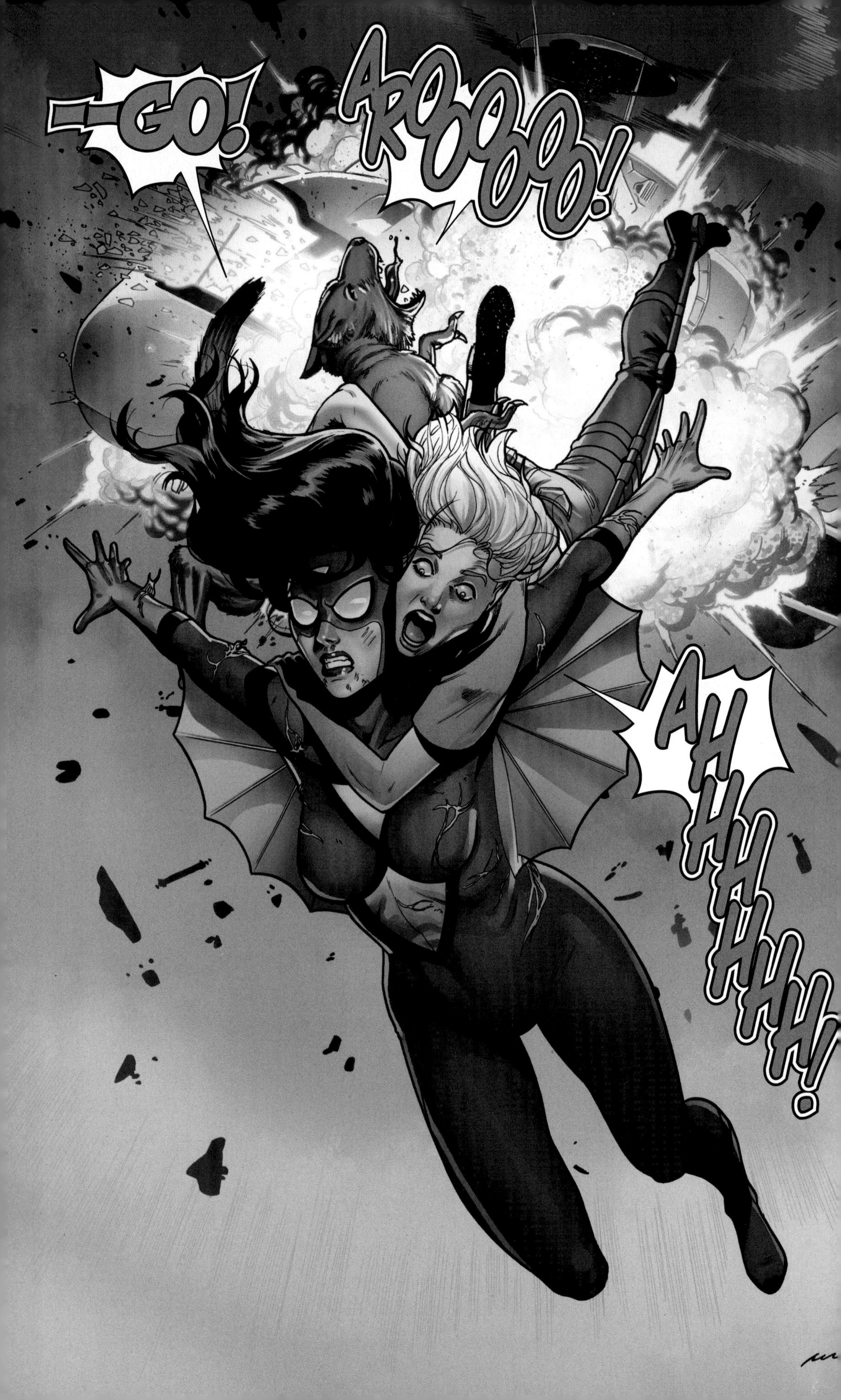
--GO!
AROOOOOO!
AHHHHHH!

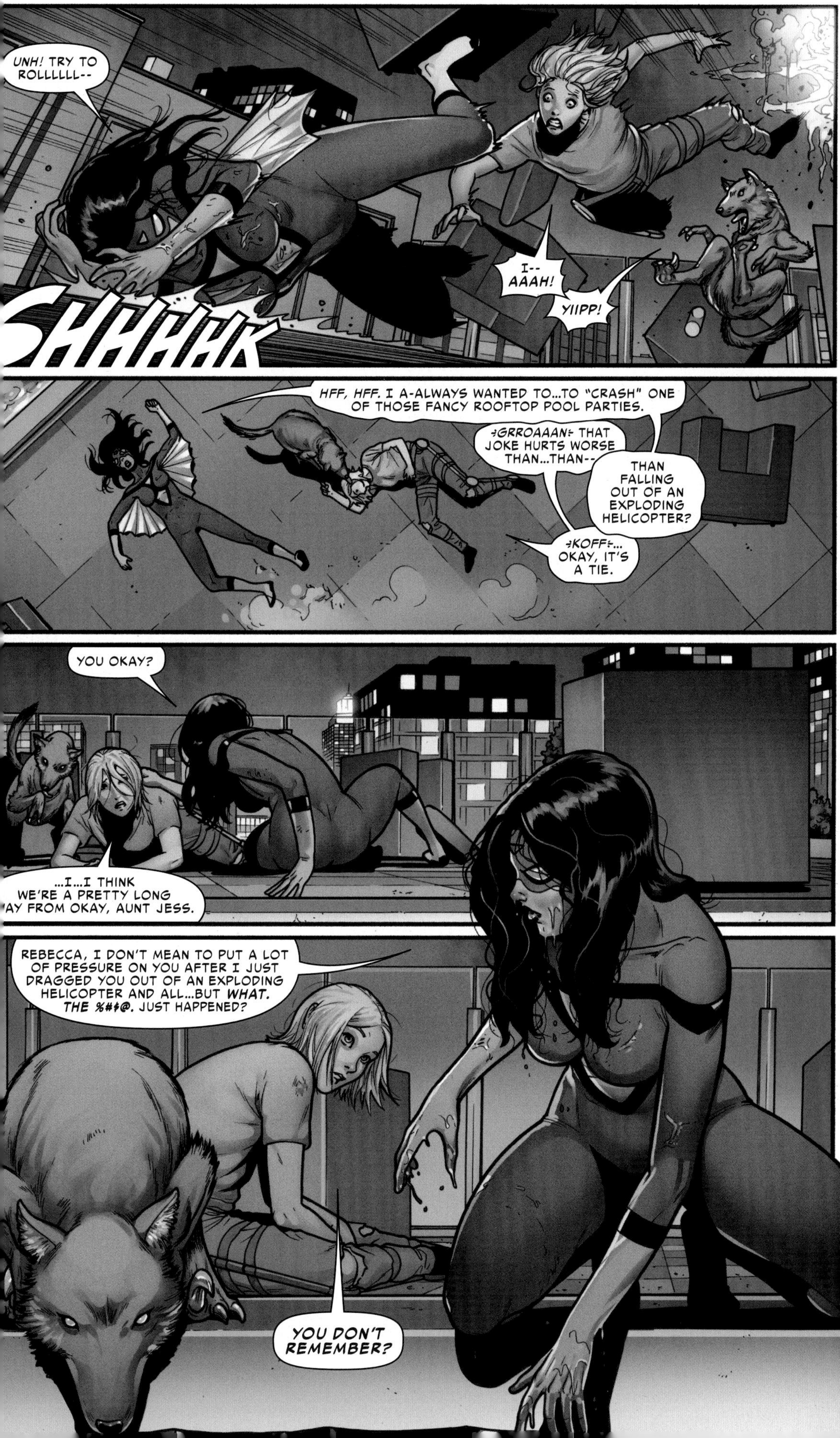
UNH! TRY TO ROLLLLLLL--
SHHHHK
I-- AAAH!
YIIPP!
HFF, HFF. I A-ALWAYS WANTED TO...TO "CRASH" ONE OF THOSE FANCY ROOFTOP POOL PARTIES.
⊰GRROAAAN⊱ THAT JOKE HURTS WORSE THAN...THAN--
THAN FALLING OUT OF AN EXPLODING HELICOPTER?
⊰KOFF⊱... OKAY, IT'S A TIE.
YOU OKAY?
...I...I THINK WE'RE A PRETTY LONG AY FROM OKAY, AUNT JESS.
REBECCA, I DON'T MEAN TO PUT A LOT OF PRESSURE ON YOU AFTER I JUST DRAGGED YOU OUT OF AN EXPLODING HELICOPTER AND ALL...BUT WHAT. THE %#$@. JUST HAPPENED?
YOU DON'T REMEMBER?

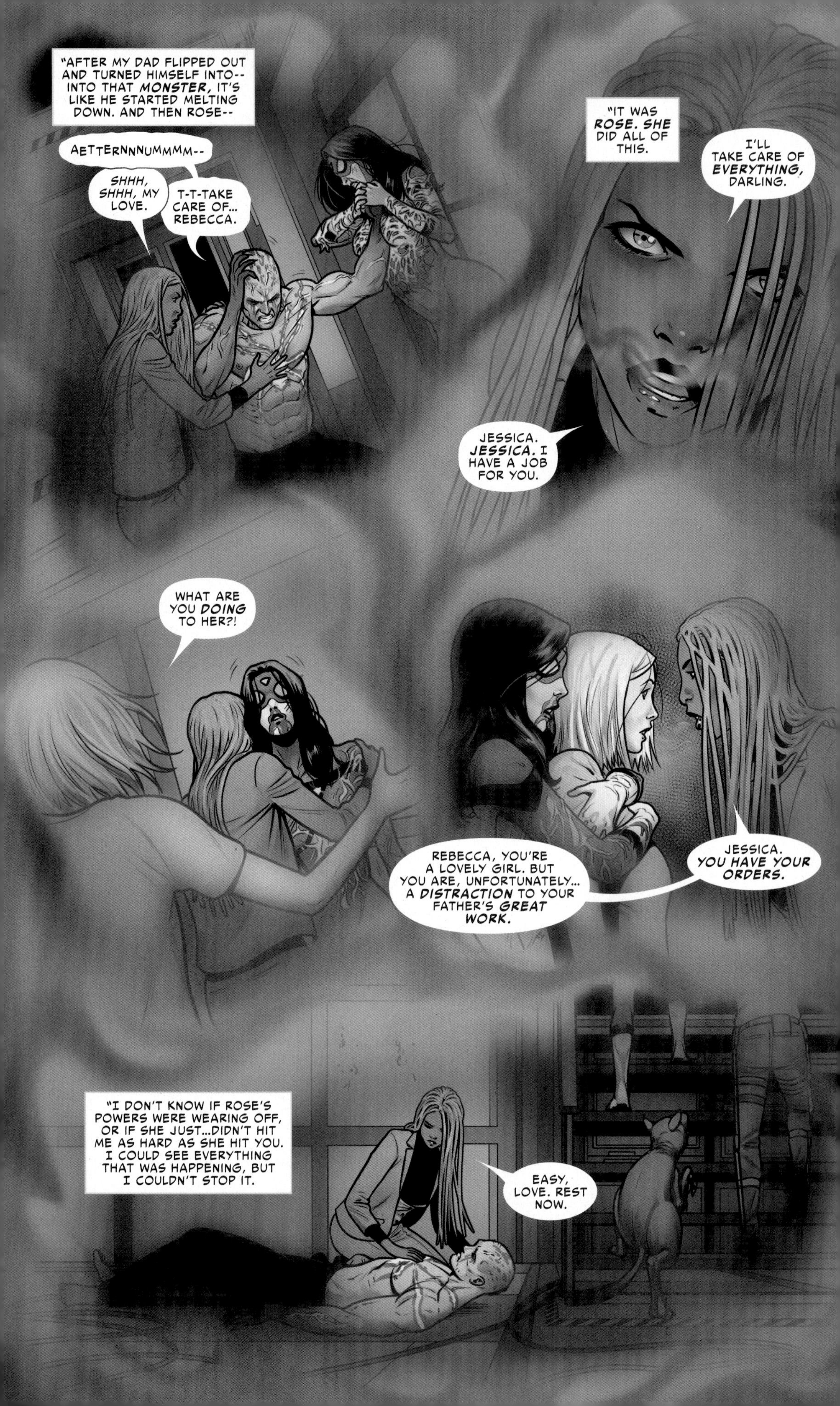

"AFTER MY DAD FLIPPED OUT AND TURNED HIMSELF INTO--INTO THAT MONSTER, IT'S LIKE HE STARTED MELTING DOWN. AND THEN ROSE--
AETTERNNNUMMMM--
SHHH, SHHH, MY LOVE.
T-T-TAKE CARE OF... REBECCA.
"IT WAS ROSE. SHE DID ALL OF THIS.
I'LL TAKE CARE OF EVERYTHING, DARLING.
JESSICA. JESSICA. I HAVE A JOB FOR YOU.
WHAT ARE YOU DOING TO HER?!
REBECCA, YOU'RE A LOVELY GIRL. BUT YOU ARE, UNFORTUNATELY... A DISTRACTION TO YOUR FATHER'S GREAT WORK.
JESSICA. YOU HAVE YOUR ORDERS.
"I DON'T KNOW IF ROSE'S POWERS WERE WEARING OFF, OR IF SHE JUST...DIDN'T HIT ME AS HARD AS SHE HIT YOU. I COULD SEE EVERYTHING THAT WAS HAPPENING, BUT I COULDN'T STOP IT.
EASY, LOVE. REST NOW.

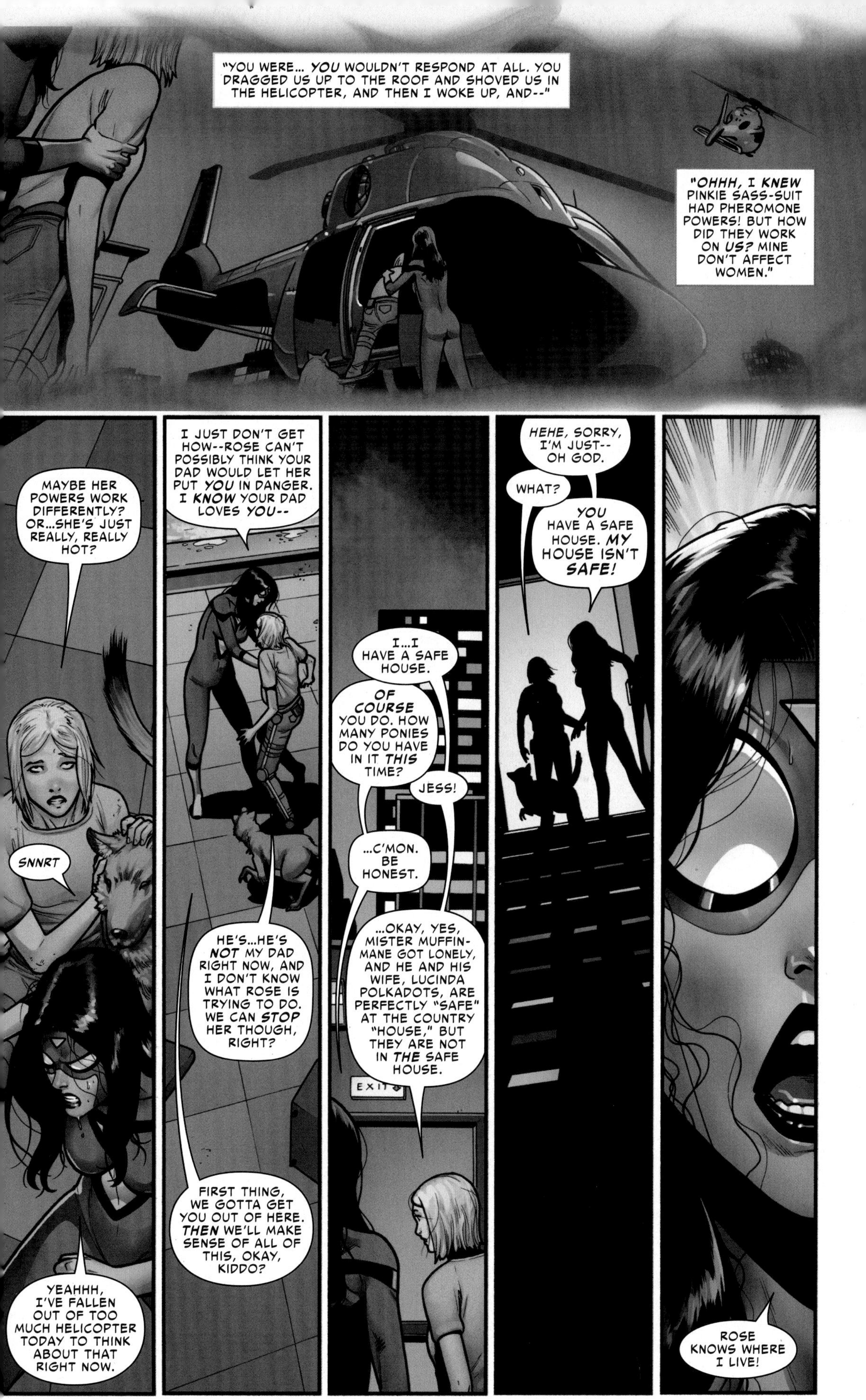

"YOU WERE... YOU WOULDN'T RESPOND AT ALL. YOU DRAGGED US UP TO THE ROOF AND SHOVED US IN THE HELICOPTER, AND THEN I WOKE UP, AND--"
"OHHH, I KNEW PINKIE SASS-SUIT HAD PHEROMONE POWERS! BUT HOW DID THEY WORK ON US? MINE DON'T AFFECT WOMEN."
MAYBE HER POWERS WORK DIFFERENTLY? OR...SHE'S JUST REALLY, REALLY HOT?
SNNRT
YEAHHH, I'VE FALLEN OUT OF TOO MUCH HELICOPTER TODAY TO THINK ABOUT THAT RIGHT NOW.
I JUST DON'T GET HOW--ROSE CAN'T POSSIBLY THINK YOUR DAD WOULD LET HER PUT YOU IN DANGER. I KNOW YOUR DAD LOVES YOU--
HE'S...HE'S NOT MY DAD RIGHT NOW, AND I DON'T KNOW WHAT ROSE IS TRYING TO DO. WE CAN STOP HER THOUGH, RIGHT?
FIRST THING, WE GOTTA GET YOU OUT OF HERE. THEN WE'LL MAKE SENSE OF ALL OF THIS, OKAY, KIDDO?
I...I HAVE A SAFE HOUSE.
OF COURSE YOU DO. HOW MANY PONIES DO YOU HAVE IN IT THIS TIME?
JESS!
...C'MON. BE HONEST.
...OKAY, YES, MISTER MUFFIN-MANE GOT LONELY, AND HE AND HIS WIFE, LUCINDA POLKADOTS, ARE PERFECTLY "SAFE" AT THE COUNTRY "HOUSE," BUT THEY ARE NOT IN THE SAFE HOUSE.
EXIT
HEHE, SORRY, I'M JUST-- OH GOD.
WHAT?
YOU HAVE A SAFE HOUSE. MY HOUSE ISN'T SAFE!
ROSE KNOWS WHERE I LIVE!

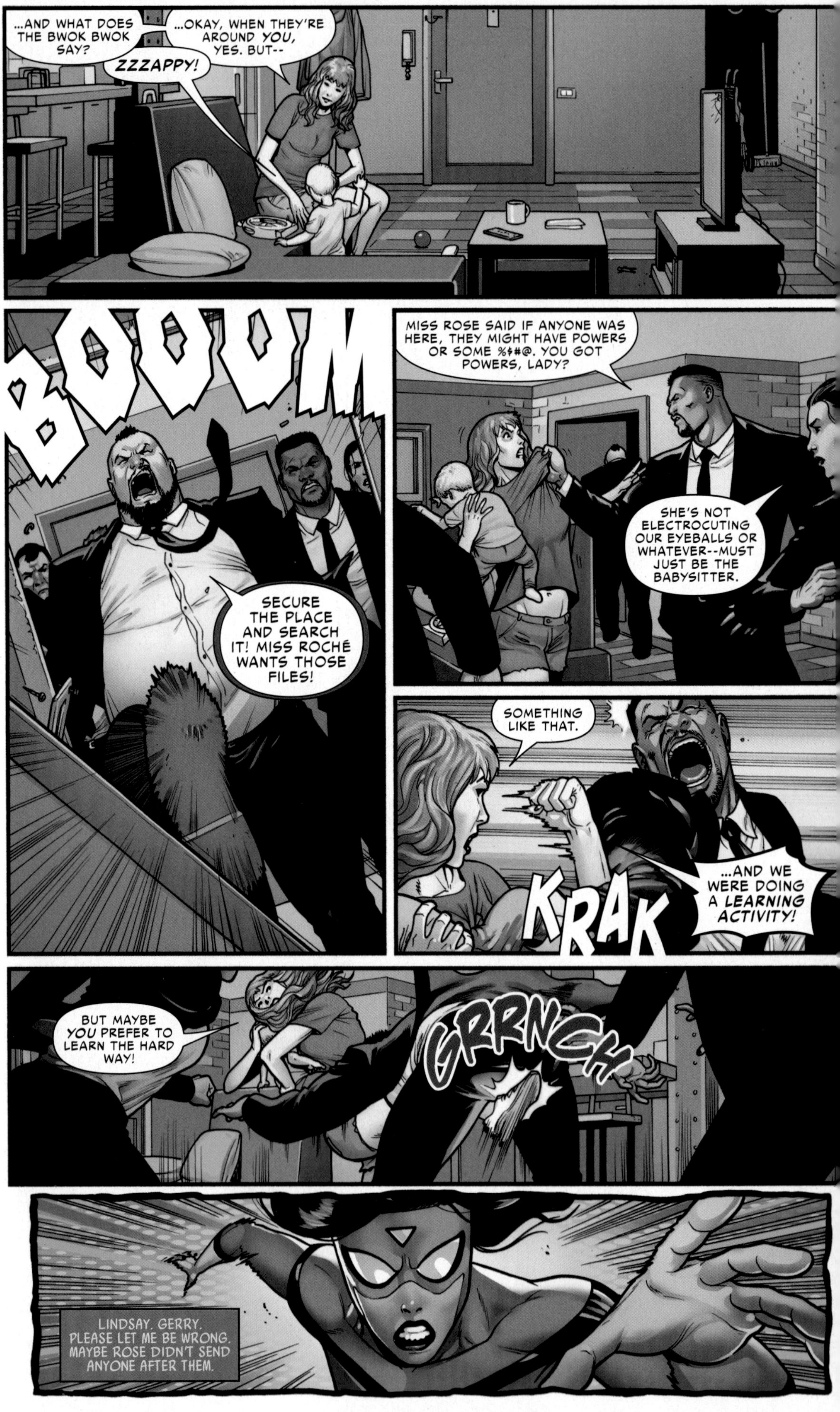
...AND WHAT DOES THE BWOK BWOK SAY?
...OKAY, WHEN THEY'RE AROUND YOU, YES. BUT--
ZZZAPPY!
BOOOM
SECURE THE PLACE AND SEARCH IT! MISS ROCHÉ WANTS THOSE FILES!
MISS ROSE SAID IF ANYONE WAS HERE, THEY MIGHT HAVE POWERS OR SOME %$#@. YOU GOT POWERS, LADY?
SHE'S NOT ELECTROCUTING OUR EYEBALLS OR WHATEVER--MUST JUST BE THE BABYSITTER.
SOMETHING LIKE THAT.
KRAK
...AND WE WERE DOING A LEARNING ACTIVITY!
BUT MAYBE YOU PREFER TO LEARN THE HARD WAY!
GRRNCH
LINDSAY. GERRY. PLEASE LET ME BE WRONG. MAYBE ROSE DIDN'T SEND ANYONE AFTER THEM.

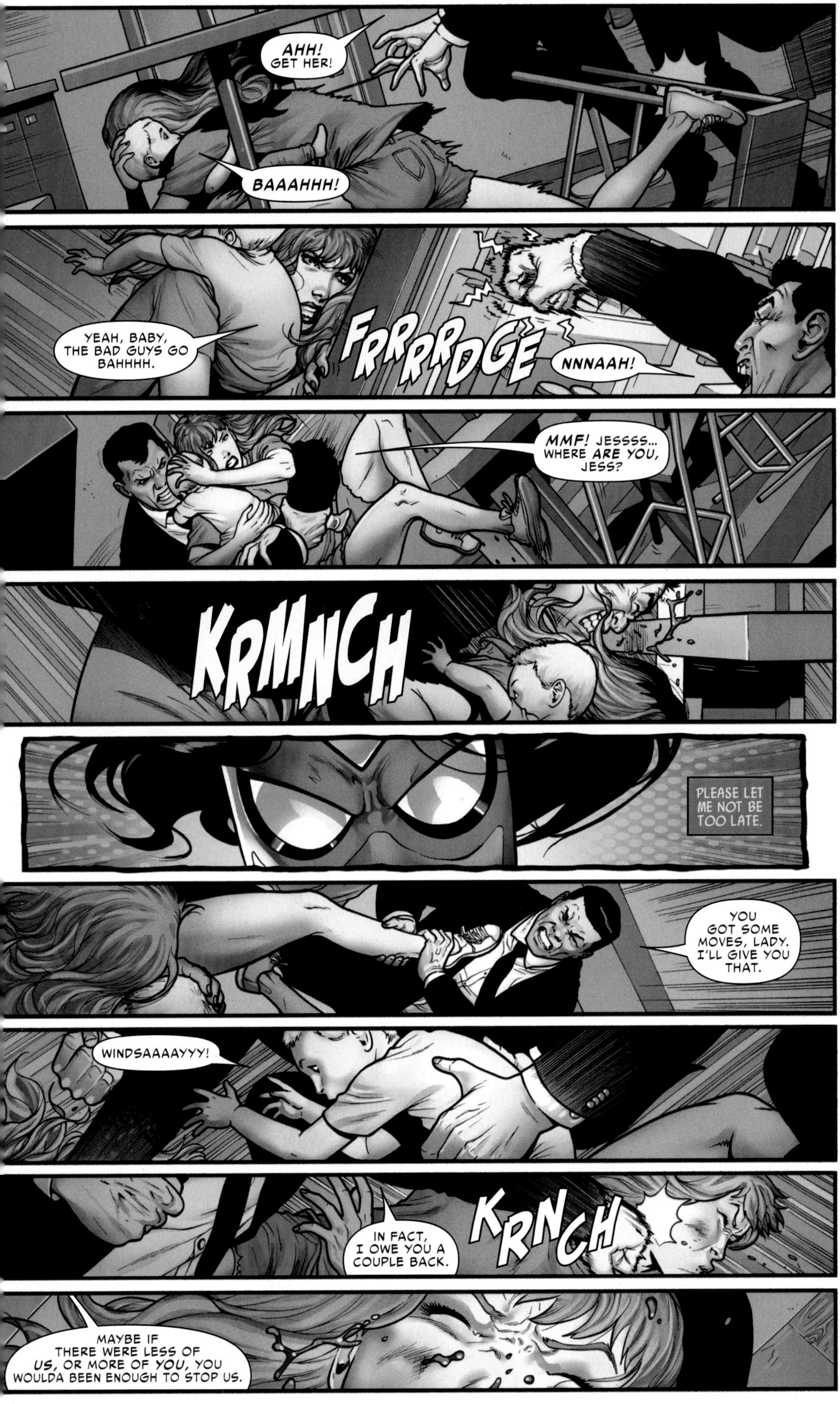
AHH! GET HER!
BAAAHHH!
YEAH, BABY, THE BAD GUYS GO BAHHHH.
FRRRRRDGE
NNNAAH!
MMF! JESSSS... WHERE ARE YOU, JESS?
KRMNCH
PLEASE LET ME NOT BE TOO LATE.
YOU GOT SOME MOVES, LADY. I'LL GIVE YOU THAT.
WINDSAAAAYYY!
IN FACT, I OWE YOU A COUPLE BACK.
KRNCH
MAYBE IF THERE WERE LESS OF US, OR MORE OF YOU, YOU WOULDA BEEN ENOUGH TO STOP US.

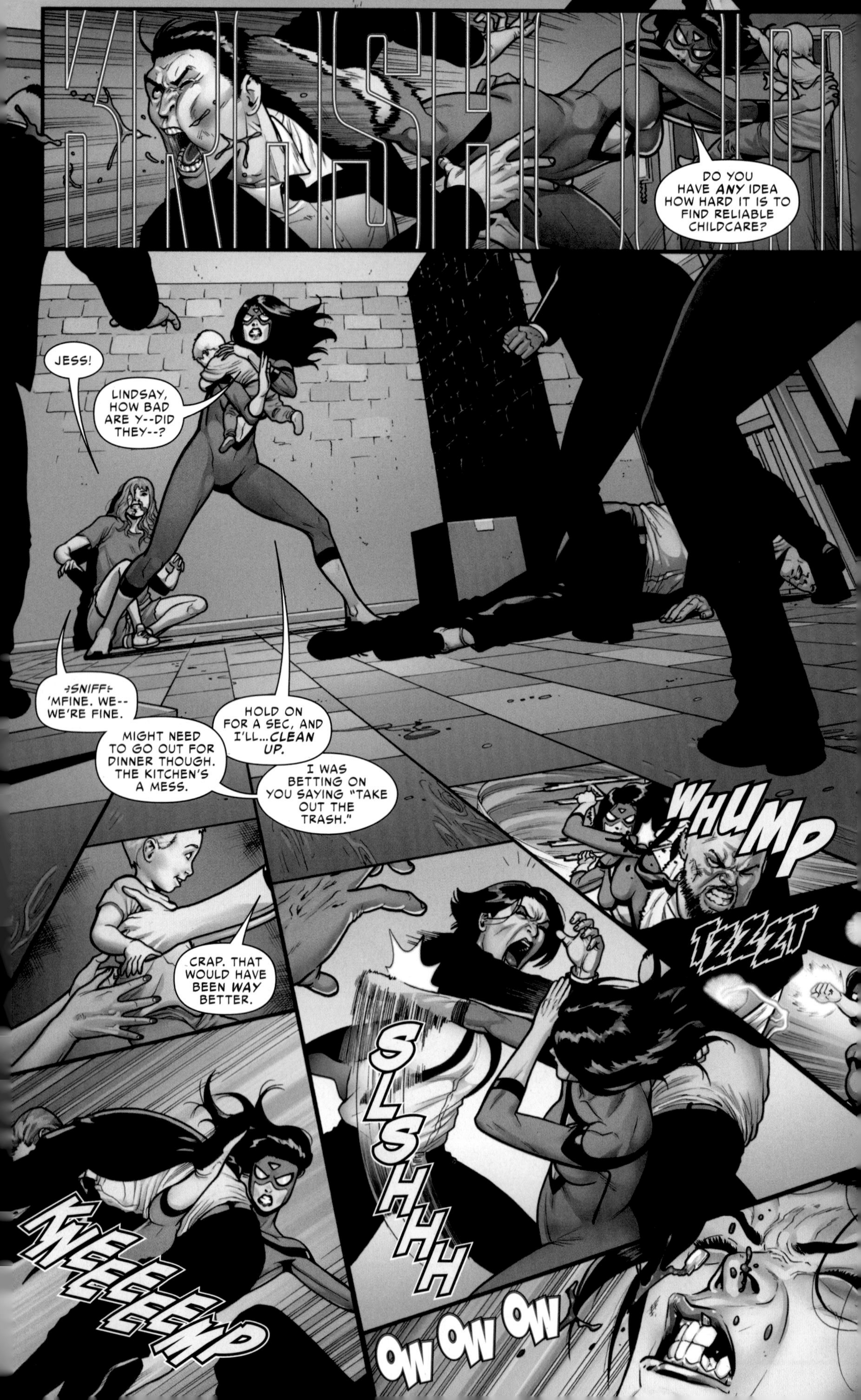
DO YOU HAVE *ANY* IDEA HOW HARD IT IS TO FIND RELIABLE CHILDCARE?
JESS!
LINDSAY, HOW BAD ARE Y--DID THEY--?
SNIFF 'MFINE. WE--WE'RE FINE.
HOLD ON FOR A SEC, AND I'LL...*CLEAN UP.*
MIGHT NEED TO GO OUT FOR DINNER THOUGH. THE KITCHEN'S A MESS.
I WAS BETTING ON YOU SAYING "TAKE OUT THE TRASH."
CRAP. THAT WOULD HAVE BEEN *WAY* BETTER.
WHUMP
TZZZT
SLSHHHH
KWEEEEMP
OW OW OW

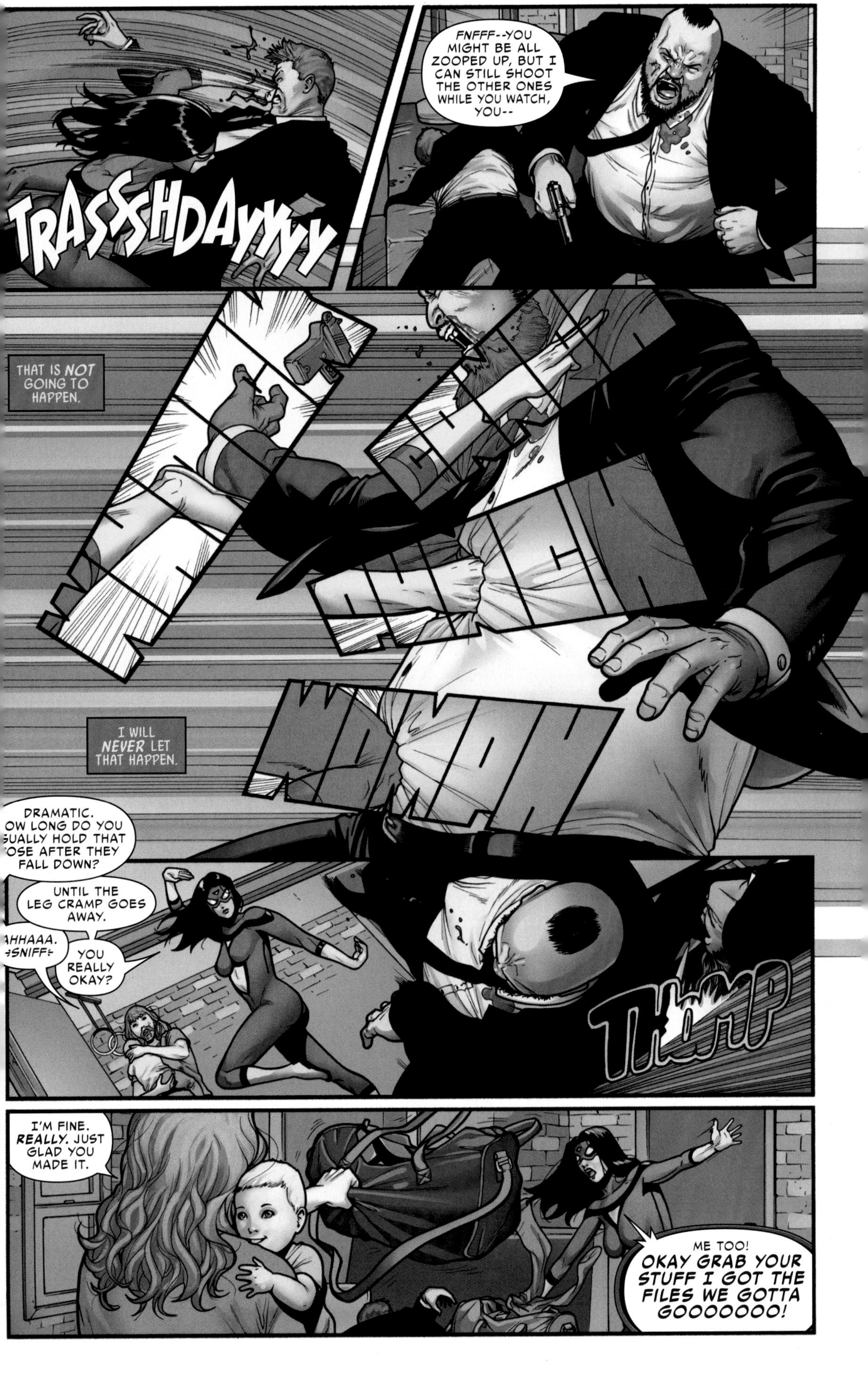
TRASSSHDAYYYY
FNFFF--YOU MIGHT BE ALL ZOOPED UP, BUT I CAN STILL SHOOT THE OTHER ONES WHILE YOU WATCH, YOU--
THAT IS NOT GOING TO HAPPEN.
I WILL NEVER LET THAT HAPPEN.
DRAMATIC.
OW LONG DO YOU
SUALLY HOLD THAT
OSE AFTER THEY
FALL DOWN?
UNTIL THE LEG CRAMP GOES AWAY.
AHHAAA.
SNIFF
YOU REALLY OKAY?
THUMP
I'M FINE. REALLY. JUST GLAD YOU MADE IT.
ME TOO! OKAY GRAB YOUR STUFF I GOT THE FILES WE GOTTA GOOOOOOO!

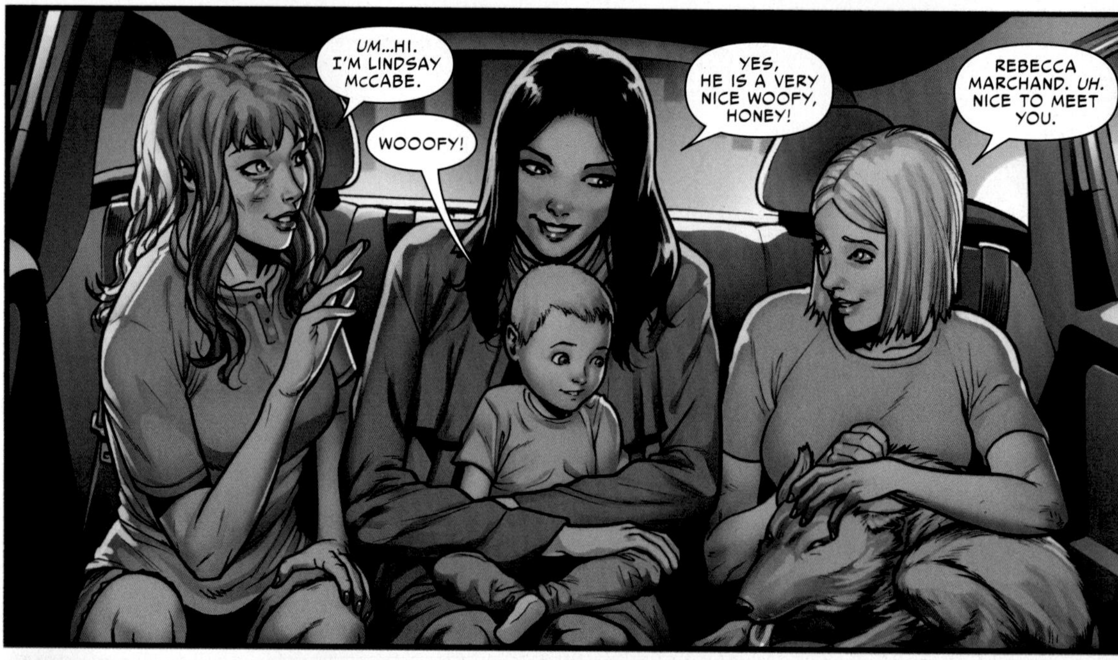
UM...HI. I'M LINDSAY McCABE.
WOOOFY!
YES, HE IS A VERY NICE WOOFY, HONEY!
REBECCA MARCHAND. UH. NICE TO MEET YOU.

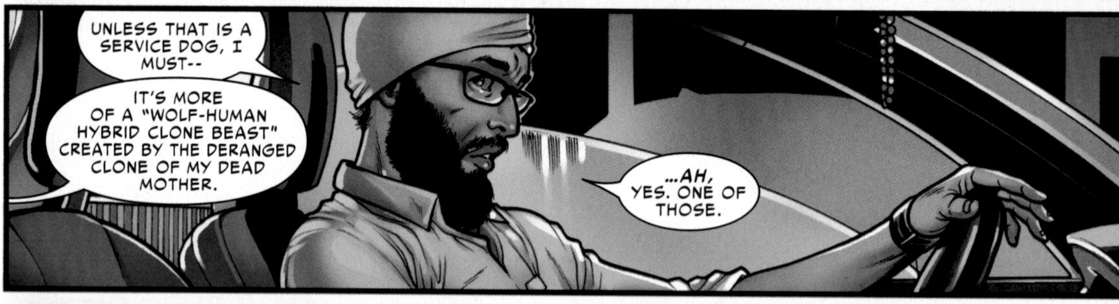
UNLESS THAT IS A SERVICE DOG, I MUST--
IT'S MORE OF A "WOLF-HUMAN HYBRID CLONE BEAST" CREATED BY THE DERANGED CLONE OF MY DEAD MOTHER.
...AH, YES. ONE OF THOSE.

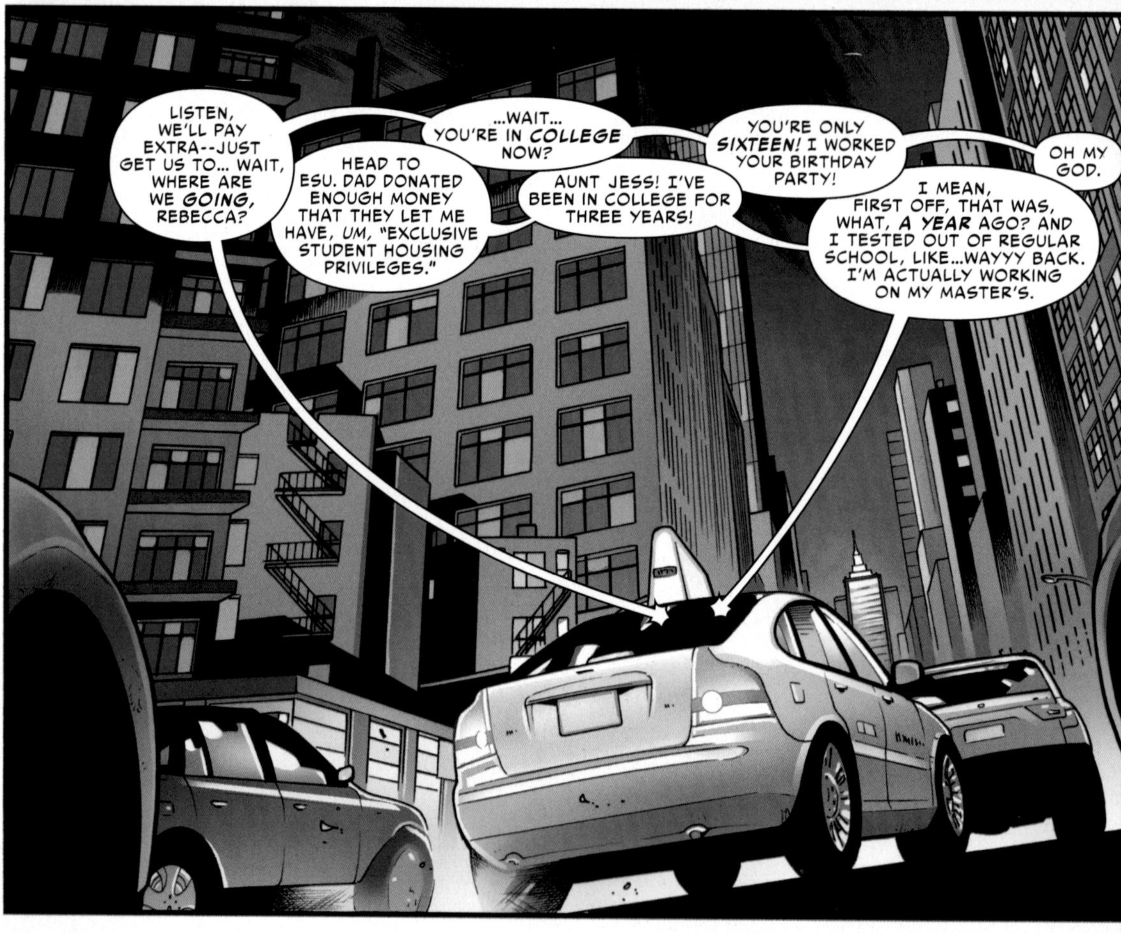
LISTEN, WE'LL PAY EXTRA--JUST GET US TO... WAIT, WHERE ARE WE GOING, REBECCA?
HEAD TO ESU. DAD DONATED ENOUGH MONEY THAT THEY LET ME HAVE, UM, "EXCLUSIVE STUDENT HOUSING PRIVILEGES."
...WAIT... YOU'RE IN COLLEGE NOW?
AUNT JESS! I'VE BEEN IN COLLEGE FOR THREE YEARS!
YOU'RE ONLY SIXTEEN! I WORKED YOUR BIRTHDAY PARTY!
I MEAN, FIRST OFF, THAT WAS, WHAT, A YEAR AGO? AND I TESTED OUT OF REGULAR SCHOOL, LIKE...WAYYY BACK. I'M ACTUALLY WORKING ON MY MASTER'S.
OH MY GOD.

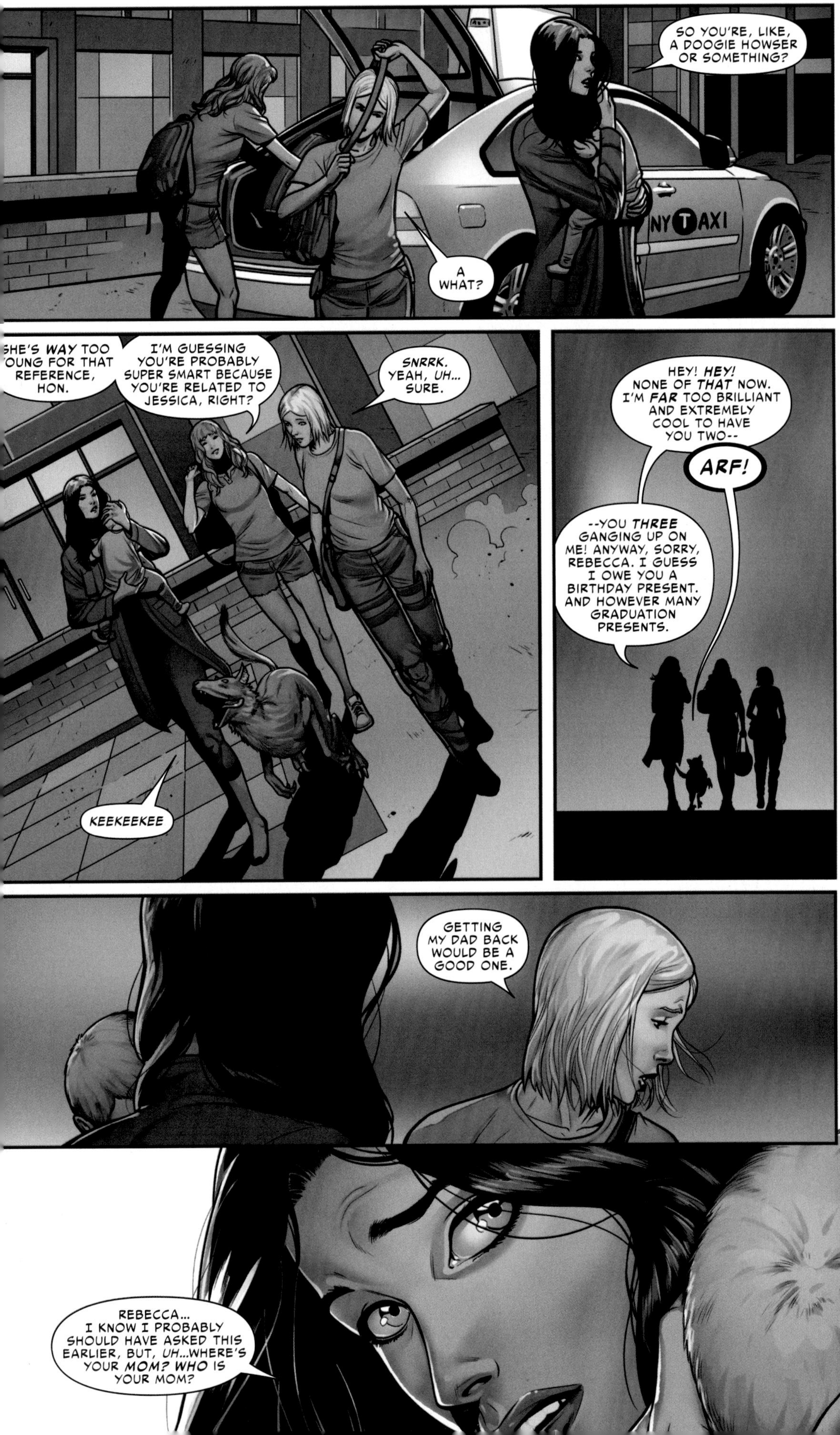

SO YOU'RE, LIKE, A DOOGIE HOWSER OR SOMETHING?
A WHAT?
SHE'S WAY TOO YOUNG FOR THAT REFERENCE, HON.
I'M GUESSING YOU'RE PROBABLY SUPER SMART BECAUSE YOU'RE RELATED TO JESSICA, RIGHT?
SNRRK. YEAH, UH... SURE.
KEEKEEKEE
HEY! HEY! NONE OF THAT NOW. I'M FAR TOO BRILLIANT AND EXTREMELY COOL TO HAVE YOU TWO--
ARF!
--YOU THREE GANGING UP ON ME! ANYWAY, SORRY, REBECCA. I GUESS I OWE YOU A BIRTHDAY PRESENT. AND HOWEVER MANY GRADUATION PRESENTS.
GETTING MY DAD BACK WOULD BE A GOOD ONE.
REBECCA... I KNOW I PROBABLY SHOULD HAVE ASKED THIS EARLIER, BUT, UH...WHERE'S YOUR MOM? WHO IS YOUR MOM?

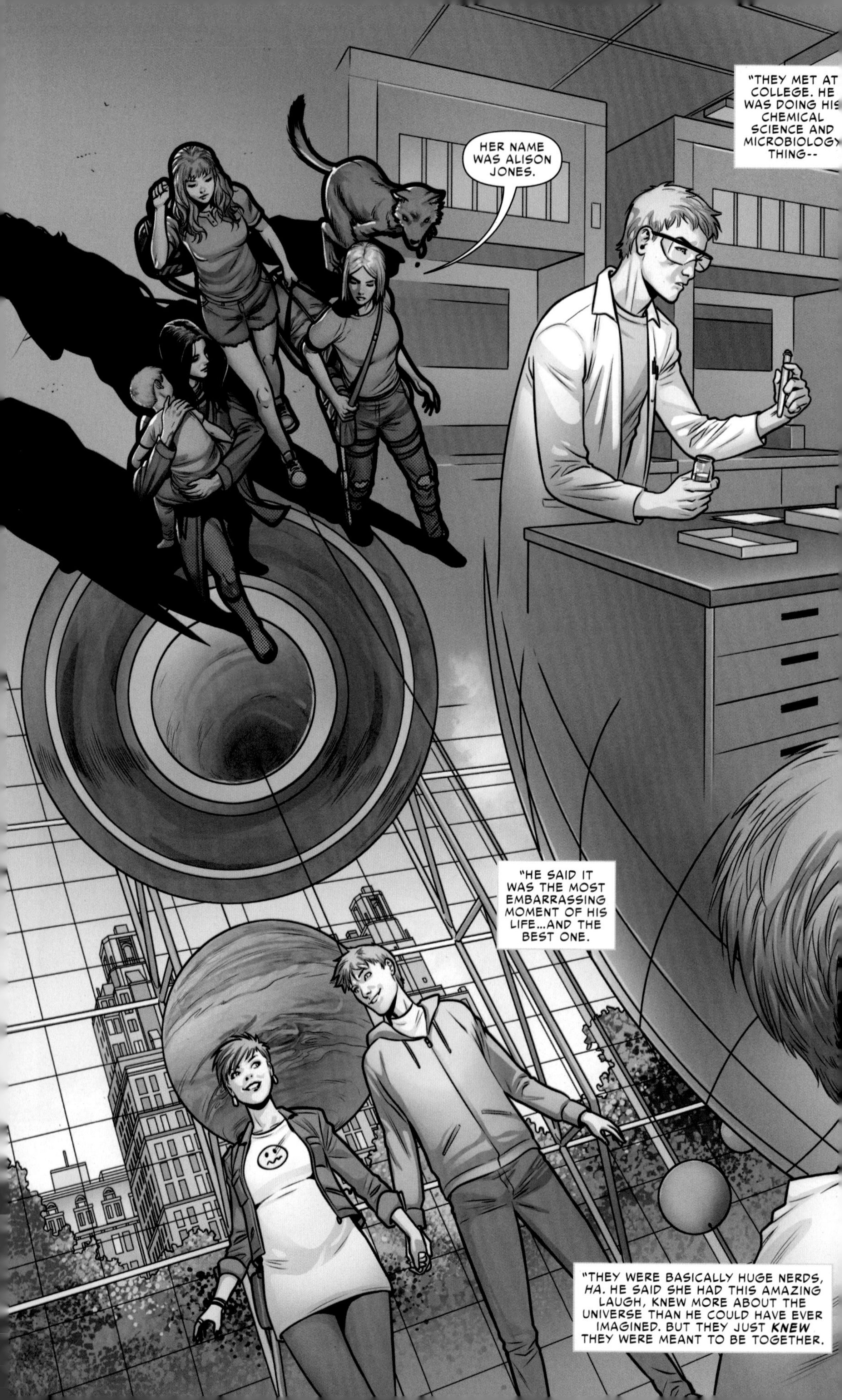
HER NAME WAS ALISON JONES.
"THEY MET AT COLLEGE. HE WAS DOING HIS CHEMICAL SCIENCE AND MICROBIOLOGY THING--
"HE SAID IT WAS THE MOST EMBARRASSING MOMENT OF HIS LIFE...AND THE BEST ONE.
"THEY WERE BASICALLY HUGE NERDS, *HA*. HE SAID SHE HAD THIS AMAZING LAUGH, KNEW MORE ABOUT THE UNIVERSE THAN HE COULD HAVE EVER IMAGINED. BUT THEY JUST ***KNEW*** THEY WERE MEANT TO BE TOGETHER.

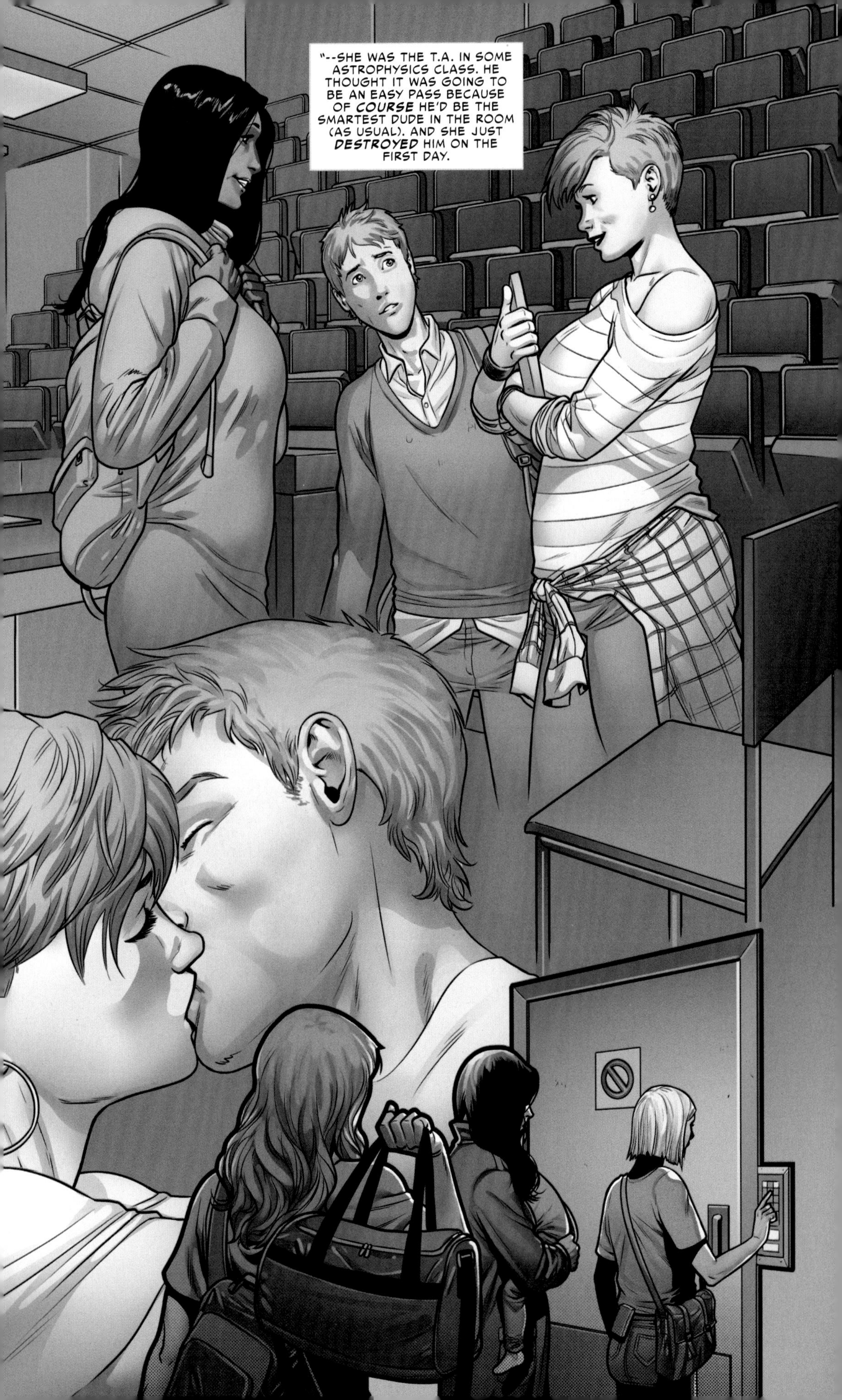
"--SHE WAS THE T.A. IN SOME ASTROPHYSICS CLASS. HE THOUGHT IT WAS GOING TO BE AN EASY PASS BECAUSE OF COURSE HE'D BE THE SMARTEST DUDE IN THE ROOM (AS USUAL). AND SHE JUST DESTROYED HIM ON THE FIRST DAY.

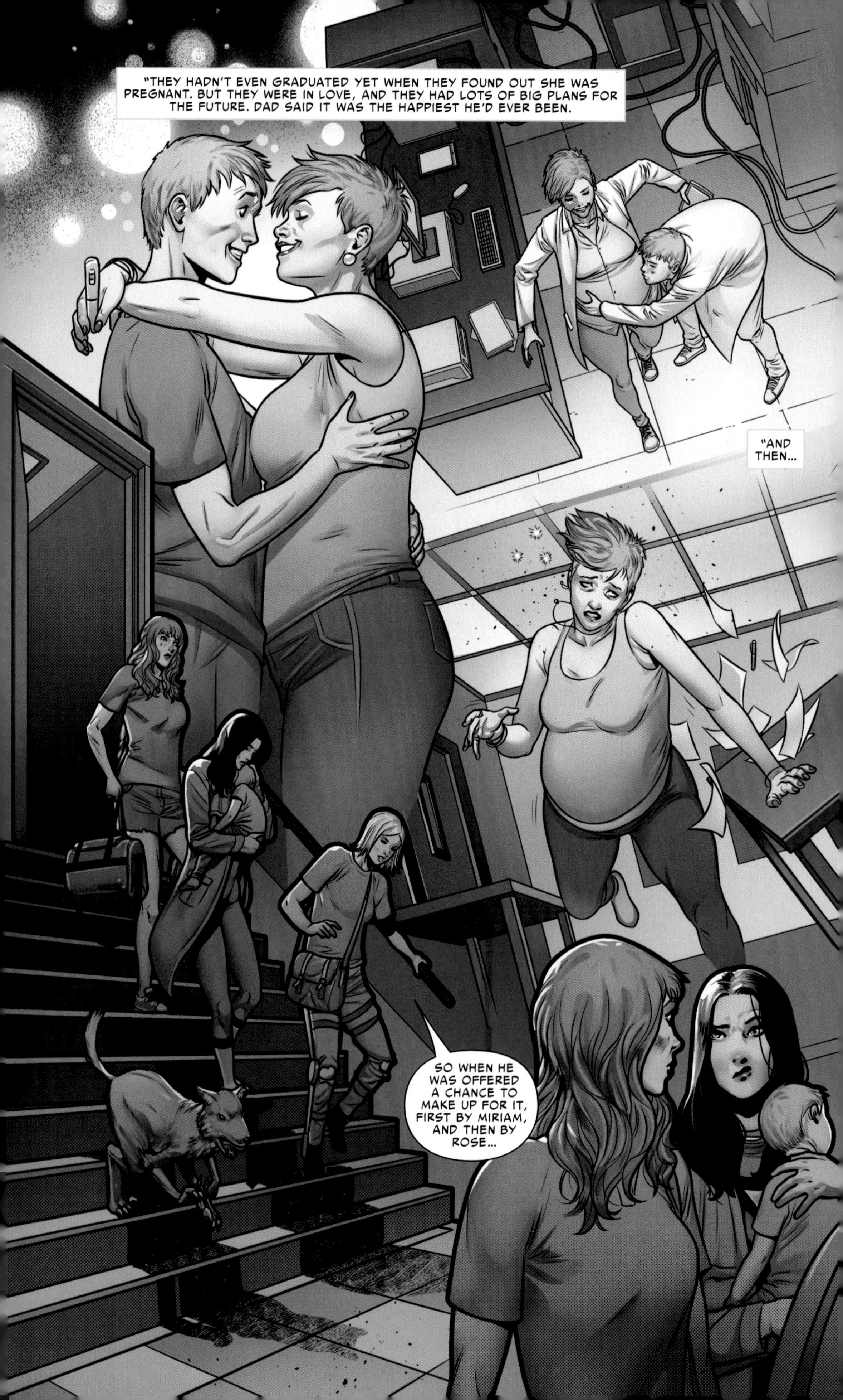
"THEY HADN'T EVEN GRADUATED YET WHEN THEY FOUND OUT SHE WAS PREGNANT. BUT THEY WERE IN LOVE, AND THEY HAD LOTS OF BIG PLANS FOR THE FUTURE. DAD SAID IT WAS THE HAPPIEST HE'D EVER BEEN.
"AND THEN...
SO WHEN HE WAS OFFERED A CHANCE TO MAKE UP FOR IT, FIRST BY MIRIAM, AND THEN BY ROSE...

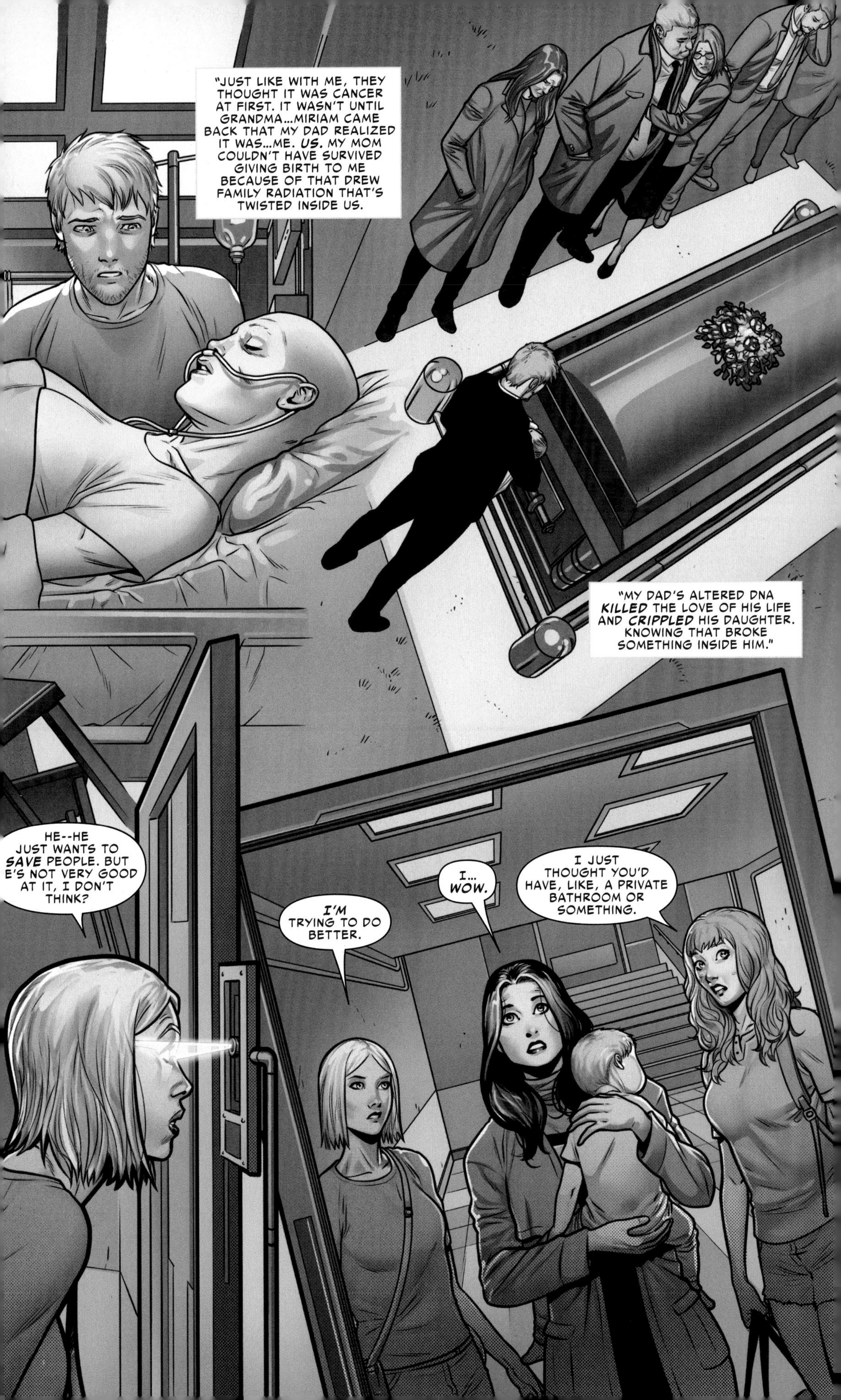

"JUST LIKE WITH ME, THEY THOUGHT IT WAS CANCER AT FIRST. IT WASN'T UNTIL GRANDMA...MIRIAM CAME BACK THAT MY DAD REALIZED IT WAS...ME. US. MY MOM COULDN'T HAVE SURVIVED GIVING BIRTH TO ME BECAUSE OF THAT DREW FAMILY RADIATION THAT'S TWISTED INSIDE US.
"MY DAD'S ALTERED DNA KILLED THE LOVE OF HIS LIFE AND CRIPPLED HIS DAUGHTER. KNOWING THAT BROKE SOMETHING INSIDE HIM."
HE--HE JUST WANTS TO SAVE PEOPLE. BUT E'S NOT VERY GOOD AT IT, I DON'T THINK?
I'M TRYING TO DO BETTER.
I... WOW.
I JUST THOUGHT YOU'D HAVE, LIKE, A PRIVATE BATHROOM OR SOMETHING.

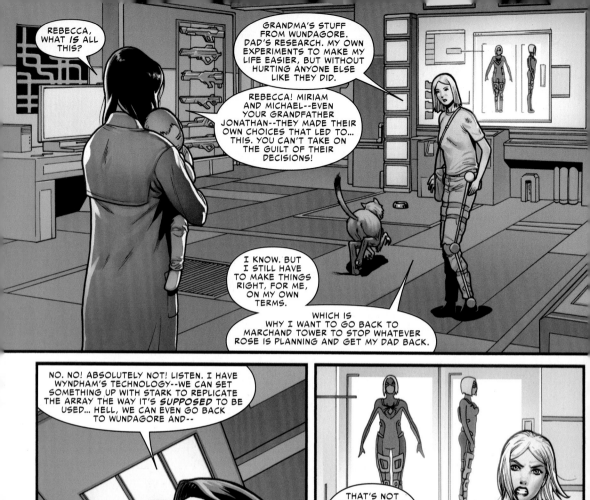

REBECCA, WHAT **IS** ALL THIS?

GRANDMA'S STUFF FROM WUNDAGORE. DAD'S RESEARCH. MY OWN EXPERIMENTS TO MAKE MY LIFE EASIER, BUT WITHOUT HURTING ANYONE ELSE LIKE THEY DID.

REBECCA! MIRIAM AND MICHAEL--EVEN YOUR GRANDFATHER JONATHAN--THEY MADE THEIR OWN CHOICES THAT LED TO... THIS. YOU CAN'T TAKE ON THE GUILT OF THEIR DECISIONS!

I KNOW. BUT I STILL HAVE TO MAKE THINGS RIGHT, FOR ME, ON MY OWN TERMS.

WHICH IS WHY I WANT TO GO BACK TO MARCHAND TOWER TO STOP WHATEVER ROSE IS PLANNING AND GET MY DAD BACK.

NO. NO! ABSOLUTELY NOT! LISTEN. I HAVE WYNDHAM'S TECHNOLOGY--WE CAN SET SOMETHING UP WITH STARK TO REPLICATE THE ARRAY THE WAY IT'S **SUPPOSED** TO BE USED... HELL, WE CAN EVEN GO BACK TO WUNDAGORE AND--

THAT'S NOT YOUR CALL TO MAKE! I DON'T **WANT** THE HIGH EVOLUTIONARY'S "CURE," AND I WANT **EVERYONE** TO STOP TRYING TO "FIX ME"!

I CAN GET MY DAD BACK JUST LIKE I AM, AND **I WILL.**

LISTEN, I PROMISE I WILL DO MY BEST TO GET BACK TO MICHAEL AND SAVE HIM, BUT I CAN'T LET YOU--

I'M NOT HELPLESS, JESS! YOU KNOW THAT! **WITH OR WITHOUT** A CURE! I CAN DO THIS! I HAVE TO. HE'S **MY DAD.**

IS THIS THE SUIT MIRIAM MADE YOU, REBECCA?

SAME MATERIAL. I HELPED GRANDMA WITH THE ORIGINAL DESIGN. THEN AFTER EVERYTHING, Y'KNOW...*BLEW UP,* I STARTED MAKING MY OWN IMPROVEMENTS.

DANG. THAT'S AMAZING! JESSICA! DID YOU SEE WHAT A GREAT SUIT SHE MADE?

*IN *SPIDER-WOMAN* #5! --LC

NOT HELPING, LINDS--

SHH! BABY! KEEP YOUR VOICE DOWN!

...FINE. I JUST DON'T THINK--

YOU ADMIT SHE'S HAD TO DEAL WITH THE CONSEQUENCES OF *EVERYONE ELSE'S* CHOICES... WHEN DOES REBECCA GET TO MAKE HER *OWN?*

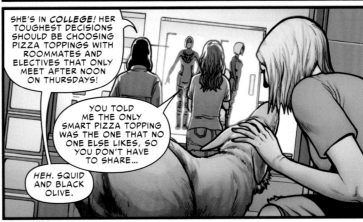

SHE'S IN *COLLEGE!* HER TOUGHEST DECISIONS SHOULD BE CHOOSING PIZZA TOPPINGS WITH ROOMMATES AND ELECTIVES THAT ONLY MEET AFTER NOON ON THURSDAYS!

YOU TOLD ME THE ONLY SMART PIZZA TOPPING WAS THE ONE THAT NO ONE ELSE LIKES, SO YOU DON'T HAVE TO SHARE...

HEH. SQUID AND BLACK OLIVE.

AND WHAT KIND OF DECISIONS DID *YOU* HAVE TO MAKE WHEN YOU WERE HER AGE, JESS?

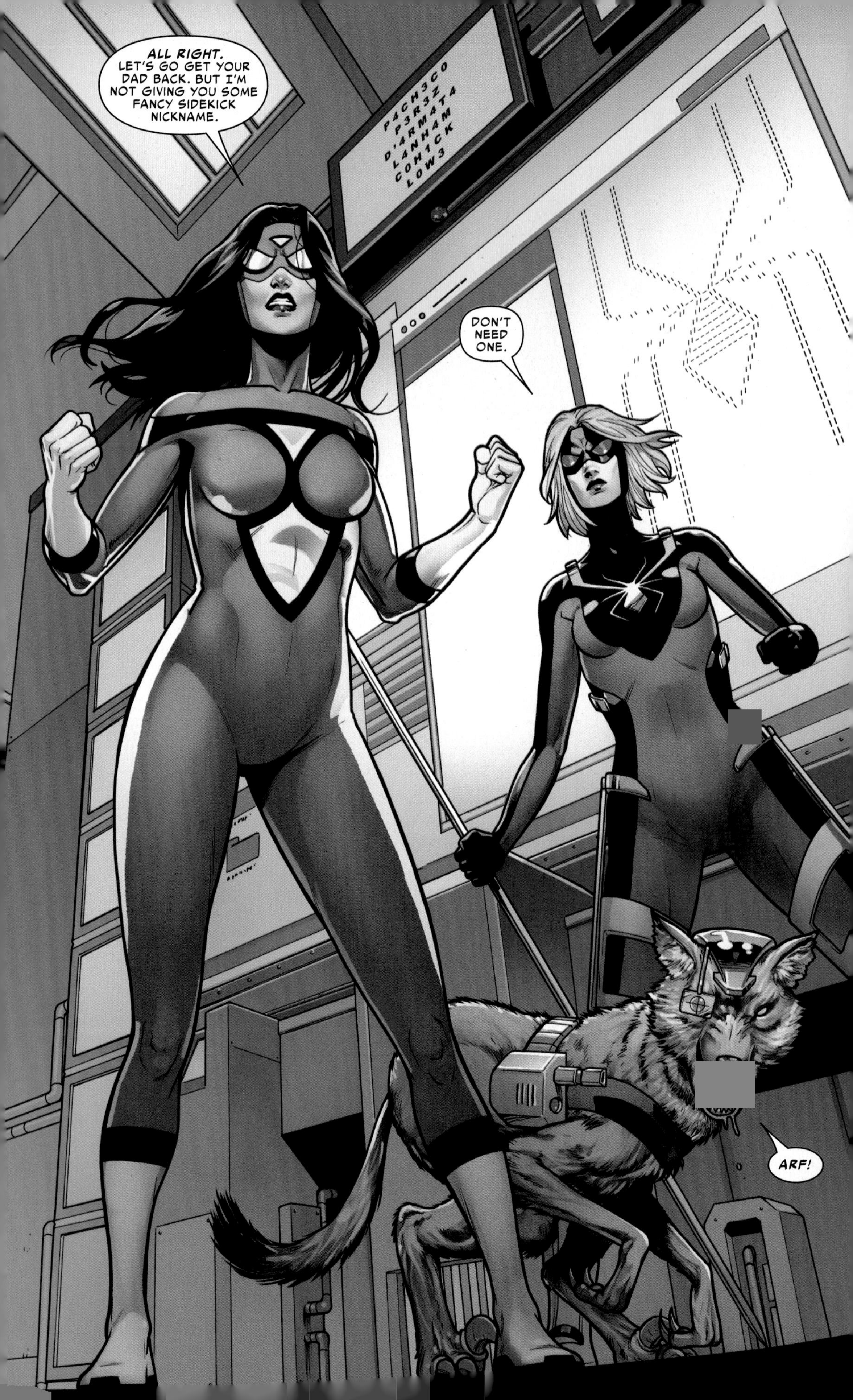
ALL RIGHT. LET'S GO GET YOUR DAD BACK. BUT I'M NOT GIVING YOU SOME FANCY SIDEKICK NICKNAME.
P4CH3CO
P3R3Z
D'ARM4T4
L4NH4M
C0H1CK
L0W3
DON'T NEED ONE.
ARF!

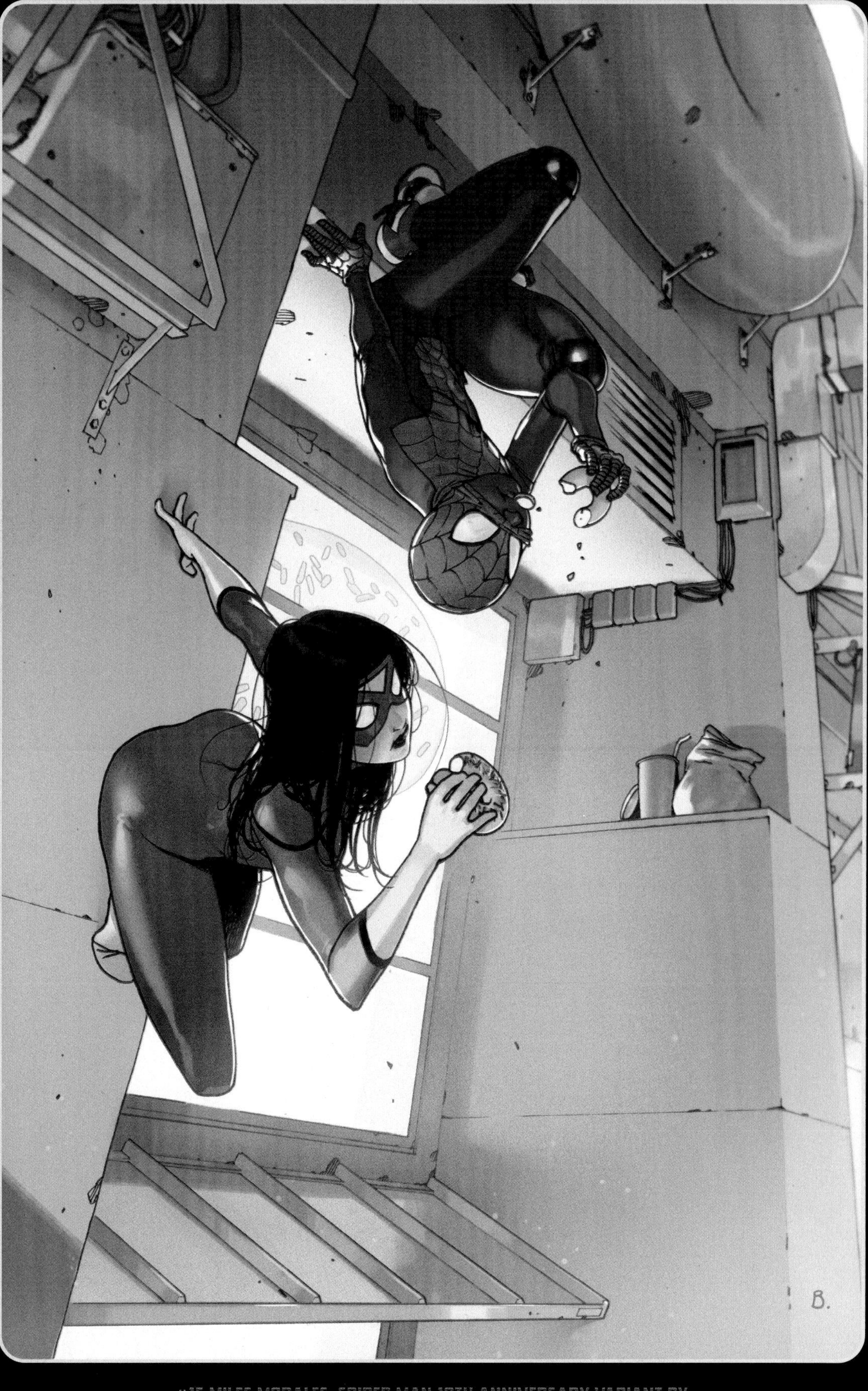
B.

#15 MILES MORALES: SPIDER-MAN 10TH ANNIVERSARY VARIANT BY
BENGAL

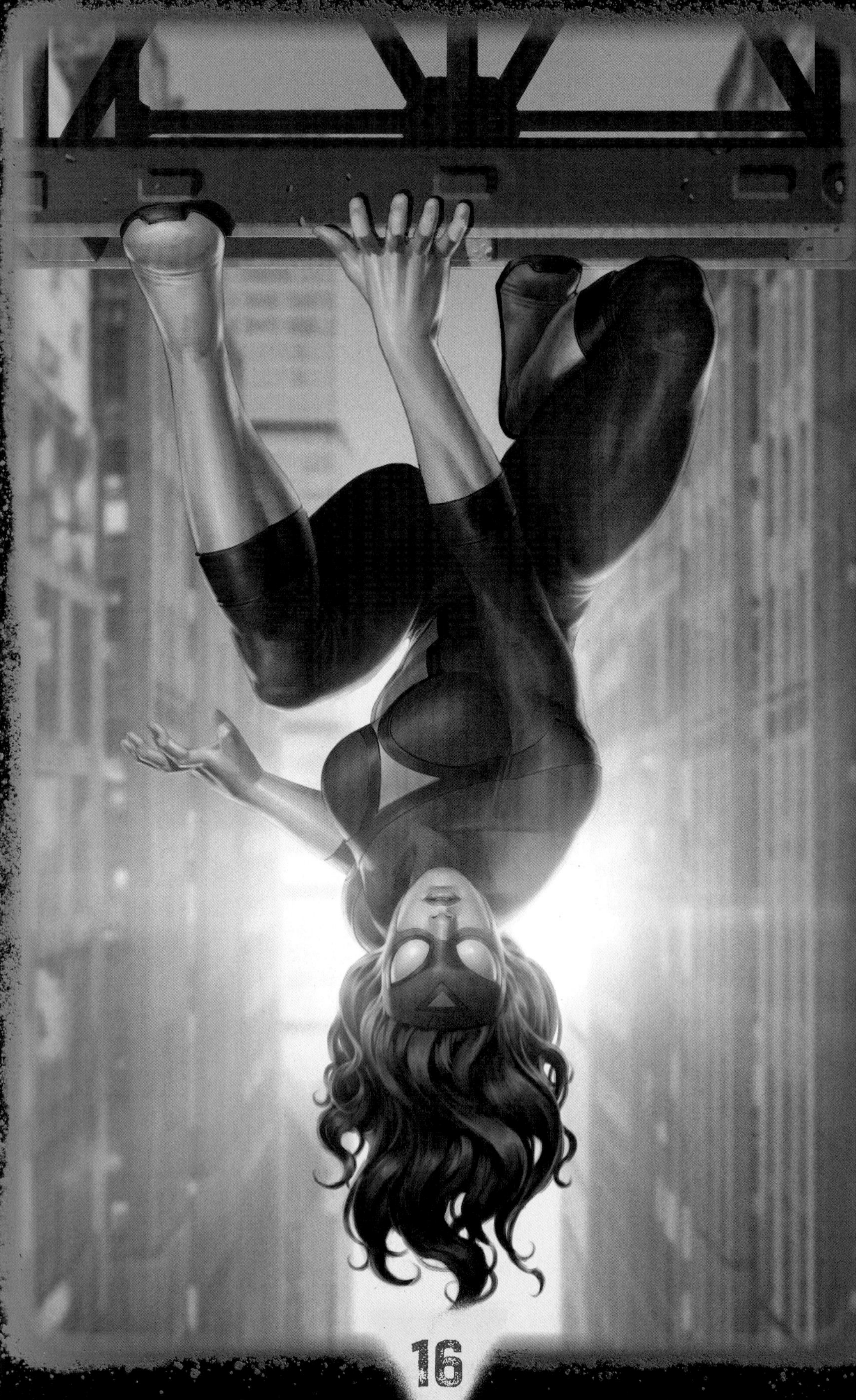

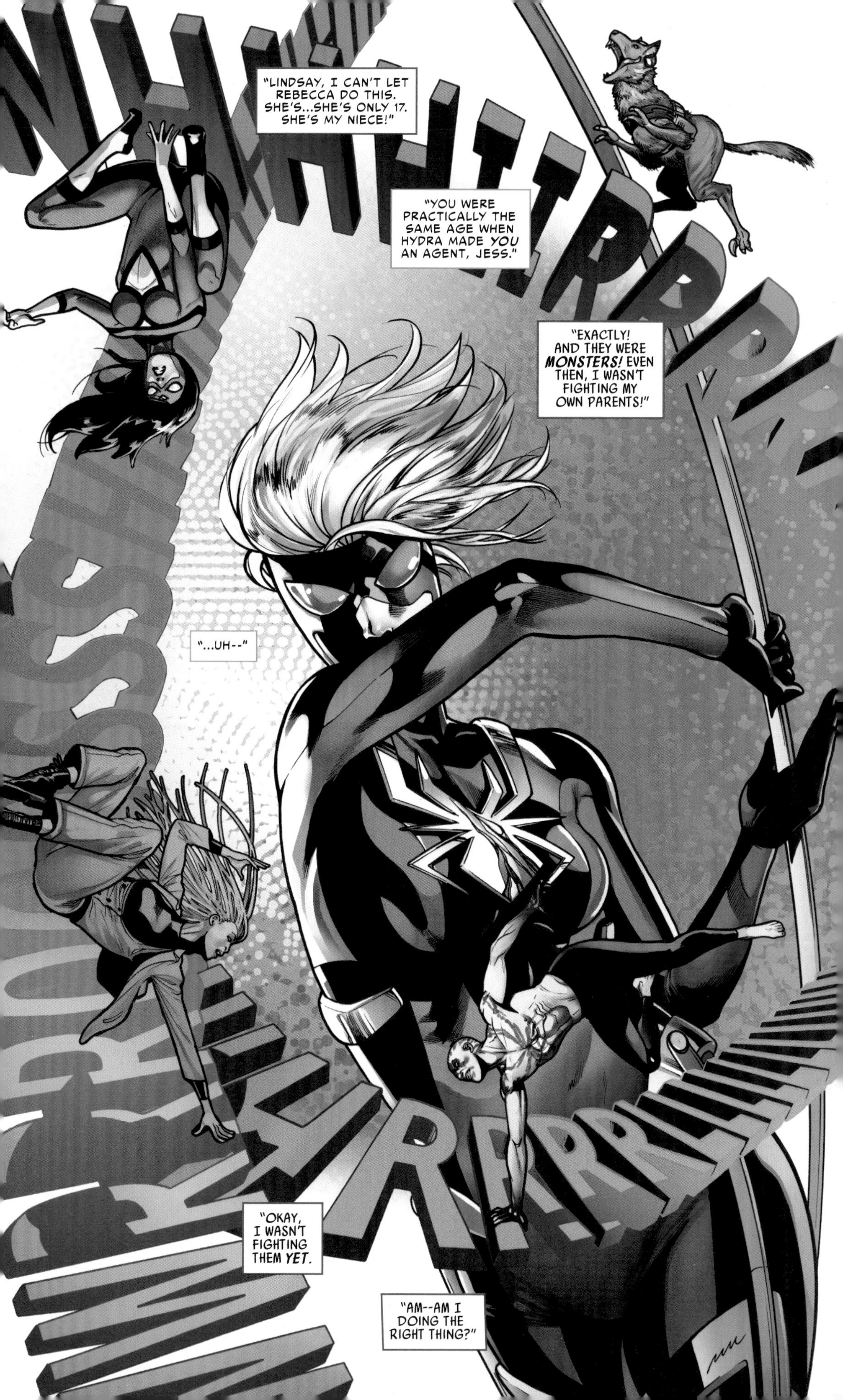
"LINDSAY, I CAN'T LET REBECCA DO THIS. SHE'S...SHE'S ONLY 17. SHE'S MY NIECE!"
"YOU WERE PRACTICALLY THE SAME AGE WHEN HYDRA MADE YOU AN AGENT, JESS."
"EXACTLY! AND THEY WERE MONSTERS! EVEN THEN, I WASN'T FIGHTING MY OWN PARENTS!"
"...UH--"
"OKAY, I WASN'T FIGHTING THEM YET.
"AM--AM I DOING THE RIGHT THING?"

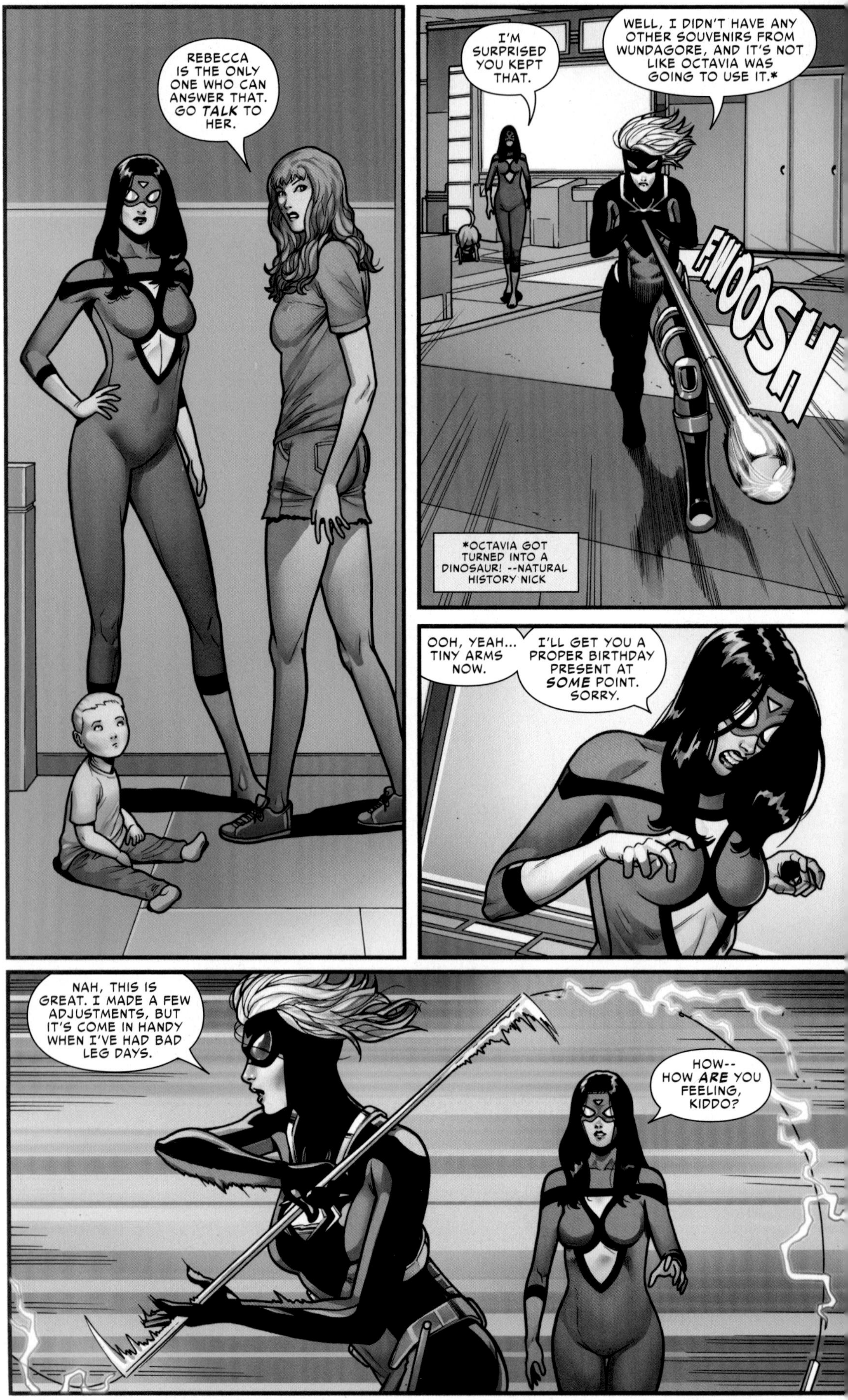
REBECCA IS THE ONLY ONE WHO CAN ANSWER THAT. GO TALK TO HER.
I'M SURPRISED YOU KEPT THAT.
WELL, I DIDN'T HAVE ANY OTHER SOUVENIRS FROM WUNDAGORE, AND IT'S NOT LIKE OCTAVIA WAS GOING TO USE IT.*
FWOOSH
*OCTAVIA GOT TURNED INTO A DINOSAUR! --NATURAL HISTORY NICK
OOH, YEAH... TINY ARMS NOW.
I'LL GET YOU A PROPER BIRTHDAY PRESENT AT SOME POINT. SORRY.
NAH, THIS IS GREAT. I MADE A FEW ADJUSTMENTS, BUT IT'S COME IN HANDY WHEN I'VE HAD BAD LEG DAYS.
HOW-- HOW ARE YOU FEELING, KIDDO?

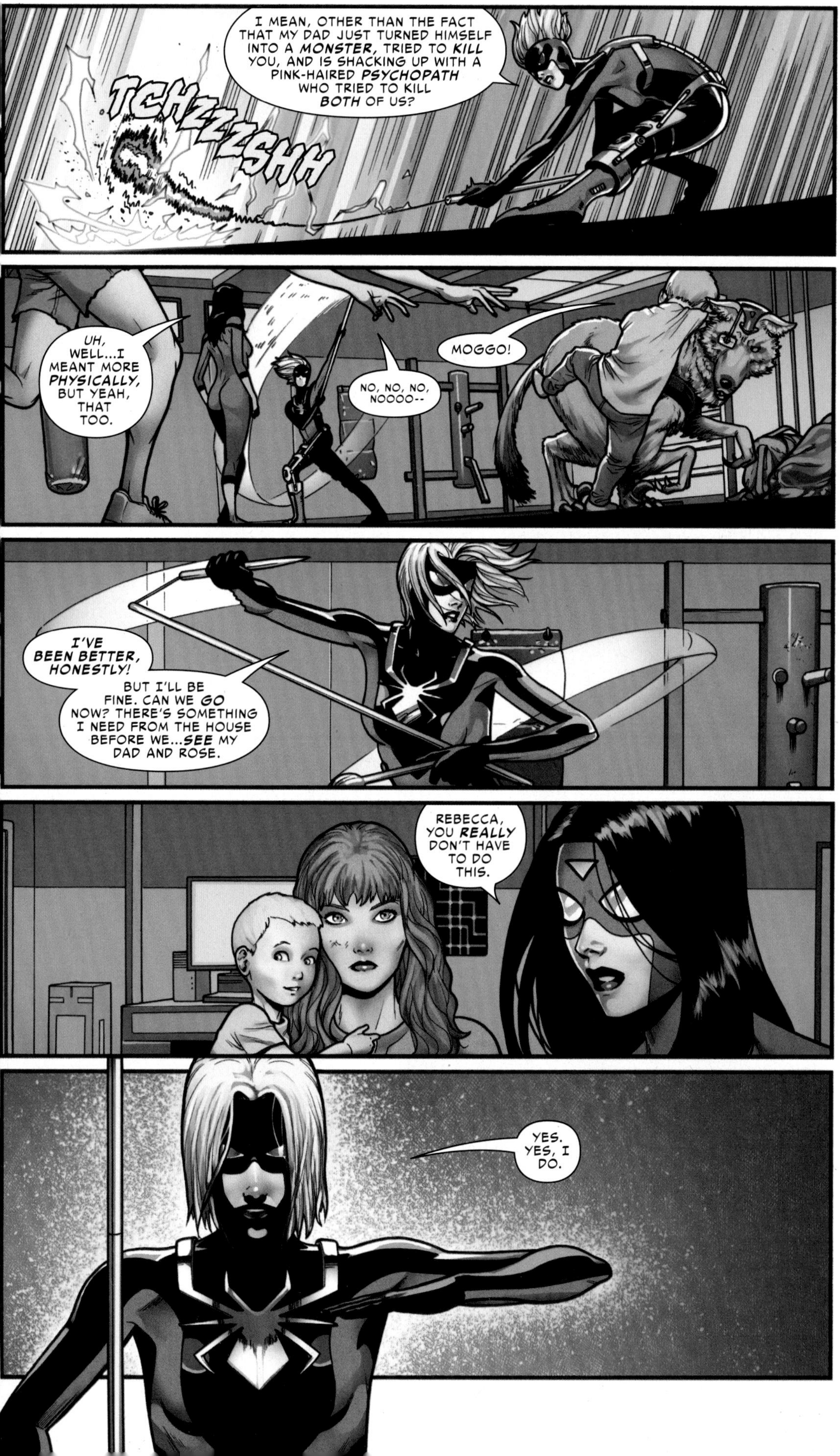

I MEAN, OTHER THAN THE FACT THAT MY DAD JUST TURNED HIMSELF INTO A MONSTER, TRIED TO KILL YOU, AND IS SHACKING UP WITH A PINK-HAIRED PSYCHOPATH WHO TRIED TO KILL BOTH OF US?
TCHZZZZSHH
UH, WELL...I MEANT MORE PHYSICALLY, BUT YEAH, THAT TOO.
NO, NO, NO, NOOOO--
MOGGO!
I'VE BEEN BETTER, HONESTLY!
BUT I'LL BE FINE. CAN WE GO NOW? THERE'S SOMETHING I NEED FROM THE HOUSE BEFORE WE...SEE MY DAD AND ROSE.
REBECCA, YOU REALLY DON'T HAVE TO DO THIS.
YES. YES, I DO.

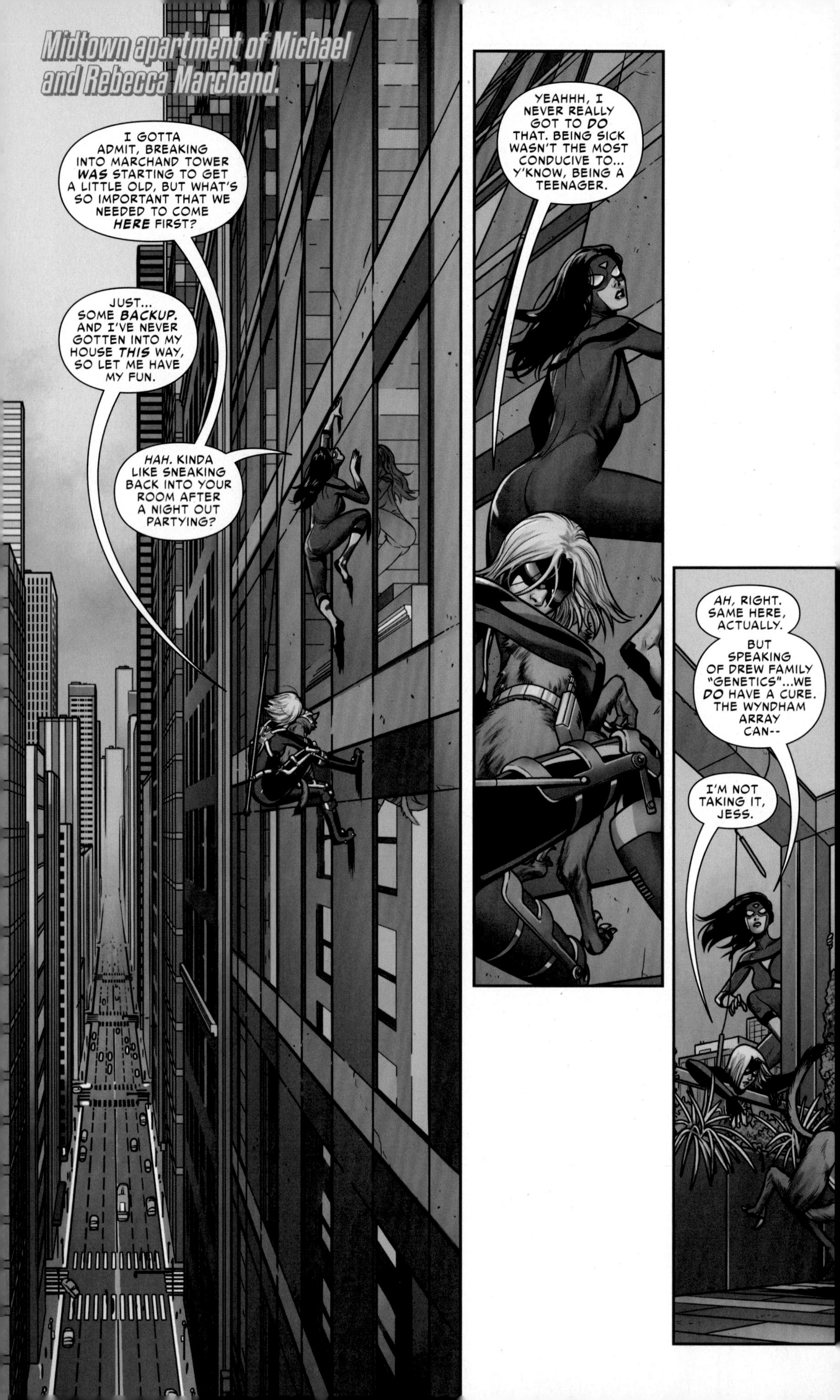

Midtown apartment of Michael and Rebecca Marchand.
I GOTTA ADMIT, BREAKING INTO MARCHAND TOWER WAS STARTING TO GET A LITTLE OLD, BUT WHAT'S SO IMPORTANT THAT WE NEEDED TO COME HERE FIRST?
JUST... SOME BACKUP. AND I'VE NEVER GOTTEN INTO MY HOUSE THIS WAY, SO LET ME HAVE MY FUN.
HAH. KINDA LIKE SNEAKING BACK INTO YOUR ROOM AFTER A NIGHT OUT PARTYING?
YEAHHH, I NEVER REALLY GOT TO DO THAT. BEING SICK WASN'T THE MOST CONDUCIVE TO... Y'KNOW, BEING A TEENAGER.
AH, RIGHT. SAME HERE, ACTUALLY.
BUT SPEAKING OF DREW FAMILY "GENETICS"...WE DO HAVE A CURE. THE WYNDHAM ARRAY CAN--
I'M NOT TAKING IT, JESS.

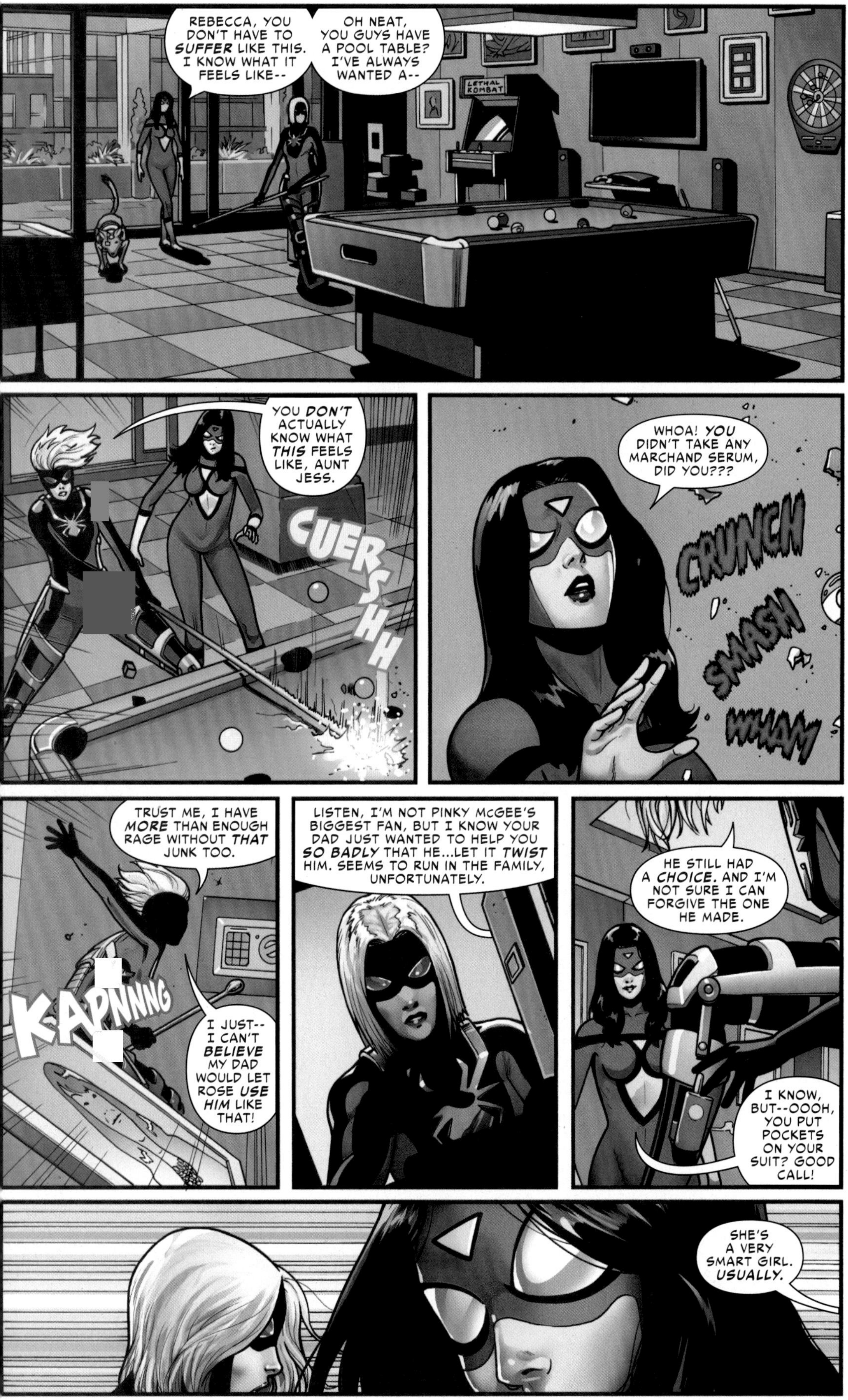
REBECCA, YOU DON'T HAVE TO *SUFFER* LIKE THIS. I KNOW WHAT IT FEELS LIKE--
OH NEAT, YOU GUYS HAVE A POOL TABLE? I'VE ALWAYS WANTED A--
LETHAL KOMBAT
YOU *DON'T* ACTUALLY KNOW WHAT *THIS* FEELS LIKE, AUNT JESS.
CUERSHH
WHOA! *YOU* DIDN'T TAKE ANY MARCHAND SERUM, DID YOU???
CRUNCH
SMASH
WHAM
TRUST ME, I HAVE *MORE* THAN ENOUGH RAGE WITHOUT *THAT* JUNK TOO.
KAPNNNG
I JUST-- I CAN'T *BELIEVE* MY DAD WOULD LET ROSE *USE HIM* LIKE THAT!
LISTEN, I'M NOT PINKY McGEE'S BIGGEST FAN, BUT I KNOW YOUR DAD JUST WANTED TO HELP YOU *SO BADLY* THAT HE...LET IT *TWIST* HIM. SEEMS TO RUN IN THE FAMILY, UNFORTUNATELY.
HE STILL HAD A *CHOICE.* AND I'M NOT SURE I CAN FORGIVE THE ONE HE MADE.
I KNOW, BUT--OOOH, YOU PUT POCKETS ON YOUR SUIT? GOOD CALL!
SHE'S A VERY SMART GIRL. *USUALLY.*

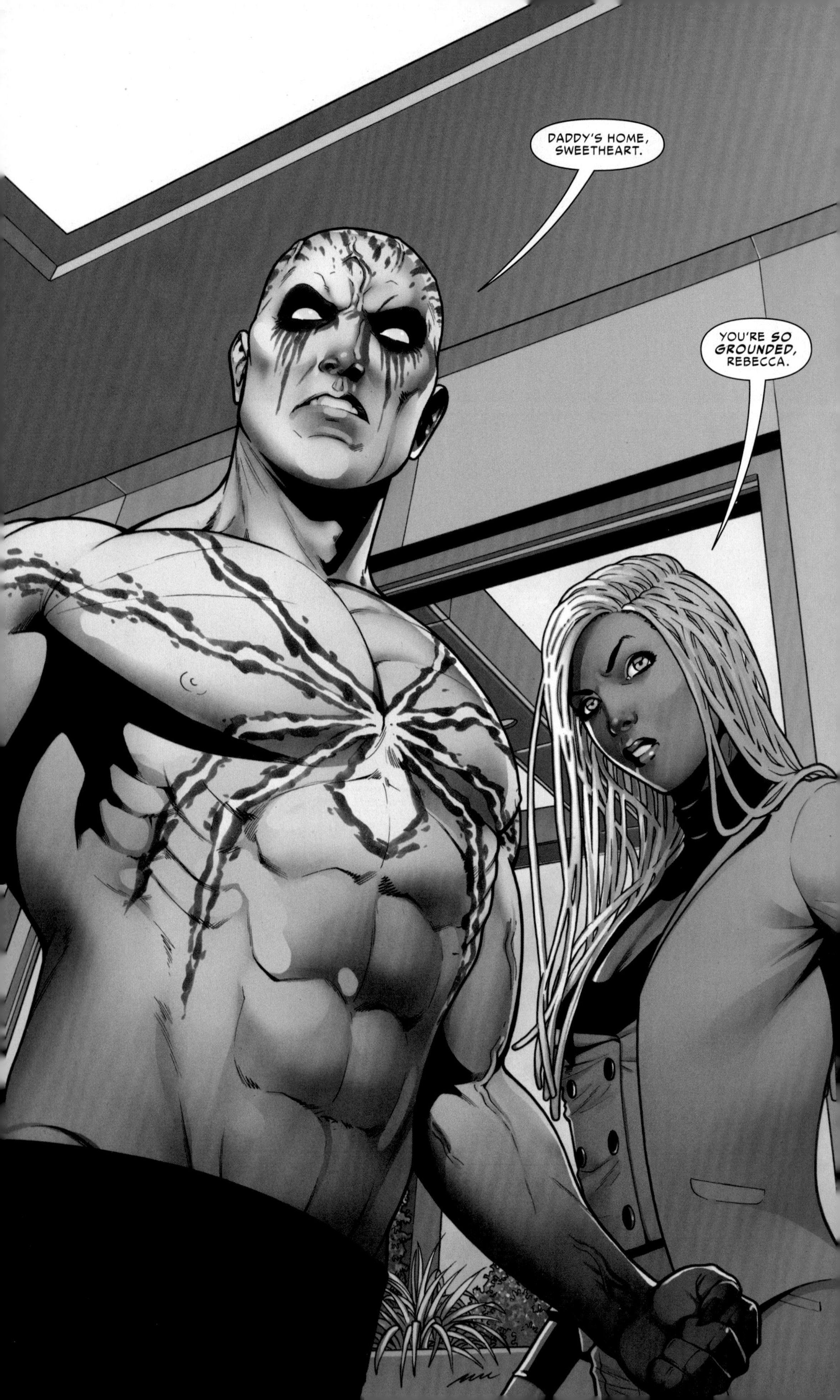
DADDY'S HOME, SWEETHEART.
YOU'RE SO GROUNDED, REBECCA.

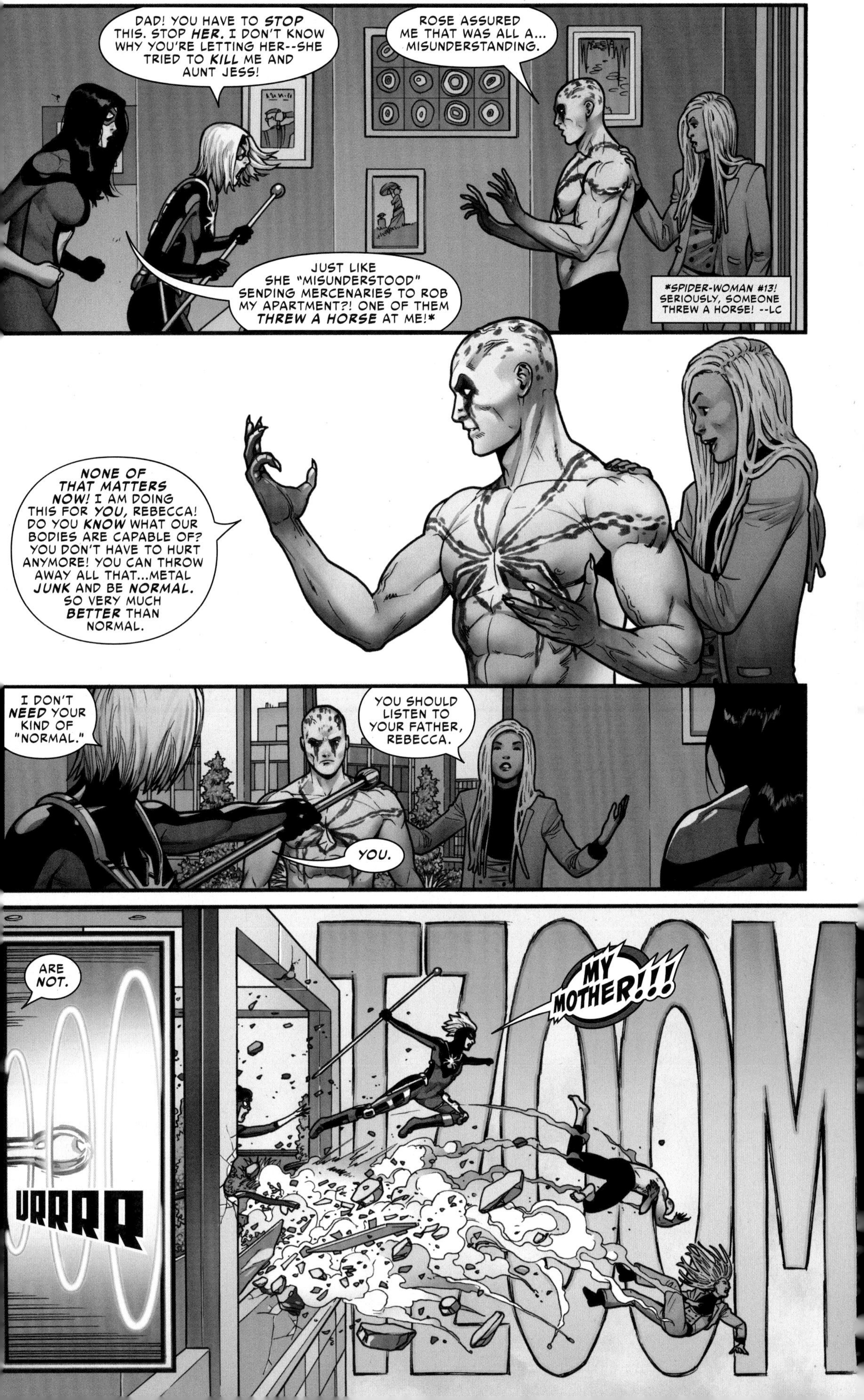
DAD! YOU HAVE TO STOP THIS. STOP HER. I DON'T KNOW WHY YOU'RE LETTING HER--SHE TRIED TO KILL ME AND AUNT JESS!
ROSE ASSURED ME THAT WAS ALL A... MISUNDERSTANDING.
JUST LIKE SHE "MISUNDERSTOOD" SENDING MERCENARIES TO ROB MY APARTMENT?! ONE OF THEM THREW A HORSE AT ME!*
*SPIDER-WOMAN #13! SERIOUSLY, SOMEONE THREW A HORSE! --LC
NONE OF THAT MATTERS NOW! I AM DOING THIS FOR YOU, REBECCA! DO YOU KNOW WHAT OUR BODIES ARE CAPABLE OF? YOU DON'T HAVE TO HURT ANYMORE! YOU CAN THROW AWAY ALL THAT...METAL JUNK AND BE NORMAL. SO VERY MUCH BETTER THAN NORMAL.
I DON'T NEED YOUR KIND OF "NORMAL."
YOU SHOULD LISTEN TO YOUR FATHER, REBECCA.
YOU.
ARE NOT.
VRRRR
MY MOTHER!!!
TOOM

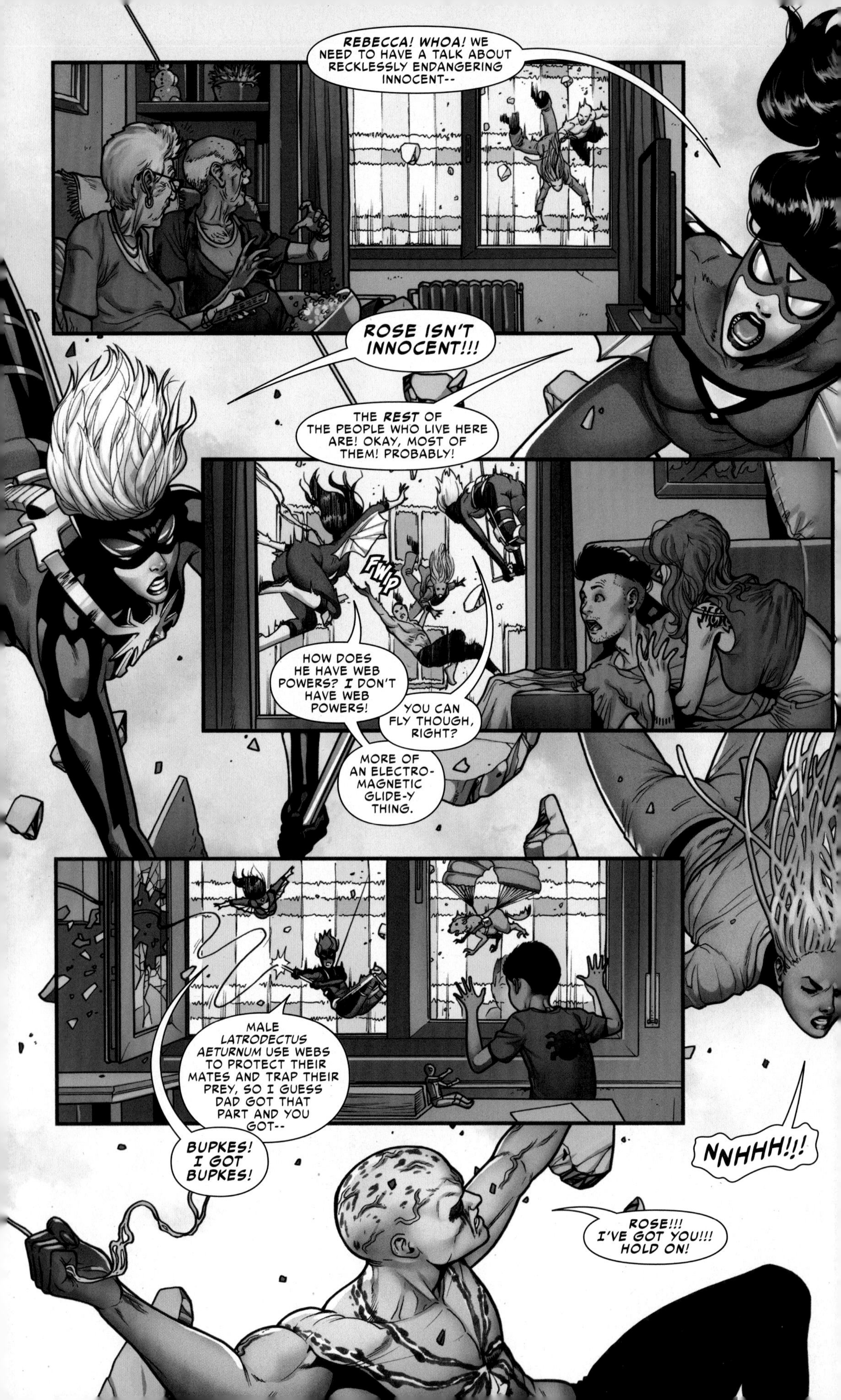

REBECCA! WHOA! WE NEED TO HAVE A TALK ABOUT RECKLESSLY ENDANGERING INNOCENT--
ROSE ISN'T INNOCENT!!!
THE REST OF THE PEOPLE WHO LIVE HERE ARE! OKAY, MOST OF THEM! PROBABLY!
FWIP
HOW DOES HE HAVE WEB POWERS? I DON'T HAVE WEB POWERS!
YOU CAN FLY THOUGH, RIGHT?
MORE OF AN ELECTRO-MAGNETIC GLIDE-Y THING.
MALE LATRODECTUS AETURNUM USE WEBS TO PROTECT THEIR MATES AND TRAP THEIR PREY, SO I GUESS DAD GOT THAT PART AND YOU GOT--
BUPKES! I GOT BUPKES!
NNHHH!!!
ROSE!!! I'VE GOT YOU!!! HOLD ON!

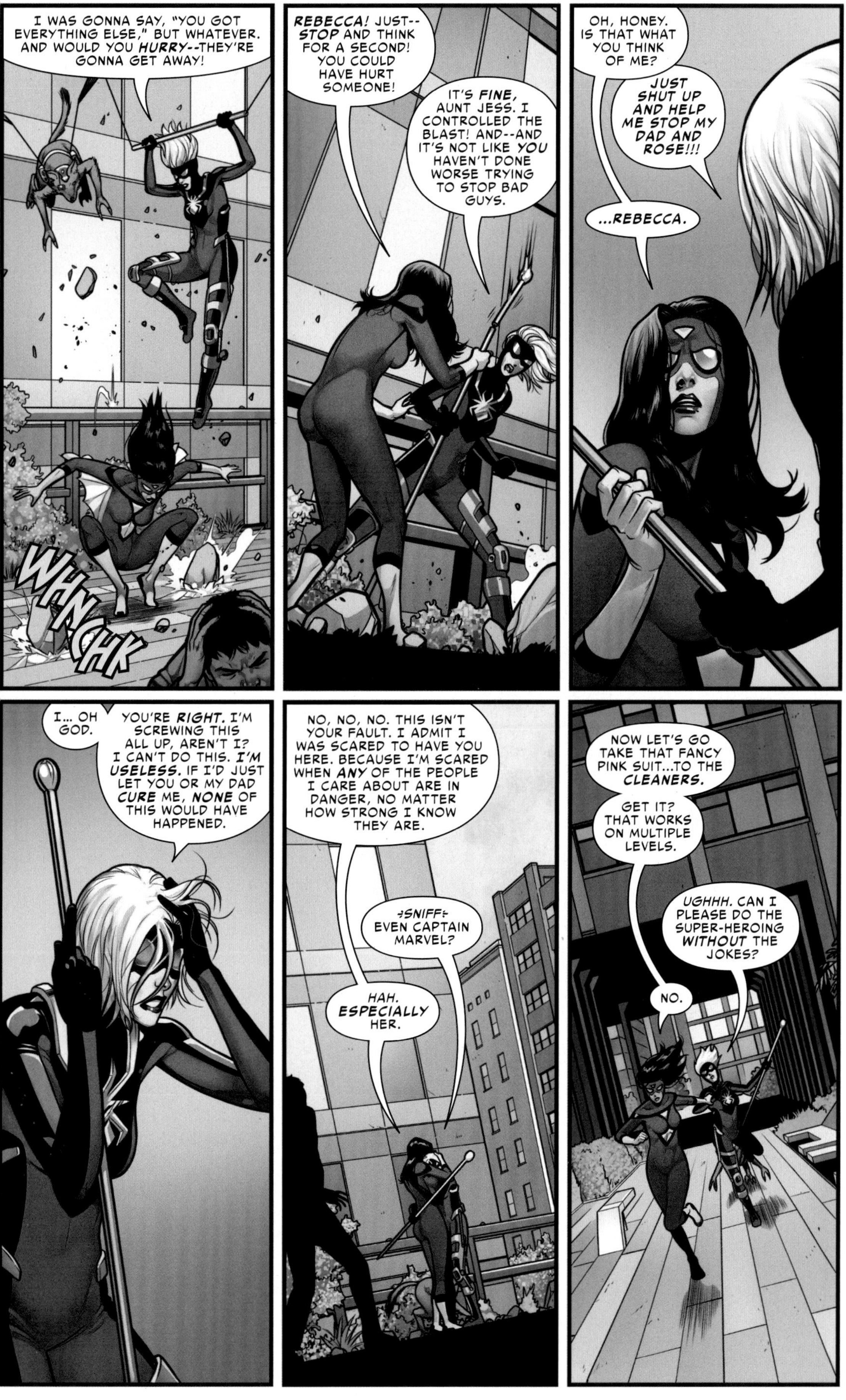
I WAS GONNA SAY, "YOU GOT EVERYTHING ELSE," BUT WHATEVER. AND WOULD YOU HURRY--THEY'RE GONNA GET AWAY!
WHNCHK
REBECCA! JUST--STOP AND THINK FOR A SECOND! YOU COULD HAVE HURT SOMEONE!
IT'S FINE, AUNT JESS. I CONTROLLED THE BLAST! AND--AND IT'S NOT LIKE YOU HAVEN'T DONE WORSE TRYING TO STOP BAD GUYS.
OH, HONEY. IS THAT WHAT YOU THINK OF ME?
JUST SHUT UP AND HELP ME STOP MY DAD AND ROSE!!!
...REBECCA.
I... OH GOD.
YOU'RE RIGHT. I'M SCREWING THIS ALL UP, AREN'T I? I CAN'T DO THIS. I'M USELESS. IF I'D JUST LET YOU OR MY DAD CURE ME, NONE OF THIS WOULD HAVE HAPPENED.
NO, NO, NO. THIS ISN'T YOUR FAULT. I ADMIT I WAS SCARED TO HAVE YOU HERE. BECAUSE I'M SCARED WHEN ANY OF THE PEOPLE I CARE ABOUT ARE IN DANGER, NO MATTER HOW STRONG I KNOW THEY ARE.
SNIFF EVEN CAPTAIN MARVEL?
HAH. ESPECIALLY HER.
NOW LET'S GO TAKE THAT FANCY PINK SUIT...TO THE CLEANERS.
GET IT? THAT WORKS ON MULTIPLE LEVELS.
UGHHH. CAN I PLEASE DO THE SUPER-HEROING WITHOUT THE JOKES?
NO.

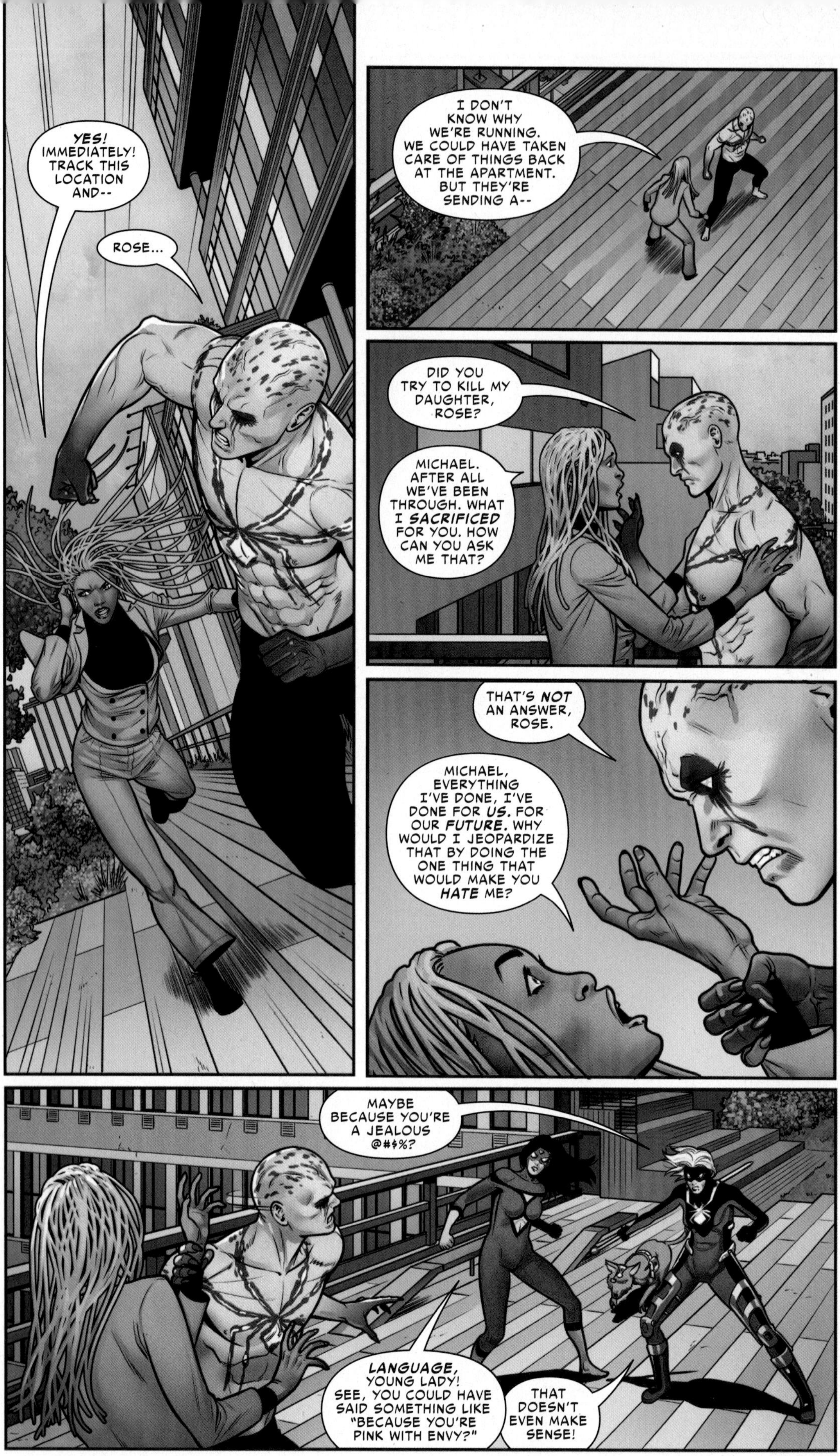
YES! IMMEDIATELY! TRACK THIS LOCATION AND--
ROSE...
I DON'T KNOW WHY WE'RE RUNNING. WE COULD HAVE TAKEN CARE OF THINGS BACK AT THE APARTMENT. BUT THEY'RE SENDING A--
DID YOU TRY TO KILL MY DAUGHTER, ROSE?
MICHAEL. AFTER ALL WE'VE BEEN THROUGH. WHAT I SACRIFICED FOR YOU. HOW CAN YOU ASK ME THAT?
THAT'S NOT AN ANSWER, ROSE.
MICHAEL, EVERYTHING I'VE DONE, I'VE DONE FOR US. FOR OUR FUTURE. WHY WOULD I JEOPARDIZE THAT BY DOING THE ONE THING THAT WOULD MAKE YOU HATE ME?
MAYBE BECAUSE YOU'RE A JEALOUS @#$%?
LANGUAGE, YOUNG LADY! SEE, YOU COULD HAVE SAID SOMETHING LIKE "BECAUSE YOU'RE PINK WITH ENVY?"
THAT DOESN'T EVEN MAKE SENSE!

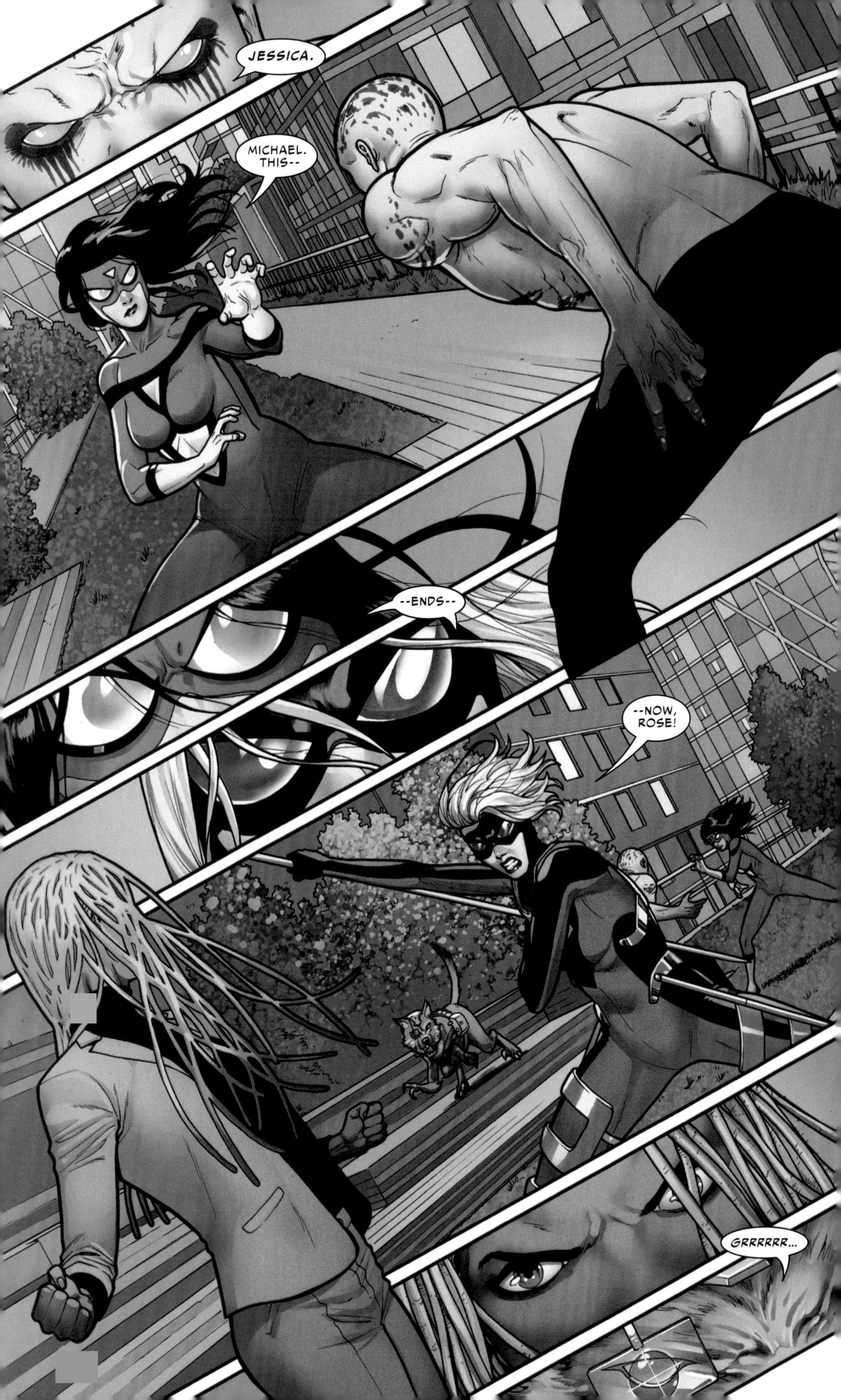
JESSICA.
MICHAEL. THIS--
--ENDS--
--NOW, ROSE!
GRRRRRR...

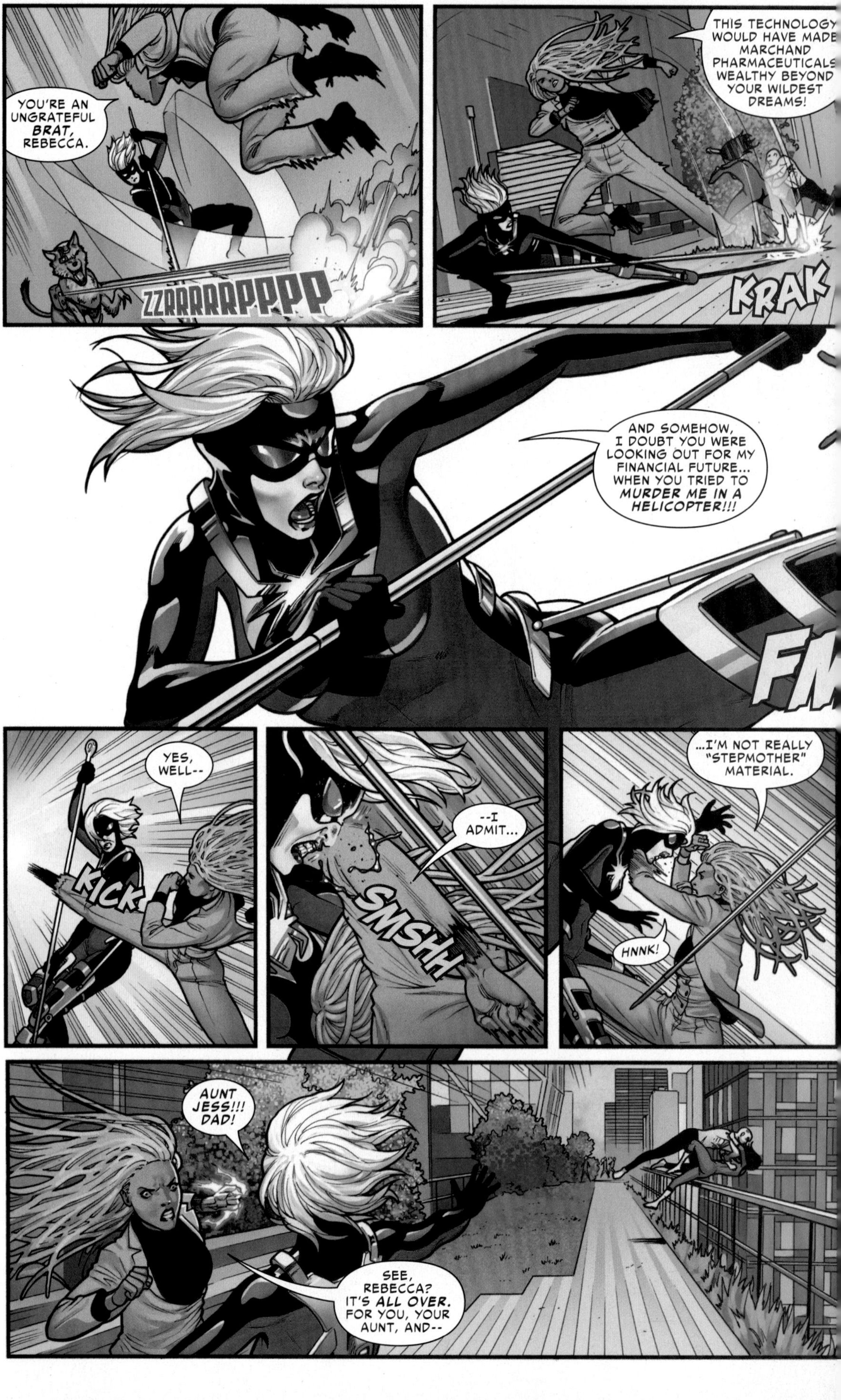
YOU'RE AN UNGRATEFUL BRAT, REBECCA.
ZZRRRRRRPPPP
THIS TECHNOLOGY WOULD HAVE MADE MARCHAND PHARMACEUTICALS WEALTHY BEYOND YOUR WILDEST DREAMS!
KRAK
AND SOMEHOW, I DOUBT YOU WERE LOOKING OUT FOR MY FINANCIAL FUTURE... WHEN YOU TRIED TO MURDER ME IN A HELICOPTER!!!
YES, WELL--
KICK
--I ADMIT...
SMSHH
...I'M NOT REALLY "STEPMOTHER" MATERIAL.
HNNK!
AUNT JESS!!! DAD!
SEE, REBECCA? IT'S ALL OVER. FOR YOU, YOUR AUNT, AND--

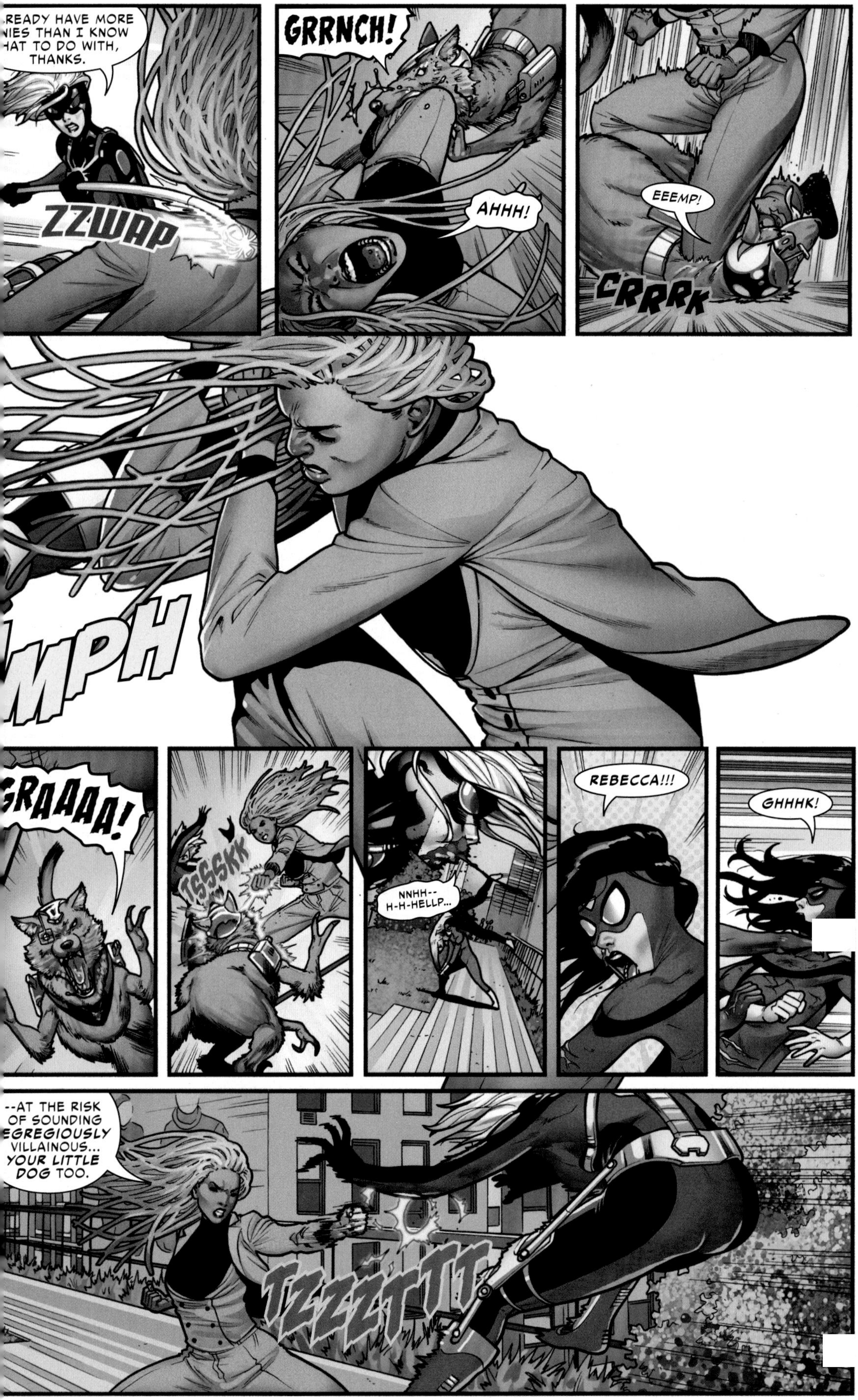

READY HAVE MORE
NIES THAN I KNOW
HAT TO DO WITH,
THANKS.
ZZWAP
GRRNCH!
AHHH!
EEEMP!
CRRRK
MPH
GRAAAA!
TSSSKK
NNHH--
H-H-HELLP...
REBECCA!!!
GHHHK!
--AT THE RISK
OF SOUNDING
EGREGIOUSLY
VILLAINOUS...
YOUR LITTLE
DOG TOO.
TZZZTTT

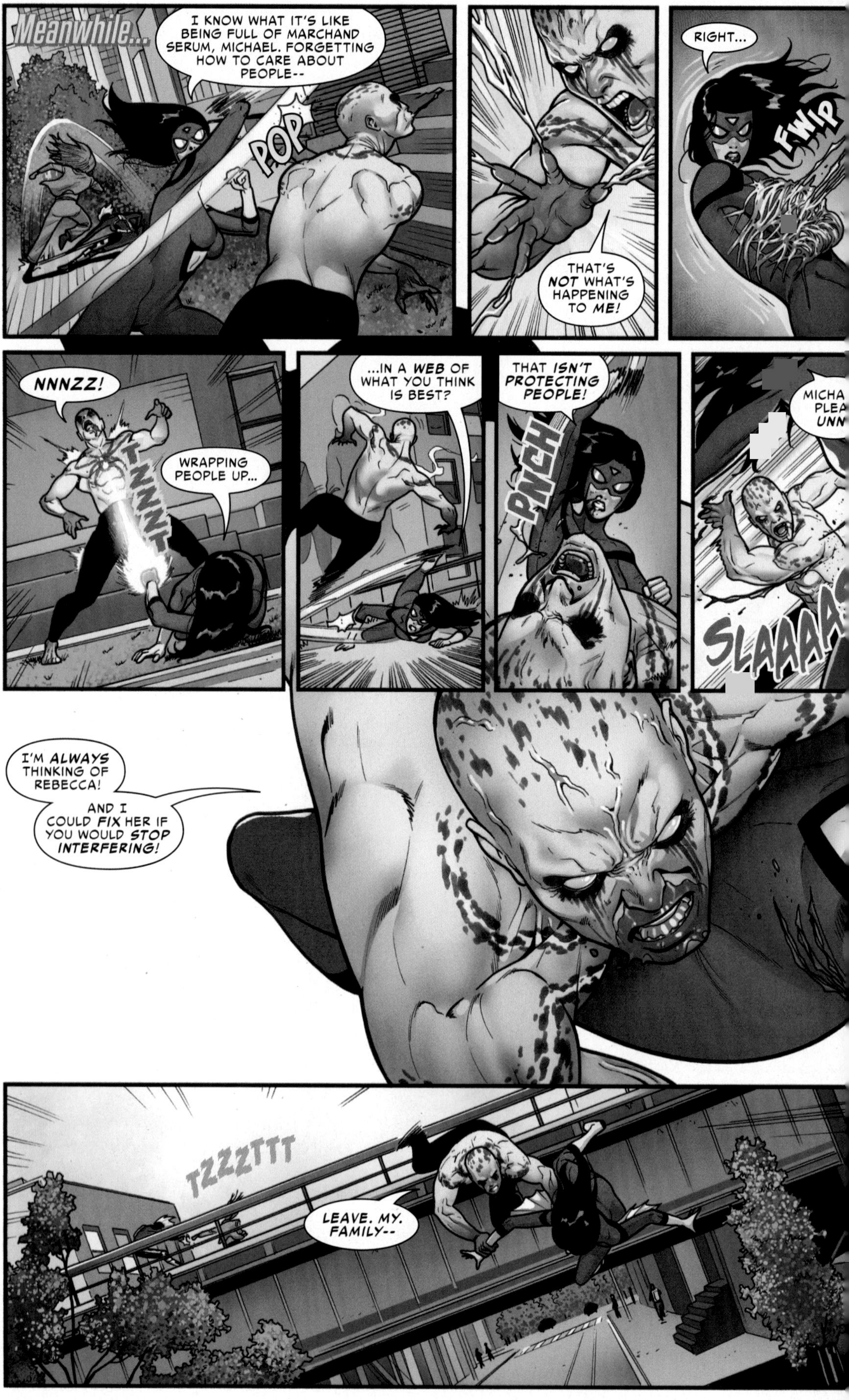

Meanwhile...
I KNOW WHAT IT'S LIKE BEING FULL OF MARCHAND SERUM, MICHAEL. FORGETTING HOW TO CARE ABOUT PEOPLE--
POP
THAT'S NOT WHAT'S HAPPENING TO ME!
RIGHT...
FWIP
NNNZZ!
TZZZZT
WRAPPING PEOPLE UP...
...IN A WEB OF WHAT YOU THINK IS BEST?
THAT ISN'T PROTECTING PEOPLE!
PNCH
SLAAAA
I'M ALWAYS THINKING OF REBECCA!
AND I COULD FIX HER IF YOU WOULD STOP INTERFERING!
TZZZTTT
LEAVE. MY. FAMILY--

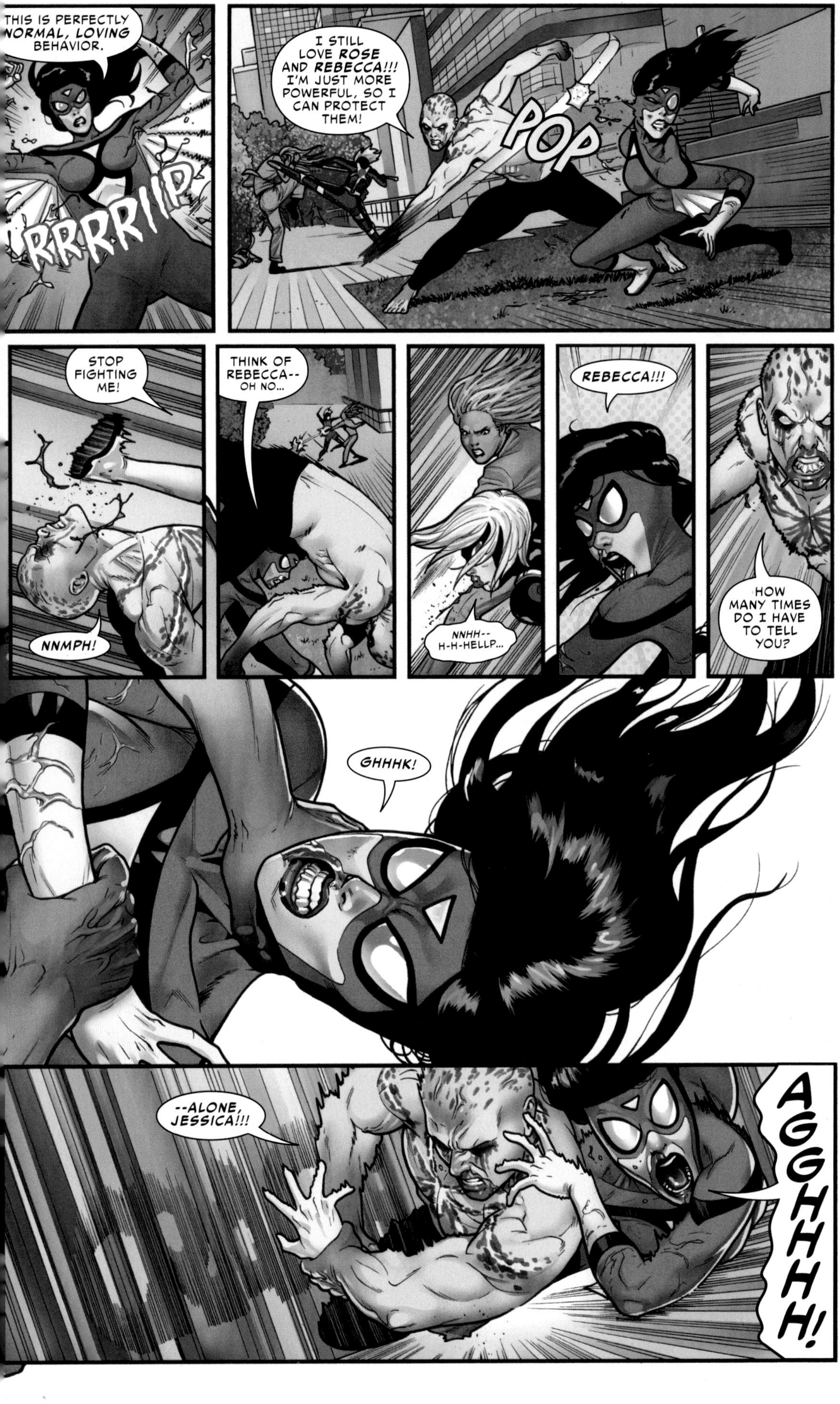

THIS IS PERFECTLY NORMAL, LOVING BEHAVIOR.
RRRRIIP
I STILL LOVE ROSE AND REBECCA!!! I'M JUST MORE POWERFUL, SO I CAN PROTECT THEM!
POP
STOP FIGHTING ME!
NNMPH!
THINK OF REBECCA-- OH NO...
NNHH-- H-H-HELLP...
REBECCA!!!
HOW MANY TIMES DO I HAVE TO TELL YOU?
GHHHK!
--ALONE, JESSICA!!!
AGGHHHH!

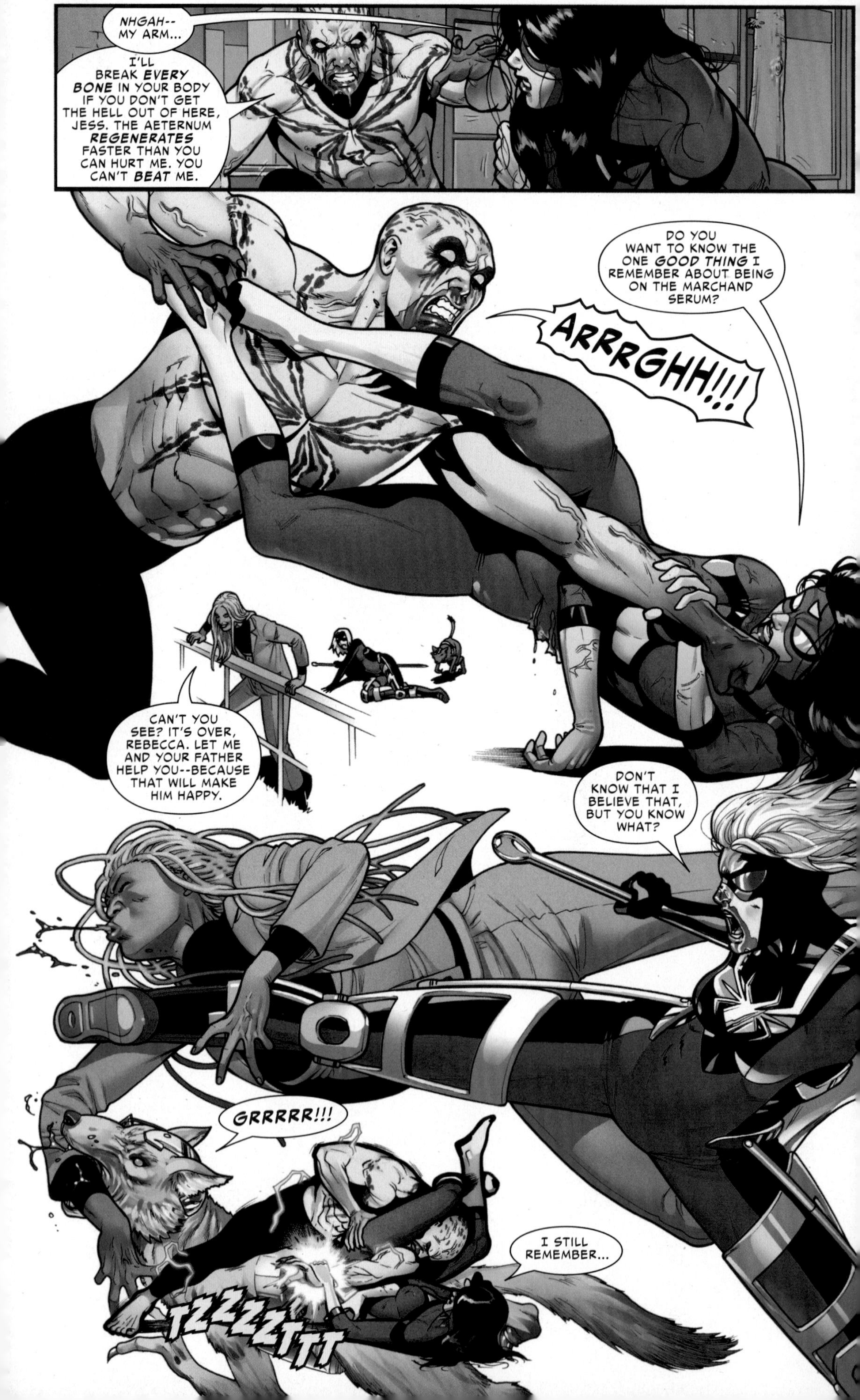

NHGAH-- MY ARM...
I'LL BREAK EVERY BONE IN YOUR BODY IF YOU DON'T GET THE HELL OUT OF HERE, JESS. THE AETERNUM REGENERATES FASTER THAN YOU CAN HURT ME. YOU CAN'T BEAT ME.
DO YOU WANT TO KNOW THE ONE GOOD THING I REMEMBER ABOUT BEING ON THE MARCHAND SERUM?
ARRRGHH!!!
CAN'T YOU SEE? IT'S OVER, REBECCA. LET ME AND YOUR FATHER HELP YOU--BECAUSE THAT WILL MAKE HIM HAPPY.
DON'T KNOW THAT I BELIEVE THAT, BUT YOU KNOW WHAT?
GRRRRR!!!
I STILL REMEMBER...
TZZZZZTTT

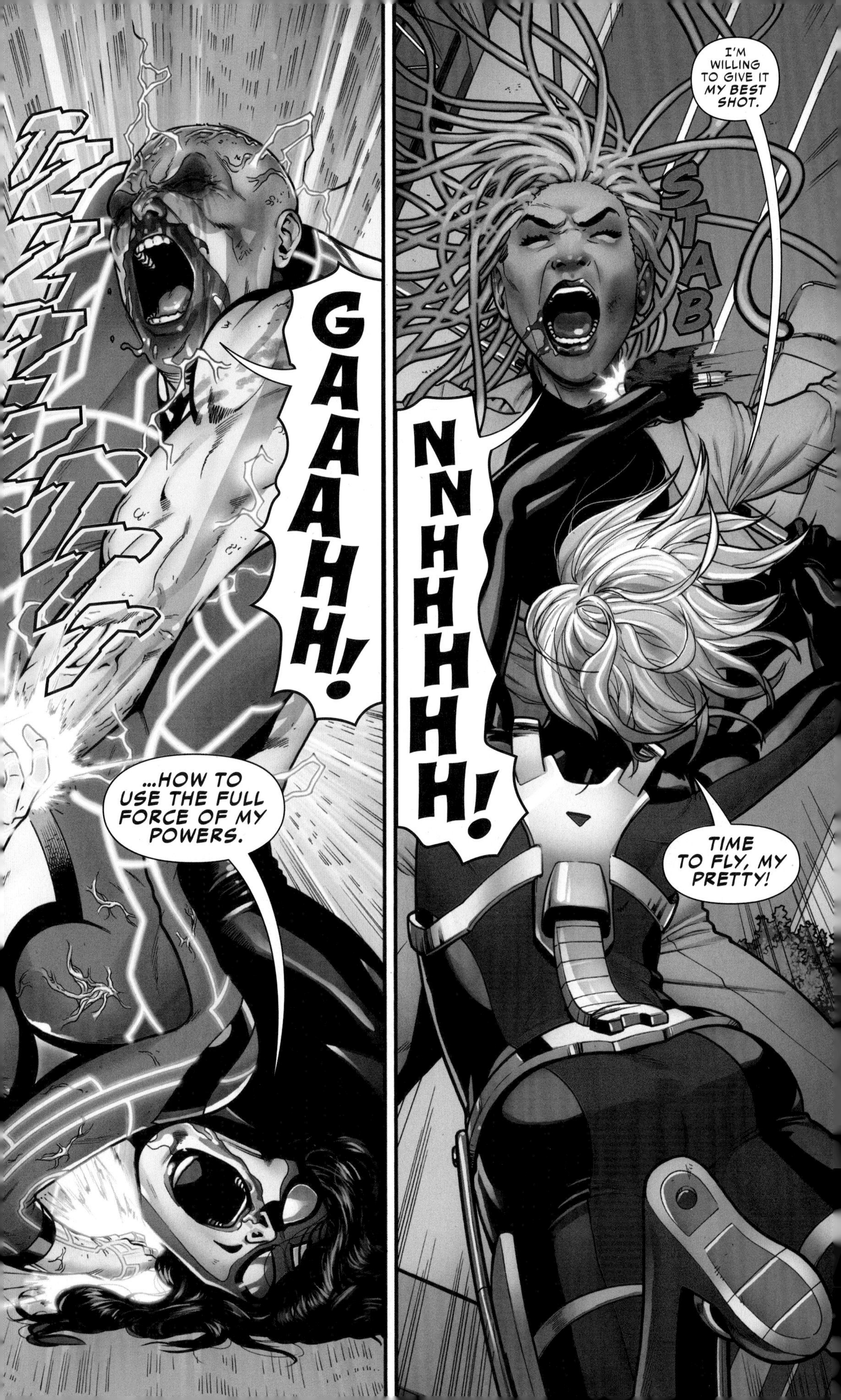
TZZZTTTT
GAAAHH!
...HOW TO USE THE FULL FORCE OF MY POWERS.
I'M WILLING TO GIVE IT MY BEST SHOT.
STAB
NNHHHHH!
TIME TO FLY, MY PRETTY!

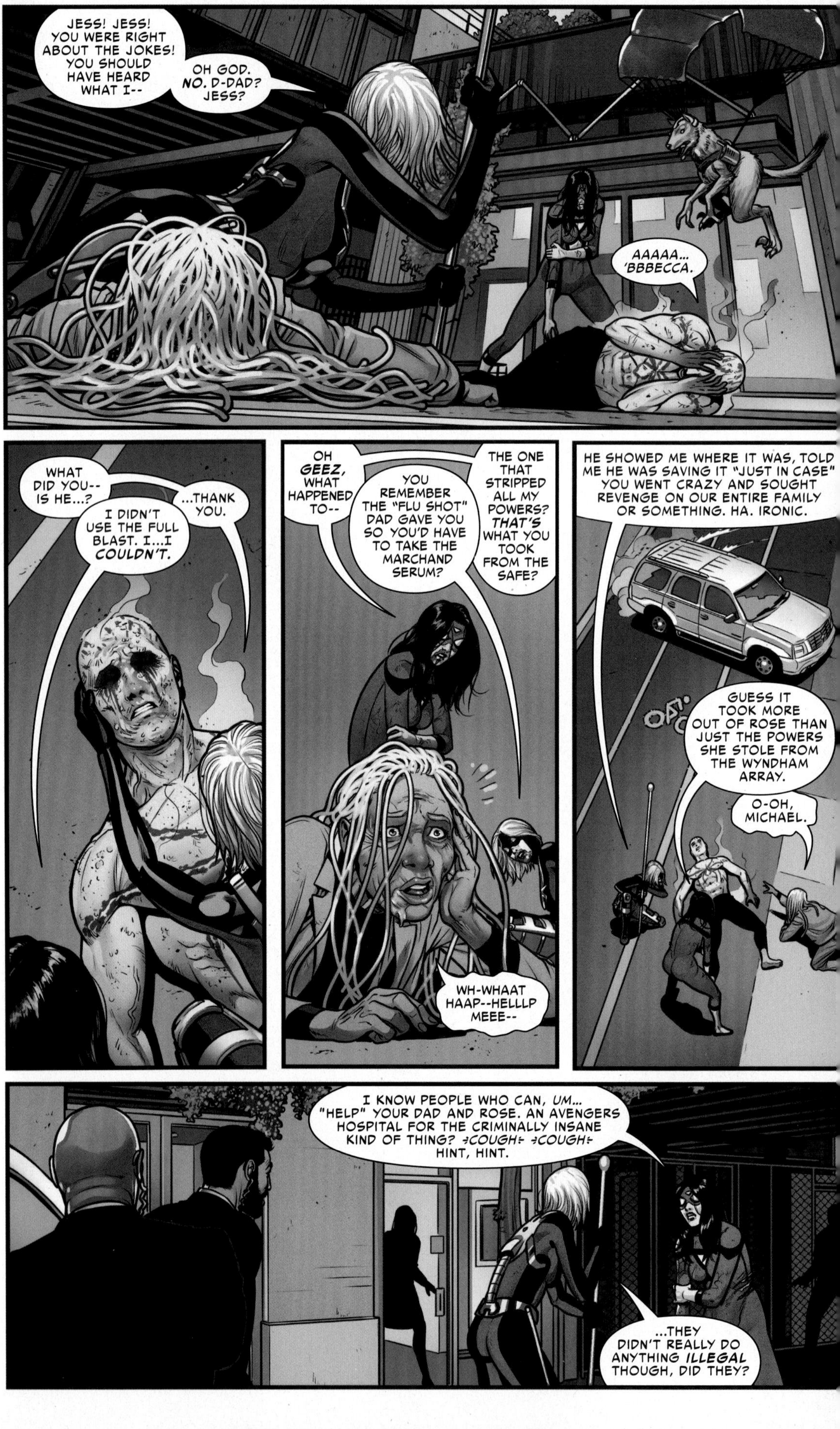
JESS! JESS! YOU WERE RIGHT ABOUT THE JOKES! YOU SHOULD HAVE HEARD WHAT I--
OH GOD. *NO.* D-DAD? JESS?
AAAAA... 'BBBECCA.
WHAT DID YOU-- IS HE...?
I DIDN'T USE THE FULL BLAST. I...I *COULDN'T.*
...THANK YOU.
OH *GEEZ,* WHAT HAPPENED TO--
YOU REMEMBER THE "FLU SHOT" DAD GAVE YOU SO YOU'D HAVE TO TAKE THE MARCHAND SERUM?
THE ONE THAT STRIPPED ALL MY POWERS? *THAT'S* WHAT YOU TOOK FROM THE SAFE?
WH-WHAAT HAAP--HELLLP MEEE--
HE SHOWED ME WHERE IT WAS, TOLD ME HE WAS SAVING IT "JUST IN CASE" YOU WENT CRAZY AND SOUGHT REVENGE ON OUR ENTIRE FAMILY OR SOMETHING. HA. IRONIC.
GUESS IT TOOK MORE OUT OF ROSE THAN JUST THE POWERS SHE STOLE FROM THE WYNDHAM ARRAY.
O-OH, MICHAEL.
I KNOW PEOPLE WHO CAN, *UM*... "HELP" YOUR DAD AND ROSE. AN AVENGERS HOSPITAL FOR THE CRIMINALLY INSANE KIND OF THING? *COUGH* *COUGH* HINT, HINT.
...THEY DIDN'T REALLY DO ANYTHING *ILLEGAL* THOUGH, DID THEY?

OTHER THAN STEALING THE WYNDHAM TECHNOLOGY, ROSE TRYING TO KILL US, AND YOUR DAD TURNING HIMSELF INTO A SUPER-POWERED MONSTER FOR POSSIBLY NEFARIOUS PURPOSES???

RIGHT. THAT.

SIGH IT'S YOUR CALL, REBECCA. I CAN GET RID OF THESE SECURITY GUYS, AND WE DO IT MY WAY, OR... OR YOU DECIDE.

REEBEECCAAA...

...SSSSORRRY, H-HONEY. JUS-JUSS WANTED. FIX YOU. HELP.

I DIDN'T NEED FIXING. I JUST NEEDED MY DAD.

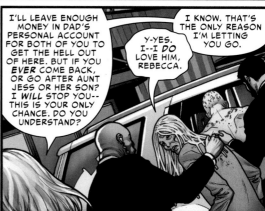

I'LL LEAVE ENOUGH MONEY IN DAD'S PERSONAL ACCOUNT FOR BOTH OF YOU TO GET THE HELL OUT OF HERE. BUT IF YOU EVER COME BACK, OR GO AFTER AUNT JESS OR HER SON? I WILL STOP YOU-- THIS IS YOUR ONLY CHANCE. DO YOU UNDERSTAND?

Y-YES. I--I DO LOVE HIM, REBECCA.

I KNOW. THAT'S THE ONLY REASON I'M LETTING YOU GO.

Y-YOU WERE RIGHT, HONEY. YOU DIDN'T NEED FIXING. YOU'RE PERFECT THE WAY YOU ARE.

SOB

I KNOW. I KNOW.

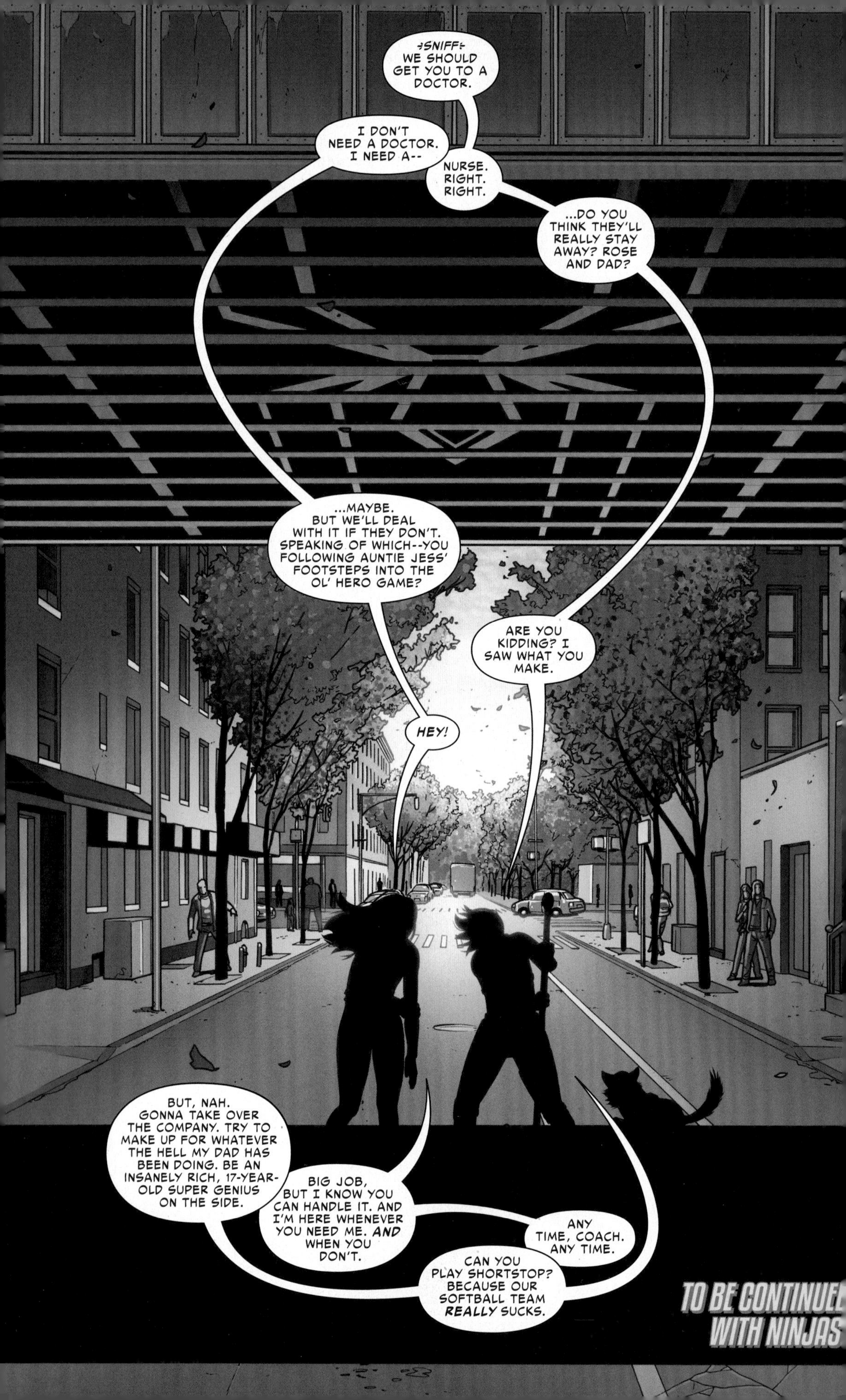

SNIFF
WE SHOULD GET YOU TO A DOCTOR.
I DON'T NEED A DOCTOR. I NEED A--
NURSE. RIGHT. RIGHT.
...DO YOU THINK THEY'LL REALLY STAY AWAY? ROSE AND DAD?
...MAYBE. BUT WE'LL DEAL WITH IT IF THEY DON'T. SPEAKING OF WHICH--YOU FOLLOWING AUNTIE JESS' FOOTSTEPS INTO THE OL' HERO GAME?
ARE YOU KIDDING? I SAW WHAT YOU MAKE.
HEY!
BUT, NAH. GONNA TAKE OVER THE COMPANY. TRY TO MAKE UP FOR WHATEVER THE HELL MY DAD HAS BEEN DOING. BE AN INSANELY RICH, 17-YEAR-OLD SUPER GENIUS ON THE SIDE.
BIG JOB, BUT I KNOW YOU CAN HANDLE IT. AND I'M HERE WHENEVER YOU NEED ME. AND WHEN YOU DON'T.
ANY TIME, COACH. ANY TIME.
CAN YOU PLAY SHORTSTOP? BECAUSE OUR SOFTBALL TEAM REALLY SUCKS.
TO BE CONTINUE[D] WITH NINJAS

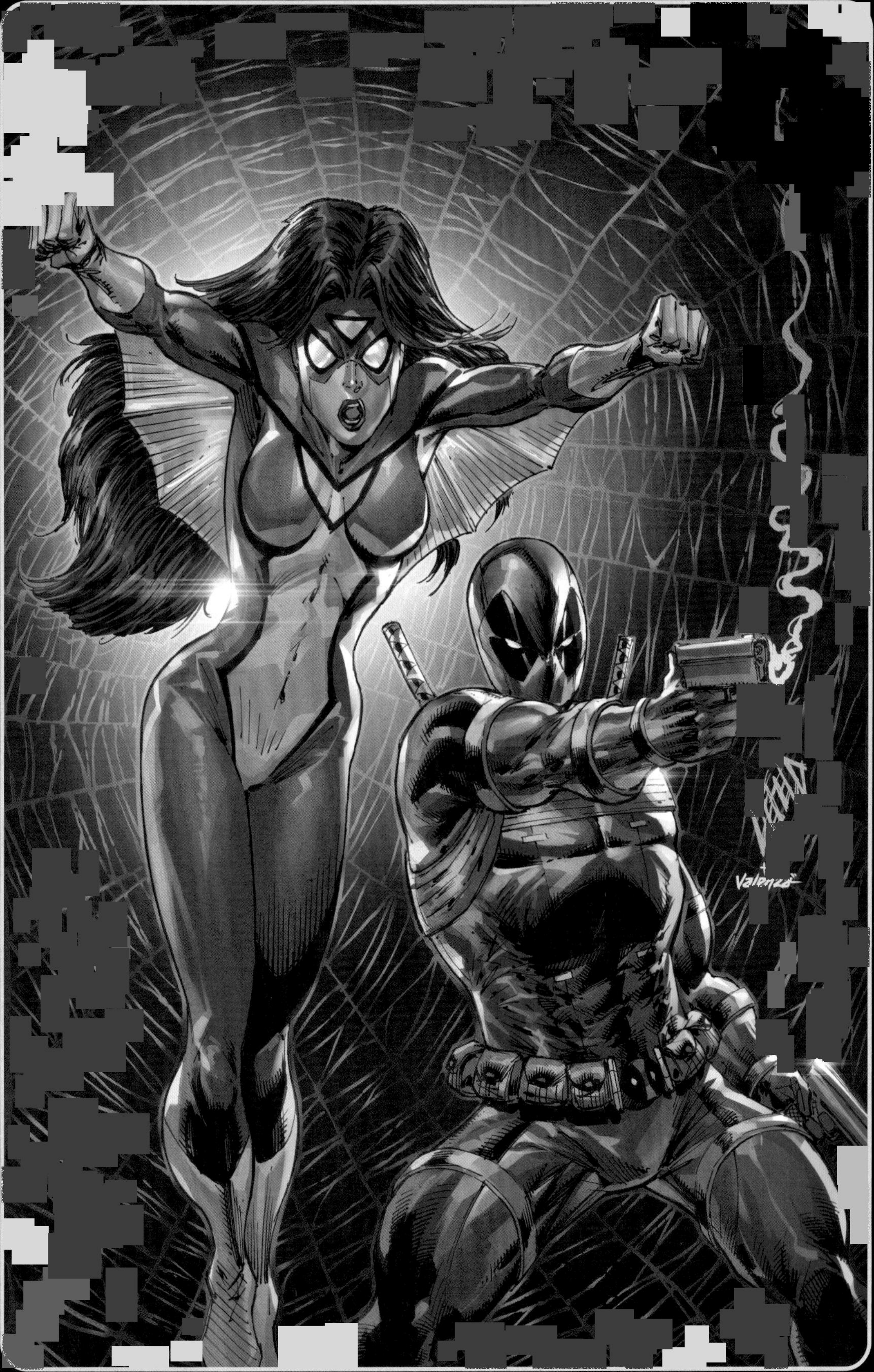
Valenza

#16 DEADPOOL 30TH ANNIVERSARY VARIANT BY
ROB LIEFELD

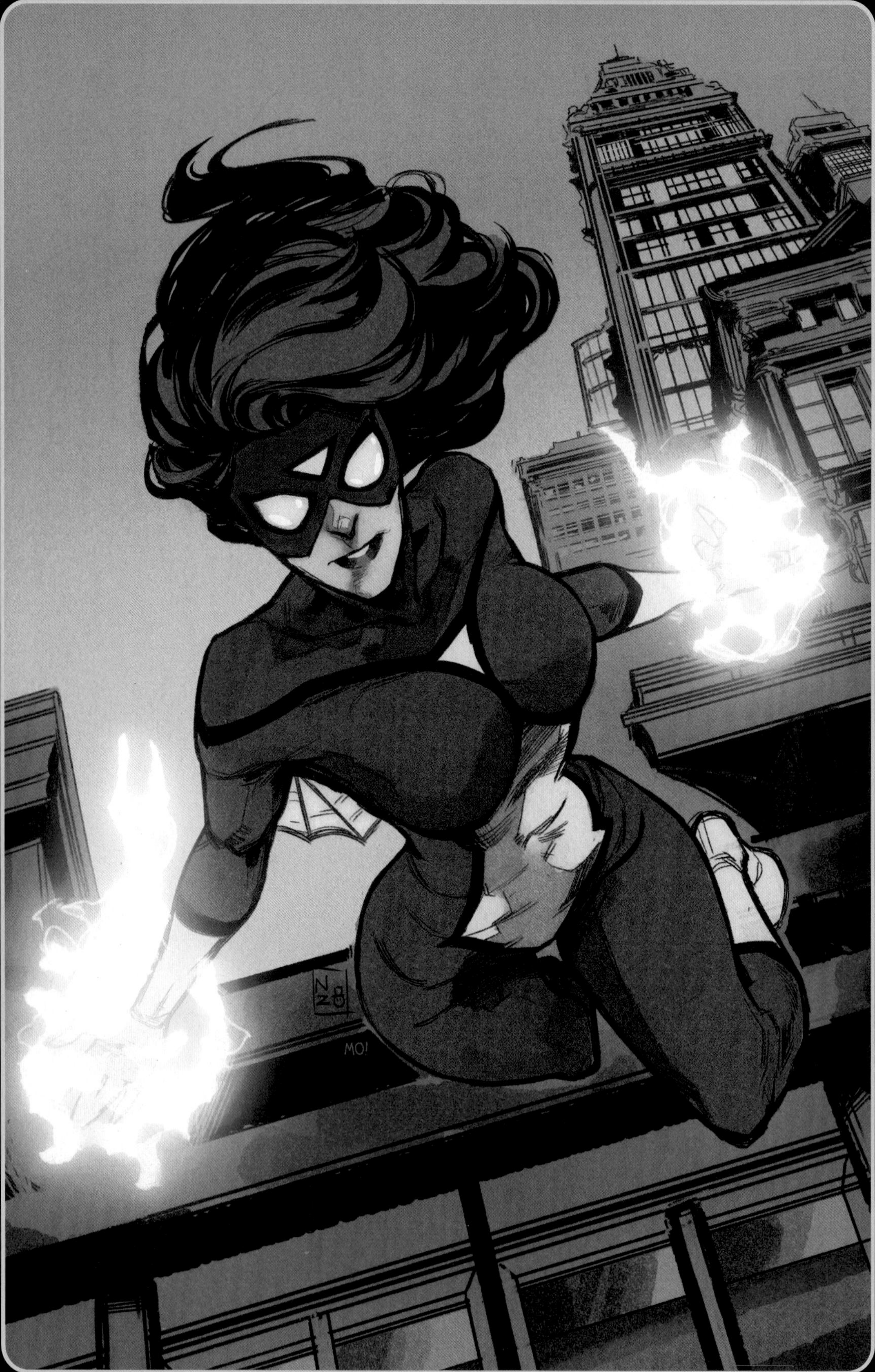
MO!

#16 VARIANT BY
NABETSE ZITRO & MORRY HOLLOWELL